Program design

For Hélène

Program Design
Third edition

PETER JULIFF

*Head of Department of Computing
& Quantitative Methods*

*Victoria College
Burwood Campus*

PRENTICE HALL

New York   London   Toronto   Sydney   Tokyo   Singapore

Typeset by Monoset Typesetters, Strathpine, Queensland
Printed and bound in Australia by Impact Printing, Brunswick, Victoria
Cover design by Denny Allnutt, Surry Hills, New South Wales

1 2 3 4 5 93 92 91 90
ISBN 0-13-728916-2

National Library of Australia
Cataloguing-in-Publication Data

Juliff, P. L. (Peter Laurence), 1938–
    Program design.

    3rd ed.
    Bibliography.
    Includes index.
    ISBN 0-13-728916-2

    1. Electronic digital computers — Programming.
    2. Algorithms. I. Title.

005.1

Library of Congress
Cataloguing-in-Publication Data

Juliff, Peter Laurence, 1938–
    Program design.

    1. Electronic digital computers — Programming.
    2. Structured programming. I. Title.

QA76.6.J84   1989   005.1'2   89-23134
ISBN 0-13-728916-2

Prentice Hall, Inc., Englewood Cliffs, New Jersey
Prentice Hall of Australia Pty Ltd, Sydney
Prentice Hall Canada, Inc., Toronto
Prentice Hall Hispanoamericana, SA, Mexico
Prentice Hall of India Private Ltd, New Delhi
Prentice Hall International, Inc., London
Prentice Hall of Japan, Inc., Tokyo
Prentice Hall of Southeast Asia Pty Ltd, Singapore
Editora Prentice Hall do Brasil Ltda, Rio de Janeiro

 PRENTICE HALL

A division of Simon & Schuster

Contents

Preface

The material in this edition represents an extension of that in the second edition. There has been more emphasis placed on the formal declaration of data associated with procedures.

An increasing number of students of programming are being introduced to the craft by means of languages requiring a formal definition of local and global data. Even for those languages where such scope rules are weak, the design of programs and their component processes will benefit from a more rigorous design of data than has been used in previous editions of this book.

Largely because of the formality used in dealing with data and procedures, the treatment of algorithm design has been extended from one to two chapters. In addition, an introductory treatment of data normalization and relational database design has been included together with an additional Appendix on dBASE 111.

Because of the selection of this book as a recommended text for examinations held by the Australian Computer Society (ACS), questions at the end of each chapter have been updated to reflect the type of questions asked on past ACS papers.

As with past editions, I hope that the treatment of program design in this book will be of value to students and practitioners alike. I have tried to maintain simplicity of style in preference to a more academic approach to the material covered and have attempted to cover the practical aspects of software design as they affect day-to-day problems facing programmers in a production environment.

I would like to thank my colleagues at Victoria College and throughout Australia and present and past students for their suggestions for improvements on past editions. I am indebted to Don Fraser for his revision of the material in this book, and to Jaki Grosvenor for her art work.

Peter Juliff,
Head, Department of Computing and Quantitative Methods,
Victoria College,
Burwood Campus,
Burwood, Victoria, Australia.

Writing programs

Programming is not only a creative and stimulating activity but also an intellectually rigorous discipline. Without wishing to detract from its enjoyment, one must be careful to distinguish between 'amateur' and 'professional' programming. I do not use the term 'amateur' in a perjorative sense but rather to describe persons who write programs mostly for their own use and enjoyment. Such persons are usually primarily concerned with producing a correct solution to a relatively small problem and not with the elegance of the algorithm, its ability to be maintained or its documentation. Professional programmers, on the other hand, will be concerned with a relatively large and complex problem and must consider many more criteria than simply solving the problem correctly. Their work will be primarily for use by other people with whom the programmer has no contact and who may be called on to modify or enhance the programs to meet their changing requirements over a period of many years.

It is my intention to address the professional programmer and to urge amateur programmers to adopt the same disciplined approach to their work.

1

I would like to make some assertions about programming:

- Programming is an inherently difficult and demanding task.
- Coding, the expression of the solution in a particular programming language, is only one small facet of programming and arguably not the most important one.
- Programming is a discipline to which certain principles may be applied independent of computer type, language or application.
- There are objective criteria for good programs; it is not a matter of personal aesthetics.
- Despite the appearance of correctness of solution as a *sine qua non*, the prime criteria in judging a program are structure and style rather than 'cleverness' of the algorithm.
- Given that programs process data, an understanding of the nature and structure of the data is an essential prerequisite to the construction of any program.
- A programmer must be familiar with as many techniques as possible, aware of their pros and cons and able to recognize situations for their application (modified where necessary).

The first of these precepts will be self-evident to any programmer. I will elaborate on the rest in this book.

The first section of the book deals with the construction of algorithms. They are first considered at a micro, or individual level to formulate guidelines for elegance of construction. Consideration is then given to their grouping to comprise a program, that is, in terms of their structure within the program as a whole and their communication with one another. By this means I hope to illustrate that the process is recursive in that the rules relating to the construction of any individual routine are just as applicable to the overall program itself.

The second section relates to the construction and processing of data structures. Algorithms are inextricably interwoven with the data which they process and their structure arguably should be modeled on that of the processed data.

In this book algorithms are expressed in pseudocode which I regard as the best of the contemporary methods for their formulation. Pseudocode is a method of expressing program algorithms in English statements which are connected by a limited number of control/sequence rules. It is sometimes referred to as Structured English, and its format will be explained in Chapter 1.

Notation

In an attempt to free the text from the syntax of any specific programming language, I have adopted a notation which is similar to that used in most contemporary programming texts. The notation also partly conforms to the syntax of many programming languages.

The symbols used are:

+ addition
− subtraction
∗ multiplication
/ division
= assignment
:} a point in an algorithm where detailed statements have been omitted for brevity

Hence, instead of

    Put zero in TOTAL

I have adopted

    TOTAL=0

which may be read as 'TOTAL is assigned a value of zero', and instead of the more colloquial

    Add 1 to COUNTER

I have used

    COUNTER=COUNTER+1

There are places in the text where I have not adhered strictly to these conventions, but the meaning of the non-standard procedures should be clear.

For the sake of readability and compatibility with the format of many programming languages, I have used an underscore character in the names of many variables, believing that

    EMPLOYEE _COUNTER

is inherently more readable than

    EMPLOYEECOUNTER

1   Algorithm design

1.1   Introduction

An algorithm is a formula, a recipe, a step-by-step procedure to be followed in order to obtain the solution to a problem. To be useful as a basis for writing a program, the algorithm must:

(1) arrive at a correct solution within a finite time;
(2) be clear, precise and unambiguous; and

(3) be in a format which lends itself to an elegant implementation in a
    programming language.

Algorithm specification has traditionally been done by drawing flowcharts which are a diagrammatic representation of the steps involved.
Throughout the book, pseudocode will be used instead of flowcharts
except for a brief introduction in this chapter to illustrate the
relationship between the two techniques.

1.2   Structured programming/ software engineering

In the 1960s Professor Edsger Dijkstra of Eindhoven University was
warning programmers of the danger of the indiscriminate use of branch
instructions (GO TOs) as a means of program control. In a paper
published in Italy in 1966, Böhm and Jacopini demonstrated that no
program need consist of a combination of any more than the three
control constructs of sequence, iteration and selection. The term
'structured programming' was coined to describe a body of technique
incorporating and formalizing these concepts which until that time had
largely existed only as personal standards of particular programmers.
Further academic contributions were made by people such as Niklaus
Wirth and David Parnas who stressed that there was a discipline which
could be brought to bear in developing programs and led to a more
theoretical extension of programming technique into 'software
engineering'.
    We as programmers owe a great deal both to the academics who
contributed to such a body of knowledge and to the popularizers and
pragmaticians such as Ed Yourdon, Tom De Marco, Gerry Weinberg and
Michael Jackson who were responsible for translating the theoretical
concepts into practical techniques and heuristics which ordinary
programmers could understand and follow.

1.3   Control structures

The key to elegant algorithm design lies in limiting the control structure
to only three constructs. These are illustrated in Figures 1.1, 1.2 and 1.3
in flowchart and statement form.

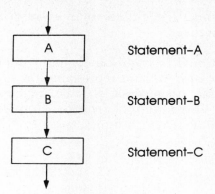

Figure 1.1 *Sequence*

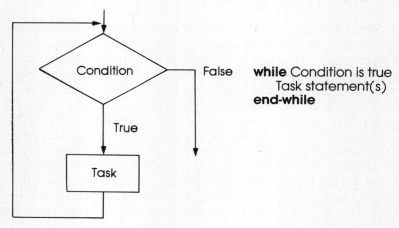

Figure 1.2 *Iteration (or repetition)*

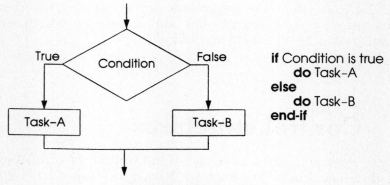

Figure 1.3 *Selection*

A variation on the construct of Figure 1.3 is shown in Figure 1.4.

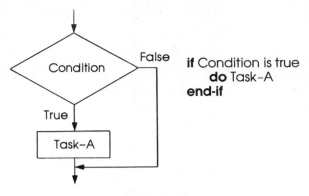

Figure 1.4

Using only the selection construct of Figure 1.4 leads to a rather complicated structure for multiple testing, as shown in Figure 1.5.

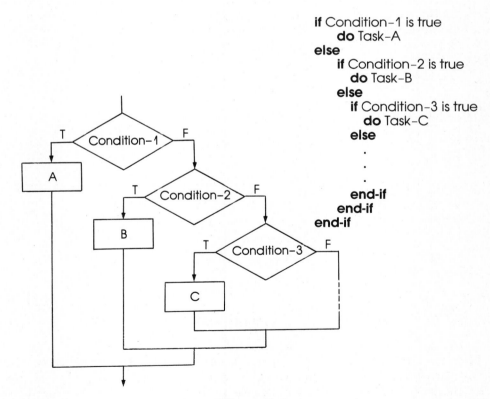

Figure 1.5

Hence, a preferable solution is that shown in Figure 1.6.

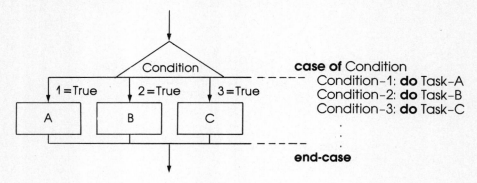

Figure 1.6

At this point, flowcharts will be abandoned as a means of expressing algorithms. Their main deficiency lies in their allowing the designer of an algorithm to develop structures which do not conform to the three control constructs listed previously and which could therefore lead to inelegant and dangerous implementation in whatever programming language is used to solve the problem. The patterns of logic in Figure 1.7, for example, are easy to depict in flowchart form.

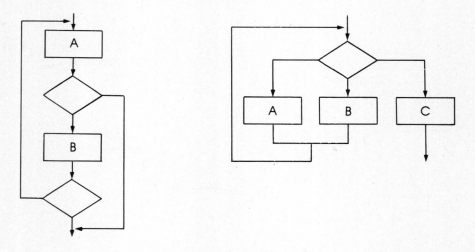

Figure 1.7

They are incapable, however, of being expressed in structured syntax in any programming language. This will not preclude their being implemented in that language, of course, but will make it possible only by the excessive use of GO TOs and their associated labels.

The advantage of using an English-like pseudocode with strictly limited control structures overcomes the two main deficiencies inherent in flowcharts:

(1) For the most part we are unable to write anything meaningful in the boxes.
(2) As stated previously, we have little effective control over the constructs which we draw, and our transgressions ultimately become embedded in the code generated from that flowchart.

1.4 Pseudocode

In contrast to the shortcomings of flowcharts, the advantages of pseudocode are:

(1) Statements are written in free English text and, although brevity is desirable, they may be as long as is needed to describe the particular operation.
(2) By providing only the three structured control concepts of sequence, iteration and selection, the technique does not permit us to use branches to labels.
(3) Many languages, such as Pascal, exist (and more are certain to follow) which have syntax that is almost identical to pseudocode and hence make the transition from design to coding extremely easy.

The conventions followed in this book for pseudocode are as follows:

(1) Individual operations are described briefly and precisely in English statements consisting of nouns and verbs.
(2) Groups of statements may be formed into modules or procedures and the group given a name, for example, Calculate Pay. Such a procedure may be executed by the statement:

>   **do** Calculate Pay

for example:

>   input employee's work details
>   **do** Calculate Pay
>   print pay envelope details

(3) Sequence of operations is effected by writing instructions on consecutive lines.

(4) Iteration (the repetition of operations) is effected by a **while** . . . statement which indicates that all of the following operations until an **end-while** is encountered are to be repeated while that condition is true. The condition is tested immediately before executing the group of statements for the first time and thereafter immediately before each prospective iteration. Hence, if the governing condition is false when the **while** is first encountered, the subordinate instruction(s) will not be executed at all.

The following task, for example, would be executed four times:

```
Counter=4
while Counter>zero
    statement-1
    statement-2
        .
        .
        .
    Counter=Counter-1
end-while
```

Similarly, the task below would not be executed at all if Counter was already equal to Target:

```
while Counter not =Target
    statement-1
    statement-2
        .
        .
        .
    Counter=Counter+1
end-while
```

Note the use of indentations of the subordinate statements to highlight the span of control.

In the second example, if Counter was greater than the value in Target when the **while** was encountered, the group of statements could be executed indefinitely! A better control statement would have been:

```
while Counter<Target
```

Such an iteration of repetition concept is referred to as a program 'loop'.

(5) Selection is effected by the **if ... else ... end-if** for simple tests and the **case** statement for multiple tests. The **else** is not essential in a test where the action to be taken upon the condition being false is merely to avoid the action if the condition were true. The following examples should illustrate the constructs.

(a)
```
if employee's age≥18
    Adult Counter=Adult Counter+1
else
    Junior Counter=Junior Counter+1
end-if
```

(b) **if** employee's sex is female
        Female Counter=Female Counter+1
   else
      if employee's sex is male
          Male Counter=Male Counter+1
      else
          Error Counter=Error Counter+1
      end-if
   end-if

(c) **if** hours worked>40
        Overtime Counter=Overtime Counter+1
   end-if

(d) **case of** employee's Skill Code:
      'E': Engineer Counter=Engineer Counter+1
      'A': Accountant Counter=Accountant Counter+1
      'P': Programmer Counter=Programmer Counter+1
   end-case

Note again the use of statement indentation to highlight the span of control of each of the statements.

In all of the examples above, the key words associated with the constructs are in bold type, for example, **do, if ... else ... end-if, case of ... end-case** and **while ... end-while.**

1.5   Patterns of logic

While every program is likely to be unique in its procedure, there are common patterns of logic followed by the vast majority of programs. One of the major skills to be acquired by programmers is that of being able to look at a problem and recognize that it falls into a certain category. If the basic pattern of logic is familiar for that type of problem, the task of the programmer is simplified to that of recognizing the features of the new problem which are unique and fitting them into the standard framework of the procedure needed for the solution.

Most programmers, in their daily activities, tend to develop the vast majority of programs by cannibalizing previously written code rather than by commencing with a clean slate.

The following are examples of basic patterns of logic which provide the groundwork for most 'data processing' programs. Later in this book, additional general purpose algorithms will be provided for more specific problems such as sorting, file updating and processing a variety of data structures.

(1) *The most basic pattern of all*: The overwhelming majority of programs fall into a pattern of:

> Beginning
> Middle
> End

where the Middle consists of a loop which is executed until a terminating condition is encountered.

This might seem trivial but certain tasks are normally associated with each of these three components of a program and this basic pattern provides programmer with a mental check list of the things to look for in the program specification.

For example,

Section of program	*Associated tasks*
Beginning	Setting of counters and totals to an initial value (usually zero); obtaining initial values from an operator at a terminal e.g., the number of items to be processed; nominating files to be processed.
Middle	Obtaining data items to be processed from an operator at a terminal or from a file; accessing a series of elements in a table; accumulating totals and counters.
End	Output of accumulated totals and counters; releasing files which have been processed.

All of the following algorithms fit into this pattern of logic.

(2) *The counted loop*: This pattern consists of one or more operations performed a predetermined number of times. The control of the required loop will depend on a counter which may either start at the target value and be decremented to zero as the loop is repeated or may start at an initial value, usually zero or one, and be incremented until the target value is encountered.

Example 1.1

Request a positive integer from an operator at a terminal and output all of the powers of 2 from 2^1 to 2 to the power of that integer. Hence, if the input integer was 4, the program would print:

$$2 \quad (2^1)$$
$$4 \quad (2^2)$$
$$8 \quad (2^3)$$
$$16 \, (2^4)$$

Powers of 2
    accept TARGET from operator
    COUNTER=0
    while COUNTER<TARGET
        COUNTER=COUNTER+1
        output $2^{COUNTER}$
    end-while

Note that this could also have been written as:

Powers of 2
    accept TARGET from operator
    COUNTER=1
    while COUNTER not>TARGET
        output $2^{COUNTER}$
        COUNTER=COUNTER+1
    end-while

It could also have been written:

Powers of 2
    accept TARGET from operator
    while TARGET>0
        output 2^{TARGET}
        TARGET=TARGET−1
    end-while

In this last case, the powers of 2 would be output in descending order rather than ascending as the other algorithms would have provided. The value in TARGET would have been lost by the end of this algorithm whereas it would still be available for further use, if needed, in the previous two algorithms.

In terms of the most basic pattern of logic, these algorithms have a 'beginning' (the input of the target and assignment of an initial value to the counter) and a 'middle' (the counted loop) but no 'end'. As soon as the loop terminated, the problem was solved.

The following example outputs the powers of 2 as before but accumulates their total and provides an 'end' by outputing that total.

Powers of 2
```
    accept TARGET from operator
    TOTAL=0
    while TARGET>0
            VALUE=2 TARGET
            output VALUE
            TOTAL=TOTAL+VALUE
            TARGET=TARGET−1
    end-while
    output TOTAL
```

Note: VALUE was introduced in this example to save the necessity of having to compute 2^{TARGET} twice.

(3) *The indeterminate loop*: This pattern of logic executes a loop as many times (which could be zero) as is needed until a specific condition is detected.

For example, a program may need to process all of the records in a file until the end-of-file is reached. The program will not know in advance how many records that will be: indeed, there may be no records at all in the file and the end-of-file may be encountered on the first file access.

A solution to this problem will be constructed in a number of stages to illustrate the problems inherent in this pattern.

Example 1.2

Read and print all of the records on a personnel file. The file ends with a standard end-of-file sentinel.

A first attempt at a solution to this problem might be:

Print Records
```
    while end-of-file not encountered
            read next record from file
            print record contents
    end-while
```

This solution fails because the end-of-file indicator is read by the program in its operation

    'read next record from file'

and as this is immediately followed by

    'print record contents'

the output from that print operation would be unpredictable as no record had been read.

A somewhat better solution would have been:

Print Records
    while end-of-file not encountered
        read next record from file
        if end-of-file not encountered
            print record contents
        end-if
    end-while

In this second case, the print operation is avoided when the end-of-file sentinel is read but only at the expense of introducing two tests for the end-of-file each time through the loop—once in the **while** and again in the **if**.

The best solution involves a 'priming' read, achieved by executing the first read operation prior to entering the loop and repeating the read just prior to each successive iteration:

Print Records
      read record from file
    while end-of-file not encountered
        print record contents
        read next record from file
    end-while

This pattern also caters for the empty file situation in that if the priming read discovers the end-of-file, the processing loop is not executed at all. This priming operation is sufficiently important to be stated as a basic pattern of logic in its own right:

(4) *The priming operation*: The concept of a priming operation applies to any situation in which a series of data items is to be processed, any of which may be discovered to be the one which terminates the processing.

Example 1.3

A large table holds, in each of its elements, the salary of a person in a particular company. The precise number of such persons, and therefore of such salaries, is unknown but the last salary is followed by a dummy value of 999999 to indicate that no more data follows.

An algorithm is required to calculate and print the average of all these salaries.

Average Salary
```
    TOTAL=0
    COUNTER=0
    access (first) SALARY
    while SALARY not = 999999
          TOTAL = TOTAL + SALARY
          COUNTER = COUNTER + 1
          access (next) SALARY
    end-while
    if COUNTER = 0
      AVERAGE = 0
    else
      AVERAGE = TOTAL / COUNTER
    end-if
    print AVERAGE
    stop
```

The test for COUNTER = 0 at the end of this algorithm was inserted to guard against the case in which the table had no real salaries at all, only the dummy value of 999999. In such a case it would be dangerous to compute an average by dividing by a counter of zero, as many programming languages will abort a program if this is attempted.

Example 1.4

Construct an algorithm to read a series of integers until the number 99 is encountered and calculate and print the total of all the integers read which are greater than 50.

Selective Total
```
    TOTAL = 0
    read INTEGER
    while INTEGER not = 99
          if INTEGER > 50
            TOTAL = TOTAL + INTEGER
          end-if
          read INTEGER
    end-while
    print TOTAL
    stop
```

Note the use of a priming read in this example.

Example 1.5

A file contains records relating to the products sold by a particular company. Each record holds the product identification number, product name and a series of six values representing the number of items of that product sold in each of the preceeding six months, e.g.,

14765 WHEELBARROWS 4, 6, 2, 0, 3, 7

The file ends with a standard end-of-file sentinel.

Construct an algorithm to read each of the records on the file and print its product name and the average number of units sold per month in the last six months. (This average will be the sum of the six monthly sales divided by 6).

Product Sales
```
    read product record from file
    while end-of-file not encountered
            TOTAL = sum of 6 sales values
            AVERAGE = TOTAL / 6
            print PRODUCT_NAME, AVERAGE
            read product record from file
    end-while
    stop
```

1.6   Algorithm construction

At this point we will consider only simple algorithms, essentially only those needed for a single task. In a later chapter we will consider the means of assembling a large number of tasks to form a complex structure.

The best method of illustrating the procedure of algorithm construction is by the use of a series of examples of increasing complexity.

Example 1.6

Construct an algorithm which will place in AREA the area of a triangle bounded by sides of length A, B and C. Should the dimensions given be such that they would be impossible to construct a triangle (e.g., A=10, B=3, C=2) the content of AREA is to be zero.

Area of triangle
```
    S=½*(A+B+C)
    if (S − A) ≤ 0
    or (S − B) ≤ 0
    or (S − C) ≤ 0
        AREA=0
    else
        AREA= √S*(S − A)*(S − B)*(S − C)
    end-if
```

Example 1.7

Construct an algorithm to read a series of integers, the first of which indicates the number of integers to follow (e.g., 5, 3, 19, 6, 82, 4) and compute and print their total and average. Exclude the first number from the total and average calculations.

Total and Average
```
read 1st number and place in COUNTER_A and COUNTER_B
TOTAL = 0
while Counter_A > 0
    read INTEGER
    TOTAL = TOTAL + INTEGER
    COUNTER_A = COUNTER_A - 1
end-while
if COUNTER_B > 0
    AVERAGE = TOTAL/COUNTER_B
else
    AVERAGE = 0
end-if
print TOTAL and AVERAGE
stop
```

Example 1.8

Construct an algorithm to compute the tax payable on an employee's gross pay according to Table 1.1. The gross pay is in GROSS_PAY, the number of dependants is in DEPENDANTS and the result of the calculation is to be placed in TAX.

Table 1.1

Gross wage	Fewer than three dependants	Three or more dependants
$100 or less $100.01 to $250 Over $250	Tax=nil Tax=15% of gross Tax=35% of gross	Tax=nil Tax=10% of gross Tax=25% of gross

Tax Calculation
```
if GROSS PAY ≤ $100
    Tax_RATE = 0
else
    if GROSS_PAY ≤ $250
        if DEPENDANTS < 3
            TAX_RATE = 15
        else
            TAX_RATE = 10
        end-if
```

```
        else
            if DEPENDANTS < 3
                TAX_RATE = 35
            else
                TAX_RATE = 25
            end-if
        end-if
    end-if
    TAX = GROSS_PAY * TAX_RATE/100
```

Example 1.9

Construct an algorithm to examine 20 numbers in a table, or array, and place in TALLY a count of those over 100.

This example requires the use of a form of notation which will allow the items to be referenced by their position in the table. This is normally done by the use of an index or subscript, for example:

(1) NUMBER (4), NUMBER (16), etc. refer to specific table elements; and
(2) NUMBER (INDEX) refers to whichever table element is currently indicated by the value held in the variable INDEX.

```
Examine Table
    TALLY = 0
    INDEX = 1
    while INDEX ≤ 20
        if NUMBER (INDEX) > 100
            TALLY = TALLY + 1
        end-if
        INDEX = INDEX + 1
    end-while
```

Example 1.10

Construct a coinage analysis algorithm to determine the number of notes/coins of each denomination needed to be put in an employee's pay envelope so as to pay the value of NET_PAY in as few notes/coins as possible. Assume that a table exists of the format shown below containing the value in cents of each note or coin to be used and a corresponding counter to contain the number of that note or coin to be placed in the pay envelope. The coinage denominations and counters may be addressed as DENOMINATION and COUNTER respectively, with a suitable subscript. Assume that all COUNTERs start with zero as their content.

DENOMINATION	2000	1000	500	200	100	20	10	5	2	1
COUNTER	0	0	0	0	0	0	0	0	0	0
	1	2	3	4	5	6	7	8	9	10

Coinage Analysis
```
REMAINDER = NET_PAY
INDEX = 1
while REMAINDER > 0
    divide REMAINDER by DENOMINATION (INDEX) placing
        quotient in COUNTER (INDEX) and remainder in REMAINDER

    INDEX = INDEX + 1
end-while
```

1.7   Postscript— Nassi–Schneiderman diagrams

One other means of avoiding flowcharts to represent algorithms is the use of Nassi-Schneiderman (N–S) diagrams. In essence, these are structured flowcharts without the use of arrows to direct the flow of logic. The logic flow from one operation to the next is achieved by abutting the following operation to the boundary of the preceding operation. By this device and by the use of a limited set of symbols, N–S diagrams enforce the adoption of the structured concepts of sequence, iteration and selection. The symbols used are illustrated in Figure 1.8, and Figure 1.9 illustrates the solution to Example 1.4.

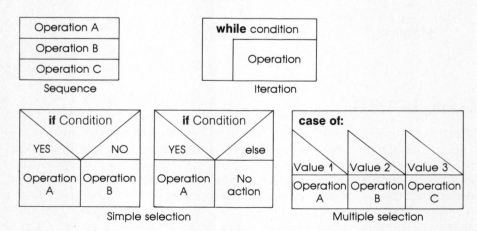

Figure 1.8

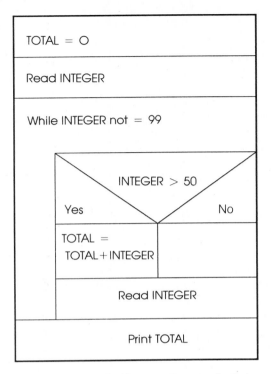

Figure 1.9 *Solution to Example 1.4*

1.8   Conclusion

Algorithm design consists of specifying the steps required to reach the solution of a problem. If the algorithm is to lead to an elegant program, it must be specified by the use of a limited number and type of control structures, those of sequence, iteration and selection.

The use of these constructs allows any module to be constructed without resorting to branches and internal labels.

The specification of the algorithm using pseudocode rather than a diagrammatic format such as a flowchart will allow for freer expression of the tasks involved and ensure that the structured programming concepts are adhered to.

1.9   Review questions

(1) Write an algorithm to read three numbers and output them in ascending sequence, for example, input: 12, 9, 10; output: 9, 10, 12.

(2) An algorithm is required to read a series of numbers and ensure that they are in ascending sequence. Some numbers may be duplicated and this is to be regarded as acceptable by the algorithm. The numbers need not be consecutive and the series ends with the number 999. The algorithm is to terminate by outputting one of the two following messages:

SEQUENCE CORRECT
OR
SEQUENCE ERROR

(3) An algorithm is required to input a series of numbers and output the highest and lowest values found. The series will end with 999 and this value is not to be included in the calculations.

For example, for the series:

6, 100, −35, 47, 0, 203, −16, 999

the output would be: Max 203
                        Min −35

(4) An algorithm is required to input 10 pairs of numbers and to output the higher number in each pair. If the values in any pair are equal, either number may be output.

For example, for the numbers:

6, 10, 12, 8, 13, 13, ...

the output would be: 10, 12, 13, ...

(5) An algorithm is required to input a series of three or more numbers. The first two numbers will be a lower and upper limit respectively and the algorithm is to output the total of all of the following numbers which fall between these two limits. The numbers end with a value of 999 which is not to be included in the calculations.

For example, for the following series of numbers:

10, 30, 16, 4, 42, 10, 25, 30, 999

the answer would be: 41 (i.e., 16 + 25).

(6) An array holds 100 numbers. An algorithm is required to output the number of times the value zero occurs in the array.

(7) An algorithm is required to calculate the factorial of any given positive number.

   The factorial of a number, X, is calculated as:

```
if X = 0,
   X! (factorial X) = 1
if X > 0
   X! = 1 * 2 * 3 * .... * X
```

   Hence, 4! = 1 * 2 * 3 * 4 = 24

Your algorithm is to accept X from a terminal operator and display X!

(8) An algorithm is required to read a series of numbers and to count the number of times a number is followed by an exact multiple of itself, e.g., 3 followed by 12 or 5 followed by 15. The series will end with the number 0. At the end of the input values, the accumulated counter is to be output.

   For example, if the following numbers were input:

   4, 13, 3, 9, 36, 5, 15, 7, 21, 70, 0

the counter would be output as 4
(3 and 9, 9 and 36, 5 and 15, 7 and 21).

(9) An algorithm is required to print a depreciation schedule for an asset such as a motor vehicle. The algorithm is to accept from a terminal operator the value of the asset and the annual rate of depreciation (expressed as a percentage). The depreciation calculation to be used is a reducing balance method whereby the depreciation for each year is calculated as a percentage of the initial value of the asset less the accumulated depreciation to date.

   The following example should illustrate the method to be used:

   Input: $5000, 10%

   Output:

Year	Depreciation for year	Asset value at end of year
1	500	4500
2	450	4050
3	405	3645

and so on.

The algorithm must terminate when the value of the asset at the beginning of a year has been reduced to less than 15% of its original value.

(10) An algorithm is required to input a series of numbers, their value being from 1 to 5 inclusive. The algorithm is to output the frequency of occurrence of each number. The series ends with a value of 999.

For example, for the series:

1, 4, 3, 5, 1, 3, 4, 1, 5, 4, 999

the output would be: 1 : 3
2 : 0
3 : 2
4 : 3
5 : 2

(11) Write an algorithm to read a series of positive integers, the last being 99, and place in ANSWER the length of the longest run of sequential values. For example, if the input was:

3, 5, 15, 20, 1, 9, 16, 35, 82, 46, 39, 58, 99

the result placed in ANSWER should be 5 (i.e., the sequence 1, 9, 16, 35, 82).

(12) An algorithm is required to calculate a repayment schedule for a loan.

Input data will consist of:

Principal	—the amount to be borrowed
Interest Rate	—the annual rate of interest charged on the loan.
Monthly Repayment	—the amount, consisting of principal and interest, to be repaid each month.

Interest is to be calculated monthly on the balance of the principal outstanding. The amount by which the principal is reduced each month is the difference between the Monthly Repayment and the interest charge for that month.

Your algorithm should:
 (i) accept the input data from a terminal operator;

(ii) check that the Monthly Repayment is in fact sufficient to cover the interest charge and allow for a reduction of the principal each month; and

(iii) print a listing containing, for each month;

Month Number
Monthly Repayment
Interest Paid
Principal Repaid
Balance of Principal Remaining.

(Remember that for the last month, the total to be paid may be less than the standard Monthly Repayment.)

(13) Two arrays, ARRAY1 and ARRAY2, each have 50 elements containing positive integers in no particular sequence. Write an algorithm to place in COUNTER the number of elements in ARRAY1 which contain a value which matches a value in one of the elements of ARRAY2.

(14) An array holds 50 numbers. All of the numbers are greater than zero and many of the values are repeated several times in the array. An algorithm is required to output the value which occurs most often. In the case of a tie, output any one of the tied values.

For example, for the following subset of the numbers:

10, 8, 6, 10, 3, 8, 17, 6, 25, 8, ...

the most often occurring value is: 8.

2 Procedures and data

2.1 Introduction

In the previous chapter, all of the algorithms examined were sufficiently simple to be able to be expressed as a single procedure. Very few, if any, real programs are that straightforward.

A typical working program will consist of some hundreds or thousands of statements and it is essential to break the total procedure required into smaller modules. This 'decomposition' is required both for ease of understanding and efficiency of operation and maintenance.

In this chapter we will look at algorithms which consist of several modules, or procedures, and consider the factors which influence their design.

2.2   Rationale for modularity

To provide a focus for the concepts involved in algorithm decomposition, consider the case of a payroll program. Ignoring, for the moment, the fact that real payroll systems will normally comprise a large number of interrelated programs to process the data involved, our program will be one in which data is entered relating to the period worked by our employees, pay and tax calculations are made and pay slips are printed to accompany the employees' wages.

It would be possible to encompass all of those tasks in a single algorithm consisting of one very large module. However, the subsequent reader of the algorithm would find considerable difficulty in determining whereabouts in the procedure certain checks were made or calculations done. Amending the algorithm to incorporate, for example, a new method of paying overtime or a new tax formula would be an extremely onerous task. Making use of some of the sections of the algorithm in other similar programs would be virtually impossible. For all of these reasons, the construction of our single payroll procedure would be a disaster.

There are a number of criteria to guide a programmer in the decomposition of a problem into smaller self-contained procedures:

(1) *Ease of understanding*: The text in this book is broken into chapters, sections and paragraphs to enable the material to be understood and digested in identifiable portions. A reader may choose a single portion of the text and strive to understand that alone without having to be burdened with the remainder of the material. An author may choose to amend, enhance or replace a single section without having to consider the book in its entirety.

There is a considerable amount of journalism involved in writing programs. The purpose of the programmer's code is not only to instruct an electronic device on how to solve a problem. It is also to inform future programmers (including the original author) as to how the problem was solved. If another programmer is unable to understand the code, the program will become a liability rather than an asset to its users.

In the interest of ease of understanding, each program module should be small enough to be comprehended by a subsequent maintenance programmer and should deal with a single task in the operation of the program. For example, in our payroll program, one would expect individual procedures involved with such tasks as:

- inputing the employees' data on hours worked, rates of pay, etc.;
- computing overtime or penalty loadings;
- calculating the taxation deduction;
- printing the pay slips.

(2) *Efficiency of maintenance*: To some extent, this goes hand-in-hand with ease of understanding. If a maintenance programmer is able to understand what a program does and how it is done, the task of maintenance is much simplified. However, other points to consider are:

- Each module, or procedure, must relate to a single, self-contained task.
- Each procedure must be self-explanatory in its operation or must contain sufficient comments to enable it to be understood.
- No procedure should have any side-effect on any other procedure, i.e., it should accomplish its own task and do nothing more.
- Each procedure should be as isolated as possible from the rest of the program and have clear lines of communication with its 'manager'. (This will be dealt with in more detail when the scope of data is discussed.)

The test of success in this aspect of module design is that a procedure, such as the tax formula in our payroll example, should be able to be removed and replaced by an amended procedure (i.e., a different set of tax calculations) without any amendments being required to the other sections of the program.

An excellent practical example of this in engineering terms is our ability to remove and replace a faulty car battery without having to consider whether this will have some unforeseen effects on, say, the gearbox or clutch assembly. The function of the battery is clearly defined (to provide a source of electric current) and its interface with the rest of the car is also clearly understood (the two terminal leads). Given these design criteria, the maintenance can be carried out by someone who knows next to nothing about the other operations of the car.

(3) *Elimination of redundancy*: Many programs contain functions which are common to a number of separate tasks. For example, our payroll data may contain the date of the start of the pay period, the date of the end of that period and the date on which the pay was to be distributed to the employees. Each of these dates would need to be checked to ensure that it was a valid calendar date, i.e., month from 1 to 12 and the day valid for that month. It should be obvious that we do not want to have to code three separate date check procedures. We will need a single date check procedure to which we can pass the three dates in turn and which will validate each one and indicate whether or not it is acceptable.

Any task which is performed more than once in a program should be the subject of a separate procedure. This procedure should be written in a sufficiently generalised manner as to be able to cope with its several invocations providing that, at each calling, it is given enough information to determine its precise operation at that time.

A practical example of this on a large scale is a file sorting program. Such a program can be called to sort any file provided that, at each calling, it is told such information as the name of file, the size of the records, the size and position of the sort key(s) and the direction of the sort.

(4) *Reusable code*: Tasks are not only commonly repeated within one program, they are common to number of programs. The date check procedure referred to above would be found in a large percentage of all commercial programs. The extension of the principle of making it reusable in a single program is that of making it reusable among several programs. Typically, a programming organization will have a library of such common procedures which may be copied into any program which requires that task to be done. This places an additional responsibility on the author of such procedures to ensure that the task is encapsulated into a module comprising its own data and procedures and which can be incorporated into any program requiring that function.

2.3   Data in programs

So far we have concentrated on the principles of constructing the procedural aspect of an algorithm. The data items used by the algorithm have been somewhat secondary in importance and merely introduced when needed by the procedure.

As Niklaus Wirth, one of the co-designers of the language Pascal, stated in the title of his book, *Programs = Algorithms + Data Structures*. The study of programming is of necessity as much concerned with the understanding of the nature and structure of data as it is with the structure and logic of algorithms. Programs are written to process data, and the programmer must have a clear understanding of this, the program's raw material.

Most formal programming languages require the names of data items to be declared prior to their use in the algorithm. In addition to their names, the type of data which they will contain must normally be declared. Once this type has been declared, any attempt by the program to assign to that item data of a different type will be regarded as an error and may result in the premature termination of the program. This principle is referred to as 'data typing' and is a key feature of most current programming languages.

Data within programs may be used as single items, such as counters and totals, or as group items, such as arrays and records. It will be profitable at this stage to examine some of the more important aspects of each of these categories.

2.4   Elementary items

Elementary, or single, data items may be considered under a number of headings.

Type

Although some contemporary languages allow programmers to invent their own data types and define their related operations, there are a number of traditional data types found in most languages:

(1) *Integer*: Integers are numeric data items which are positive or negative whole numbers, for example, 1, 47, −193. Some programming languages place restrictions on the magnitude of integers which may be used in instructions. These restrictions are usually dependent on the size of the memory location of the computer on which the language may run.

   Integers may be held within the computer's memory as a pure binary number or in a coded format such as ASCII, EBCDIC, BCD or packed decimal. Although the method of internal storage may affect the efficiency of a program, it will not have any bearing on the results of the use of such data items.

(2) *Fixed point*: Fixed point data items are numbers which have an embedded decimal point but are essentially held within the computer in the same representation as for integers. For example, in translating an instruction involving the multiplication of an item by a fixed point value of 1.5, a compiler would typically generate the code necessary to multiply by an integer value of 15 and divide by the scaling factor of 10. Because whole decimal numbers can be represented with greater accuracy than fractions by a computer which works internally in binary, fixed point representation will give more accurate results to computations than will floating point representation.

(3) *Real*: Real, or floating point, data items are numbers which are held as binary fractions by a computer. The numbers are reduced to a normalized form consisting of a mantissa and an exponent, for example:

Number	Mantissa	Exponent
12.3 $(=0.123 \times 10^2)$	.123	2
123000 $(=0.123 \times 10^6)$	.123	6
.000123 $(=0.123 \times 10^{-3})$	.123	−3

Floating point representation of data is used to overcome the restrictions placed on the magnitude of numbers by the size of a computer's memory locations; however, they do not give the same precision of arithmetic because of the inability of the binary numbering system to represent a large proportion of decimal fractions as exact binary values (just as 1/3 cannot be represented exactly as a decimal fraction).

Another problem that affects the accuracy of floating point numbers is that of round-off errors occurring during arithmetic operations or because of the restriction placed on the number of bits allocated to hold the value of the number at any time during the execution of a program. The problem may be appreciated by using decimal values (for ease of illustration) and considering a situation in which only five digits are permitted for holding the mantissa of any floating point number.

In such a case, it is obvious that any value requiring more than five digits must be stored as an approximation. Hence, the value 247308 must be held as a mantissa of .24731 (after rounding) and an exponent of 6. The value will therefore be used in the program as equivalent to 247310. The round-off error so caused is an absolute error of 2 (247310 − 247308) and a relative error of 0.000008 (2/247308). This relative error is certainly small but several such errors taken together in a program or multiplied by large factors may result in a significant loss of accuracy.

Such errors may also occur as a result of arithmetic operations on values with differing numbers of fractional places. For example, consider the addition 1234.5 + 0.031627. Given the suggested limitation of a five-digit mantissa, this addition would become (.12345, 4) + (.31627, −1) where, in each case, the first value in the parentheses is the normalized mantissa and the second is the exponent. In order to achieve the same effect as the alignment of decimal points when performing the addition manually, the two exponents in the floating point addition must be made equal at the larger value. This will mean an adjustment to the mantissa of the value for which the exponent is altered. The addition now becomes (.12345, 4) + (.0000031627, 4). This would produce an answer, again restricted by the five-digit limit on the mantissa, of (.12345, 4) which is equivalent to the value 1234.5. Given that the true value of the result would have been 1234.531627, the absolute error is .031627 and the relative error is .000026 (.031627/1234.531627).

Once again the absolute and relative errors are small, but the multiplier effect of using such values in repetitive calculations and/ or in combination with other such values may result in an error which becomes significant to the result of the operation of a program.

(4) *Character*: Character data, sometimes referred to as 'string' data, may consist of any digits, letters or symbols which the internal coding system (e.g., ASCII, EBCDIC) of the computer is capable of representing. Many programming languages require character data to be enclosed by quotation marks when used in instructions, for example: PRINT 'HAPPY NEW YEAR'.

(5) *Boolean*: Boolean data items are used as status indicators (flags, switches) and may contain only one of two possible values: True or False. It is immaterial to the programmer what the internal representations of True and False are. The only allowable operations on Boolean items, sometimes called logical items, are setting them to True or False and testing them for those values.

Usage

There are two basic methods of using data items in a program:

(1) *Constants*: A constant is a specific value or character string used explicitly in an operation, for example:

```
multiply . . . by 47.5
add 1 to . . .
if . . . = 13
print 'PLEASE INPUT TODAY'S DATE'
```

(2) *Variables*: A variable is a symbolic name assigned to a data item by the programmer. The actual location in the computer's memory used to hold that item is immaterial and its contents vary from time to time as a result of the program's operation, for example:

```
add . . . to TOTAL
if RECORD_TYPE = . . .
print MESSAGE
```

2.5   Data aggregates

Data aggregates, or groupings, may be classified as hierarchical or tabular, the usual categories being:

(1) *Files*: A file is a collection of logical entities, or records, relating to one aspect of a computer system; for example, customers, products, motor vehicles, invoices, and so on. Records may be accessed by serially reading through the file, starting at the first record, or by directly locating a required record, depending on the storage medium used.

(2) *Records*: A record is a collection of elementary items, or fields, comprising one logical entity, that is, one customer, one product, one motor vehicle, and so on. The elementary items may be of differing types and sizes and can be accessed through a unique name assigned by the programmer. In addition, some programming languages allow the assignment of a symbolic name to the record as a whole.

(3) *Arrays*: An array, or table, is a collection of elementary items, each of which is the same type, has the same size and is accessed by the same name. Items in a table are distinguished from one another by the use of a subscript or index indicating the position of the element in the array, for example:

ITEM (6), ELEMENT (23)

The subscript may be a variable and may then be used to access any item within the valid bounds of the array, for example:

ITEM (COUNTER), ELEMENT (INDEX)

(4) *Strings*: A string is essentially a stream of characters containing no inherent internal structure. A reader, for example, may look at the character string ITISWETONTHEMAT and discern several discrete words. The separation is from the reader's recognition of character patterns forming certain words rather than from any indication within the character string itself.

   For a program to effect the same separation, it would need to have a dictionary of words with which it matched the characters in the string. Such a program may come to the conclusion that the words contained in the string are IT IS WE TON THEM AT.

2.6   Data declaration and typing

From this point onwards, the specification of an algorithm will contain a formal declaration of the names and types of all variables used within it. This procedure will introduce a further degree of formality to the specification of a program and will assist in the transition from pseudocode to most programming languages.

   The data items will be declared in a section of the algorithm headed 'local data' and the procedure will be enclosed within a 'begin . . . end' pair.

For example, a restatement of Example 1.7 would now appear as:

```
Total and Average
   local data
        COUNTER_A, COUNTER_B, TOTAL, INTEGER: integer
        AVERAGE : real
   begin
        read 1st number and place in COUNTER_A and COUNTER_B
        TOTAL = 0
        while Counter_A > 0
            read INTEGER
            TOTAL = TOTAL + INTEGER
            COUNTER_A = COUNTER_A − 1
        end-while
        if COUNTER_B > 0
            AVERAGE = TOTAL/COUNTER_B
        else
            AVERAGE = 0
        end-if
        print TOTAL and AVERAGE
   end
```

In this example the **local data** consist of four items declared to be integers and one as a real, or floating-point, item. As discussed earlier in this chapter, other types could have been character or boolean.

2.7   Parameters and the scope of data

As stated earlier in this chapter, only extremely simple algorithms consist of a single procedure. The vast majority of programs are constructed from a number of task-orientated procedures. In the course of performing its operations, a module may call upon the services of a subordinate module (via a **do** pseudocode construct) to help in its required task. This called module may in turn call upon a further subordinate and so on. This 'nesting' of called procedures, or subroutines, is the means by which a procedural hierarchy is created within a program.

The question which now arises is whether a called, subordinate, procedure has access to the same data items which were declared in the calling procedure. If lower level procedures do have access to data declared at higher levels, that data is referred to as 'global' data. Data items which are accessable only by the procedures in which they were declared are referred to as 'local' data.

For the purpose of our pseudocode, global data for any set of procedures will be declared before the first of those procedures. This will reinforce the concept that such data does not belong to any one of those procedures but is available to all of them. Global variables will not need to be passed as parameters between procedures as all procedures automatically have access to whichever of the global variables they need.

In the interest of module reusability and ease of maintenance, data should normally be declared as local rather than global. The range of procedures to which a particular data item is accessable is known as the 'scope' of that data item.

Given that the scope of most data will be limited to the procedure in which it was declared, a means must exist by which data may be passed between calling and called procedures in order to be processed. This passing mechanism is effected by means of 'parameters'. Parameters are data items transferred from a calling module to its called, subordinate module at the time of the call. When the subordinate module terminates and returns control to its caller, the values in the parameters are transferred back to the calling procedure.

There are a variety of ways by which individual programming languages implement the mechanics of this parameter passing operation and these are discussed in Chapter 14. For the purpose of developing algorithms in pseudocode, it will be assumed that the contents of all parameter variables are passed from the calling to the called procedure at the time of the subroutine call and returned again, altered or not as the case may be, when control is passed back to the caller.

An extremely important concept to note in relation to the scope of data is that each time a procedure is invoked, its local data items are re-initialised. This means that procedures have no 'memory' from one invocation to another. Any item of data that needs to be remembered from one invocation of a procedure to the next must be stored at a higher level. This means that such items must be held in the calling procedure and passed as parameters or must be held as global data.

Therefore, each procedure call must consist of the name of the called procedure together with a list of any parameters passed to the called routine. The called routine will have, following its name, a list of parameters which it expects to receive from its caller. The names which these respective procedures give to the parameters need not be the same (although it helps reader comprehension if they are) but their number and type must be identical. In the interest of simplicity, an exception will be made to this principle of matching parameters by position rather than name in the case of global data. For the purpose of our pseudocode, global data must be given the same name in all procedures in which they are accessed.

Consider the following, somewhat artificial, example:

Example 2.1

A program is required to accept pairs of integers from an operator at a terminal and to display their sum and average. The program is to terminate when a pair of zero values is entered. For example:

INPUT	OUTPUT
10, 20	30, 15.0
14, 37	51, 25.5
0,0	

```
Total and Average
    local data
        NUMBER1, NUMBER2, SUM : integer
        AVERAGE : real
    begin
        input NUMBER1, NUMBER2
        while NUMBER1 not = 0
            or NUMBER2 not = 0
                SUM = NUMBER1 + NUMBER2
                do Compute Average (SUM, AVERAGE)
                output SUM, AVERAGE
                input NUMBER1, NUMBER2
        end-while
        stop
    end

Compute Average (SUM, AVERAGE)
    local data
        SUM : integer
        AVERAGE : real
    begin
        AVERAGE = SUM / 2
    end
```

Note that the called routine could have been written:

```
Compute Average (X, Y)
    local data
        X : integer
        Y : real
    begin
        Y = X / 2
    end
```

The passing of parameter values depends only on the position of the parameters within their respective lists. Hence, in the second example of

Compute Average above, SUM would be equated with X and AVERAGE with Y. The result will be the same as for the prior example but the readability has suffered.

In the above example, when Compute Average is called for the first time, there has been no assignment of any value to the variable AVERAGE within the Total and Average procedure. Therefore, the value passed to the AVERAGE (or Y) parameter in the called routine is indeterminate.

The following series of examples should illustrate the procedure involved in constructing algorithms composed of several modules. They will also illustrate the use of a 'value =' clause to assign a constant value to a local or global data item. This value will be permanently associated with that item for the duration of the program. This technique of assigning a descriptive name to a constant within a program will be discussed further in Chapter 5. It must be emphasized that these assigned values are not merely initial values which may then be altered as required during the running of the program. The use of the 'value =' construct is to give a name to a value which will be a constant throughout the operation of the program.

Example 2.2

A program is required to accept a group of three integers from an operator at a terminal and to output these numbers sorted into ascending order. The program will terminate when all three input numbers are zero.

For example:

INPUT	OUTPUT
6, 13, 2	2, 6, 13
79, 0, 34	0, 34, 79
0, 0, 0	

```
Process Numbers
    local data
        NUMBER1, NUMBER2, NUMBER3: integer
    begin
        input NUMBER1, NUMBER2, NUMBER3
        while NUMBER1 not = 0
            or NUMBER2 not = 0
            or NUMBER3 not = 0
            do Sort (NUMBER1, NUMBER2, NUMBER3)
            output NUMBER1, NUMBER2, NUMBER3
            input NUMBER1, NUMBER2, NUMBER3
        end-while
        stop
    end
```

Sort (LOW, MID, HIGH)
    local data
        LOW, MID, HIGH : integer
    begin
        if MID < LOW
            do Swap (MID, LOW)
        end-if
        if HIGH < MID
            do Swap (HIGH, MID)
        end-if
        if MID < LOW
            do Swap (MID, LOW)
        end-if
    end
Swap (LEFT, RIGHT)
    local data
        LEFT, RIGHT, HOLD: integer
    begin
        HOLD = LEFT
        LEFT = RIGHT
        RIGHT = HOLD
    end

Example 2.3

A program is required to input 10 integers from an operator at a terminal and to output a counter of the number of those integers whose value is greater than the average value of the input numbers. For example:

```
INPUT:     15, 6, 32, 18, 3, 48, 13, 1, 27, 20
           (Average = 183 / 10 = 18.3)
OUTPUT:    4 (i.e., the numbers 32, 48, 27, 20)
```

global data
    NUMBER (10) : integer array
    ARRAY_SIZE : integer, value = 10

Process Numbers
    local data
        INDEX, COUNTER : integer
        AVERAGE : real
    begin
        INDEX = 1
        while INDEX not > ARRAY_ SIZE
            input NUMBER (INDEX)
            INDEX = INDEX + 1
        end-while
        do Calculate Average (AVERAGE)
        COUNTER = 0
        INDEX = 1

```
    while INDEX not > ARRAY_SIZE
        if NUMBER (INDEX) > AVERAGE
            COUNTER = COUNTER + 1
        end-if
        INDEX = INDEX + 1
    end-while
    output COUNTER
    stop
end


Calculate Average (AVERAGE)
    local data
        TOTAL, INDEX : integer
        AVERAGE : real
    begin
        TOTAL = 0
        INDEX = 1
        while INDEX not > ARRAY_SIZE
            TOTAL = TOTAL + NUMBER (INDEX)
            INDEX = INDEX + 1
        end-while
        AVERAGE = TOTAL / ARRAY_SIZE
    end
```

The array NUMBER was declared as a global variable to save the necessity to create a further array in the Calculate Average subroutine and transfer the contents of the two arrays back and forth. In the above example, while each of the procedures will create its own separate variable INDEX, they will share the common array NUMBER between them.

Example 2.4

A program is required to process a file containing details of students enrolled in a college. Each student record contains an identification number, the student's name and the codes of up to four subjects in which that student is enrolled. The program is to print each student's name together with a counter of the number of subjects in which the student is enrolled. If a student is enrolled in fewer than four subjects, the unused subject codes will be blank. The file ends with a standard end-of-file sentinel. For example:

```
INPUT                                      OUTPUT
1423 JONES SCI1,  LAW1,  ART2, MTH1        JONES 4
1796 LEE    LAW2, HST2,        ,           LEE   2
1810 WHITE MTH1,  SCI2, LAW2,              WHITE 3
1937 HUNT  LAW3,        ,       ,          HUNT  1
e-o-f
```

```
global data
    STUDENT : record of
            ID : integer
        NAME : character
    SUBJECT (4) : character array

    ARRAY_SIZE : integer, value = 4
```

Student Enrollments
```
    local data
        COUNTER : integer
        EOF : boolean
    begin
        do Read Next Student (EOF)
        while EOF = false
            do Count Subjects (COUNTER)
            print NAME, COUNTER
            do Read Next Student (EOF)
        end-while
        stop
    end
```

Read Next Student (EOF)
```
    local data
        EOF : boolean
    begin
        read STUDENT
        if end-of-file is encountered
            EOF = true
        else
            EOF = false
        end-if
    end
```

Count Subjects (COUNTER)
```
    local data
        COUNTER, INDEX : integer
    begin
        COUNTER = 0
        INDEX = 1
        while INDEX not > ARRAY_SIZE
            if SUBJECT(INDEX) not = blanks
                COUNTER = COUNTER + 1
            end-if
            INDEX = INDEX + 1
        end-while
    end
```

As for the array in the preceeding example, the record structure in this
example is declared as a global variable. Its contents are shared by the
main Student Enrollments procedure and both of the called subroutines.
The Count Subjects procedure needs to access only the array of subject
codes with the record.

Example 2.5

Construct an algorithm to check the validity of a calendar date, that is:

(1) Check that the month lies between 1 and 12; and
(2) Check that the day is correct for the month concerned, including a leap year check for February.

The algorithm assumes that the date to be validated is in the format DDMMYYYY, for example, 25041983 and the three components DD, MM and YYYY are separately accessible.

If the date is found to be correct, ERROR_FOUND will be set to a value of false; otherwise it will be set to a value of true.

Note: A leap year is one which is exactly divisible by four. Century years, however, are only leap years if they are exactly divisible by 400. Hence, 1900 was not a leap year but 2000 will be.

```
Date Validation (DD,MM,YYYY, ERROR_FOUND)
    local data
        DD,MM,YYYY,LAST_DAY : integer
        ERROR_FOUND,LEAP_YEAR : boolean
    begin
        ERROR_FOUND = false
        case of MM :
            4, 6, 9, 11 : LAST_DAY = 30
            1, 3, 5, 7, 8, 10, 12 : LAST_DAY = 31
            2 : do Check Leap Year (YYYY,LEAP_YEAR)
                if LEAP_YEAR = true
                    LAST_DAY = 29
                else
                    LAST_DAY = 28
                end-if
            else : ERROR_FOUND = true
        end-case
        if ERROR_FOUND = false
            if DD < 1
            or DD > LAST_DAY
                ERROR_FOUND = true
            end-if
        end-if
    end


    Check Leap Year (YYYY,LEAP_YEAR)
        local data
            YYYY,QUOTIENT, REMAINDER : integer
            LEAP_YEAR : boolean
```

```
begin
    LEAP_YEAR = false
    QUOTIENT = YYYY / 400
    REMAINDER = YYYY - (400 * QUOTIENT)
    if REMAINDER = 0
        LEAP_YEAR = true
    else
        QUOTIENT = YYYY / 100
        REMAINDER = YYYY - (100 * QUOTIENT)
        if REMAINDER > 0
            QUOTIENT = YYYY / 4
            REMAINDER = YYYY - (4 * QUOTIENT)
            if REMAINDER = 0
                LEAP_YEAR = true
            end-if
        end-if
    end-if
end
```

In this example, the main procedure, Date Validation is itself a called subroutine. Any program wishing to make use of this to check the validity of a calendar date would need to provide the day (DD), month (MM) and year (YYYY) at the time of calling this routine and would receive in return a True or False response in ERROR_FOUND.

2.8   Conclusion

At this point we have developed a technique of specifying complex procedures and the data on which they operate. It is essential that programmers be able to describe an algorithm to solve a problem independent of the syntax of a particular programming language. One needs to be able to think **into** a programming language and not be restricted to thinking **in** one.

The essential principles for algorithm design as they have been developed so far are:

(1) All procedures must consist only of the constructs of sequence, selection and iteration.
(2) Complex procedures must be decomposed into smaller modules each centered around one specific task.
(3) The communication between modules is effected by means of parameters passed when the subordinate procedure is called.
(4) Data in programs may be local or global. Keep as much data as possible local to its own procedure rather than shared globally.

If these principles are adhered to at a pseudocode level, the subsequent transformation of the algorithm into a programming language becomes a minor task in the development of a program.

2.9   Review questions

(1) Using decimal values and a convention of holding a mantissa in four digits, calculate the absolute and relative errors associated with the following:
   (a) storing the values 10673, 23.9187, 0.039186
   (b) performing the additions
      3 478.6 + 1.39824
      2 506 + 8.206

(2) An array contains 100 integer values. An algorithm is required to place in COUNTER a count of the number of those integers which are greater than the average value of all of the integers.

(3) A file contains details of students enrolled in a college. Each student's record consists of their name, ID number, home address and term address. The term address allows for the recording of an away-from-home address during teaching periods for country and overseas students. This item is blank for most students' records.
   A program is required to read this file and print a report with a line for each student containing the student's ID number, name and home address. A second line is to be printed containing the term address of any student for whom that item is not blank. A blank line is to separate students' entries from each other in the report.
   The report is to allow for a maximum of 50 lines per page, including the blank, spacing lines. Each page is to be numbered and suitably headed. If a student's entry requires two lines and there is insufficient room left on the current page, the program is to skip to a new page and print both lines together.
   Write the pseudocode for the program to produce the report.

(4) An organization has a file of sales transactions which have accumulated during a calendar month. Each transaction record contains the customer's account number, the value of the sale and a code indicating whether the customer is local (code = 1) or interstate (code = 2). The file has been sorted into ascending sequence of account number.
   Because there may be several transactions on the file for any customer, a program is required to read the sales records and create

two output files, one containing only local sales and the other containing only interstate sales. On each of these files there is to be only one record for any customer. This record is to contain the customer's account number and the total of either the local or interstate sales for that customer. For example:

Input File	Output Files	
	Local	Interstate
.		
.		
1234, 200.00, 1		
1234, 150.00, 1	.	.
1234, 75.00, 2	.	.
1234, 80.00, 1	1234, 430.00	1234, 75.00
.	.	.
.	.	.

The input file ends with a standard end-of-file sentinel.

Write the pseudocode for a program which would read the input file and create the output files.

(5) The organization referred to in the previous question wishes to prepare a report listing the local sales for each month. The report is to consist of one line for each customer, containing the customer's account number, name and total sales. The Local Sales File is already in customer account number sequence. A Customer File exists, also in customer account number sequence, containing a record for each customer consisting of the customer's account number and name.

A program is required to read the Local Sales File and Customer File and produce the sales report. For this exercise, page changes and headings may be ignored and it may be assumed that every record on the Local Sales File will have a corresponding record on the Customer File (i.e., one with a matching account number). Note, however, that every Customer File record need not necessarily have a corresponding record on the Local Sales File. Both files will terminate with standard end-of-file sentinels.

Write the pseudocode for a program which will produce the report from the two input files.

(6) A file contains records relating to payroll data for employees in a factory. Each record consists of an employee name, their hourly rate of pay and seven values representing the hours worked on each of the days of that week. The first of these days is Monday and the last is Sunday. For example, one such record could appear as:

ARMSTRONG, 24.75, 8,8,8,8,10,0,0

This employee is paid at $24.75 per hour and has worked a total of 42 hours for the week.

The file ends with a standard end-of-file sentinel. An algorithm is required to read through the records in this file and to make the following checks on each record:

  (i) The name must not be blank.
 (ii) The hourly rate of pay must lie within the range $5.50 to $30.00.
(iii) The sum of the total hours worked for the week must be within the range 1 to 60. (The values for hours worked will be all integers.)
 (iv) The value of hours worked on any one day must not exceed 12.

   Records which pass all of these checks are to be written to an output file from which the employees' pay will eventually be calculated. Records failing any (or all) of the checks are to be printed on a report headed 'Payroll Records Rejected'. For the purpose of this exercise, no specific error message need accompany the rejected records.

(7) A program is required to remove duplicated values from a 100-element array containing employees' surnames. The names left in the array are to be in consecutive elements commencing at element 1 and unused elements are to be filled with blanks.

   The following is an example of the procedure using a 5-element array:

	Before		After
1	JONES	1	JONES
2	WALTERS	2	WALTERS
3	JONES	3	BENSON
4	BENSON	4	
5	WALTERS	5	

Write the pseudocode for this procedure.

(8) The following method, commonly called the Sieve of Eratosthenes, may be used to detect prime numbers (i.e., those with no factors other than themselves and 1).
(a) Set out the range of numbers from which primes are to be selected, for example:

1, 2, 3, 4, 5, 6, 7, 8, 9, 10, 11, 12, 13, 14, 15, . . .

(b)   Selecting 2 as the first prime, cross out every following second number, that is:

1, 2, 3, 4̸, 5, 6̸, 7, 8̸, 9, 1̸0̸, 11, 1̸2̸, 13, 1̸4̸, 15, . . .

(c)   Selecting the next number not crossed out, namely 3, cross out every following third number, that is:

1, 2, 3, 4̸, 5, 6̸, 7, 8̸, 9̸, 1̸0̸, 11, 1̸2̸, 13, 1̸4̸, 1̸5̸, . . .

(*Note*: Some will already be crossed out as a result of step (b).)

(d)   Continue step 3 in general terms. Select the next number not crossed out, n, and cross out every following nth number.

(e)   The numbers remaining, that is those not crossed out, are the prime numbers.

Write a pseudocode algorithm to implement the Sieve of Eratosthenes to select the primes from an array which should be initialized to hold the numbers from 1 to 1000. The primes found should be printed as they are found. You may assume that 'crossing out' a number can be effected by replacing it with zero in the array.

3　Program structure

3.1　Introduction

In this chapter, we will consider the techniques concerned with the specification of a complete program, each portion of which will be implemented by means of the procedures for algorithm design already covered.

3.2   Program development

The steps involved in the development of any program are:

(1) Define the problem.
(2) Construct a program design document or 'blueprint'.
(3) Code the program in a suitable programming language.
(4) Convert the coded program to a form able to be executed by the computer.
(5) Test the program with data designed to detect any errors in its operation.
(6) Prepare whatever additional documentation is needed to facilitate its comprehension and maintenance over a period of time.

In this chapter we will deal with the first two stages; in subsequent chapters we will cover the others. The 'blueprint' referred to in step 2 will comprise a structure diagram and its associated pseudocode algorithm.

3.3   Problem definition

Before any program can be constructed, the programmer must have a clear understanding of precisely what the program must do. To this end it is useful to focus on three aspects of the program: input, processing and output.

Input

What is the structure, content and format of the data which the program is to process? Is it to be created by the program itself, is it to be input via a terminal, is it to be read from a file on a storage device such as a disk or tape? Is the data to be in the form of a continuous stream of characters, is it to be entered item by item by an operator at a screen, is it to be read record by record from a file? Is the data to be alphanumeric or numeric, in which latter case, are the numbers to be integers or may they contain decimal fractions?

Processing

What is the algorithm required to do to the input to produce the desired output? What calculations are needed? Does the format of the data need to change between its input form and that in which it is to be output?

Do any validation checks need to be applied to the input data to ensure that it is acceptable? Will any additional data areas, such as tables or temporary storage items, need to be constructed? Do any counters or totals need to be accumulated?

Output

What is the structure, content and format of the required output? Is the data to be printed, displayed on a screen or written to a storage peripheral? In the case of printed output, what page headings or descriptive column headings are required? For terminal output, what is the format of the screen? How many lines? How many columns? For file output, what is the format of items, or fields, within records? The content of error messages also needs careful planning.

It is only after clarifying these considerations that the design of the program may be started.

3.4 Top-down decomposition

The key to program construction is the decomposition of the overall procedure into modules of a single, comprehensible task and the structuring of those modules to provide an elegant implementation of the solution to the problem. Unfortunately, there is no single formula which will decompose a complex program into individual tasks. The strategy, however, is one of top-down reduction of the processing until a level is reached where each of the individual processes consists of one self-contained task which is understandable and would be able to be programmed in relatively few instructions.

Without suggesting that a complete payroll procedure could be encompassed within the span of a single program, the following example should illustrate the process of decomposition. A payroll example has been chosen because of its familiarity to most readers.

The framework of the payroll situation is that an employee's work details are entered into the factory's computer system at the end of each week via a terminal, certain checks are made on the reasonableness of the data (e.g., is the employee on the payroll?, does the number of hours worked appear excessive?, etc.), the employee's pay is calculated and a coinage analysis made (i.e., how many $20, $10, $5 . . . 5¢, 2¢, 1¢ notes/coins are needed for the pay envelope?) and the employee's history record is updated with that week's earnings added to year-to-date totals.

A list is to be printed showing the gross pay, tax and net pay for each employee and, at the end of the procedure, totals of each of these three items, together with a total coinage analysis for the factory as a whole.

An examination of the overall problem would suggest the following main tasks, or modules:

(1) Obtain employee's work details from terminal operator.
(2) Check employee's details for reasonableness.
(3) Read employee's history record from the main payroll file (i.e., the master file).
(4) Calculate the pay and coinage analysis.
(5) Update the employee's history record.
(6) Print the employee's pay details.
(7) Print factory payroll totals.

The modules required to handle these fuctions need not be performed in the order listed and it is clear that those numbered 1 to 6 will be repeated as many times as there are employees while 7 will be performed once only. These are considerations which will emerge as the solution progresses.

The following points would need to be covered, when considering the generation of each module.

(1) Obtain employee's work details from terminal operator.
   • Obtain employee's identification (ID) number.
   • Obtain the hours worked each day of the pay period.
   • Request any additional data (e.g., bonus amounts, etc.) which may be relevant.
(2) Check employee's details for reasonableness.
   • Ensure that items which are numeric by nature do not have non-numeric contents.
   • Ensure that the hours worked in any day do not exceed some predetermined figure (e.g., 10 hours).
(3) Read employee's history record and validate the ID number.
   • Using the employee's ID number obtained from the terminal, retrieve the associated history record and display the employee's name on the terminal to enable the operator to confirm that the correct ID number has been entered.
(4) Calculate pay and coinage analysis. This module is an obvious candidate for further decomposition:
   (a) Calculate pay.
      • Determine the number of hours to be paid, taking into consideration overtime allowances, etc.
      • Compute gross pay by multiplying the payable hours by the employee's hourly rate of pay according to his or her history record.
      • Calculate tax payable. (This would be the task of a separate module which applied the current tax formula to the gross pay already calculated.)

- Calculate net pay by deducting tax from gross pay and adding or deducting any other relevant allowances or deductions.
(b) Coinage analysis.
    - Determine from the net pay the number of each denomination of note and coin needed to be placed in the employee's pay envelope.
(c) Accumulate factory totals.
    - Anticipating the needs of module 7 which must print the factory totals, these must be accumulated as each employee is dealt with.
(5) Update the employee's history record.
    - Add to the respective year-to-date fields in the employee's master record the gross pay, tax, net pay, etc. computed for this period.
    - Rewrite the history record to its file.
(6) Print the employee's pay details.
    - Print one or more lines as required for the employee's ID, name, gross pay, tax, net pay, etc.
(7) Print factory payroll totals.
    - Skip to a new page, print a suitable heading and print a summary of the gross pay, tax, net pay, etc., and a total coinage analysis for the factory as a whole.

This process of top-down decomposition must be continued until each module is clearly and simply defined and is felt to be of a size small enough to be implemented in a program in a module, the purpose and method of operation of which would be apparent to a reader other than the original author.

To some extent, developing a feeling for how much or how little constitutes a comprehensible module in a coded program is an iterative process. It presupposes some familiarity with programming languages which may be used and hence a programmer must expect to err initially in placing too much or too little work in an individual module. Although this skill will improve as more programs are written, it will always be better to err on the side of using too many simple modules than too few modules which are then too complex.

An example of this dilemma occurs in relation to searching a table in an attempt to find an item which may or may not be in it. A COBOL programmer anticipating the use of a SEARCH instruction may regard this task as a single operation. A BASIC or FORTRAN programmer, however, may regard it as a separate module to be implemented by a FOR . . . NEXT or a DO loop, respectively.

Although it is tempting to design an algorithm with a specific target language in mind, it is preferable to avoid the temptation and to describe the process in general terms which will then be capable of implementation in any programming language.

Having decomposed the problem into a number of individual modules, two further steps are required before a program may be coded. The first is the design of the structure of the program, that is, the relationship of the modules with one another in terms of their hierarchy and their sequence of operation. This will be dealt with in the following section of this chapter. The second step, to be covered in Chapter 4, is the concept of inter-module communication.

It may be profitable at this point to reconcile any seeming contradiction between the assertion in Chapter 1 that pseudocode is to be preferred over diagrammatic methods of presenting algorithms and the return in this chapter to representing programs diagrammatically. The purpose of a structure diagram is two-fold:

(1) The main purpose is to enable the programmer to arrive at an acceptable structure for a program by identifying its component modules and their mutual interaction.
(2) A by-product of the diagram is the semi-automatic generation of a program algorithm by implementing in pseudocode the control structures indicated in the structure diagram.

The strength of structure diagrams lies in the fact that by concentrating on structure, logic is derived automatically whereas the weakness of flowcharts lies in the fact that by concentrating on logic, structure is not derived at all.

3.5   Structure diagrams

Of the program design tools currently available, the best for determining and illustrating program structure is that of the structure diagram.

A structure diagram depicts a program's structure in terms of its hierarchy and operating sequence. It does not attempt to displace the design of individual algorithms as a description of the logic involved in the solution of the problem.

The diagram comprises a tree-like structure with the program name in the top-most box and each module in a box subordinate to its 'manager' or 'controller'. An iteration or loop construct is indicated by an arrow encompassing the lines of control drawn from a controller to its subordinates. A selection construct is obtained by the use of the diamond symbol traditionally used to represent decisions in flowcharts. Apart from these symbols, the only rules of interpretation are that hierarchy is represented from top to bottom and sequence is read from left to right.

Figures 3.1, 3.2, 3.3, 3.4 and 3.5 illustrate the relationship between the structure of an algorithm and the method of its implementation in a program.

Often a program contains a situation in which several actions are dependent on a single condition. The easiest means of indicating such a structure is by the introduction of an 'umbrella' operation encompassing the individual actions.Figure 3.4(b) illustrates the structure and two alternative expressions in pseudocode.

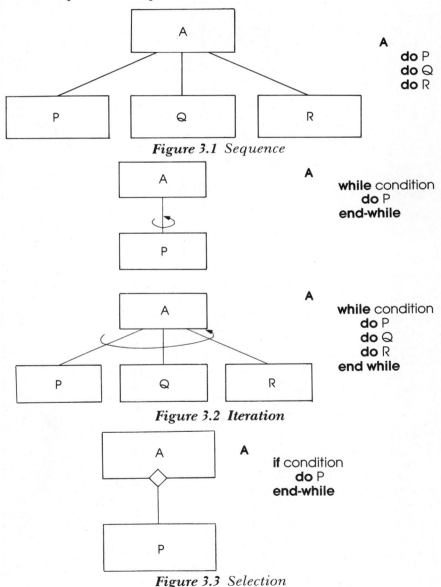

Figure 3.1 Sequence

Figure 3.2 **Iteration**

Figure 3.3 Selection

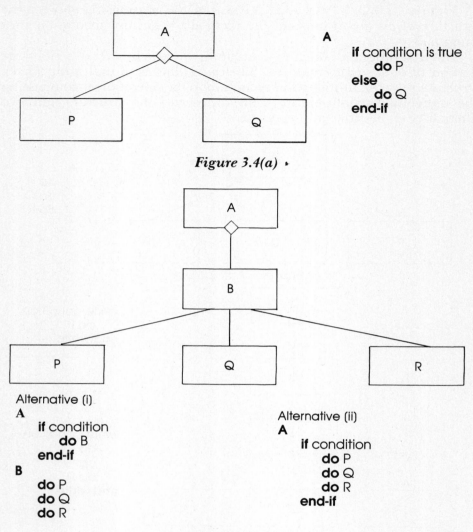

Figure 3.4(a)

Figure 3.4(b)

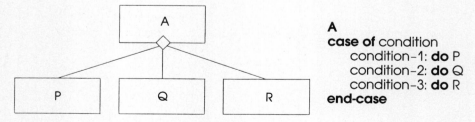

Figure 3.5

3.6   A general example

As a general example, Figure 3.6 represents the structure of an algorithm consisting of a number of modules arranged hierarchically. Such a structure may depict the solution to a complete program, as is the case in Figure 3.6, or of any portion of a program.

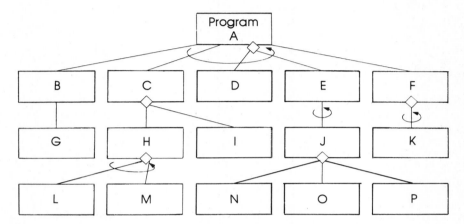

Figure 3.6

The algorithm required to implement the control structure indicated by Figure 3.6 would be:

```
Program A
    do B
    while Condition-a
        do C
        if Condition-b
            do D
        else
            do E
        end-if
    end-while
    do F
    stop

B
    .
    .
    .
    Do G
    .
    .
    .
```

```
C
    .
    .
    .
    if condition-c is true
        do H
    else
        do I
    end-if
    .
    .
    .

E
    .
    .
    .
    while condition-e
        .
        .
        .
        do J
        .
        .
        .
    end-while
    .
    .
    .

F
    .
    .
    .
    if condition-f is true
        while Condition-g
            do K
        end-while
    end if
    .
    .
    .

H
    .
    .
    .
    while condition-h
        if condition-lm is true
            do L
        else
            do M
    end-while
```

J
.
.
.

case of Condition-j
    j-1: **do** N
    j-2: **do** O
    j-3: **do** P
end-case

The principles of constructing structure diagrams and their associated algorithms are illustrated by Examples 3.1, 3.2 and 3.3.

Example 3.1: Motor vehicle enquiries

A program is required to retrieve motor vehicle registration records from a file upon receipt of a request from an operator at a terminal. The operator will supply a vehicle registration number and the program will display the details of the vehicle and its owner. An error message will be displayed if the program is unable to locate the vehicle's record.

The modules required to implement the solution are:

(1) Accept the vehicle registration number from the terminal operator.
(2) Using the registration number, attempt to retrieve the vehicle's record from its file.
(3) A successful retrieval will allow the details of the vehicle to be displayed on the screen.
(4) An unsuccessful attempt at retrieval will indicate the absence of the vehicle from the file and a suitable error message may be displayed.

On the assumption that the procedure continues until the operator initiates an abort-and-log-off procedure, Figure 3.7 illustrates a simple structure diagram for this program.

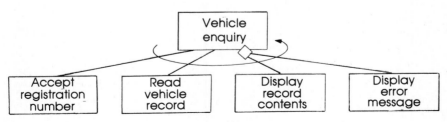

Figure 3.7

A skeleton algorithm for the implementation of this program would be constructed as:

Motor Vehicle Enquiries
    while operator is logged on
        accept vehicle registration number
        retrieve vehicle record from file
        if record is successfully read
            display record contents on terminal
        else
            display error message
        end-if
    end-while

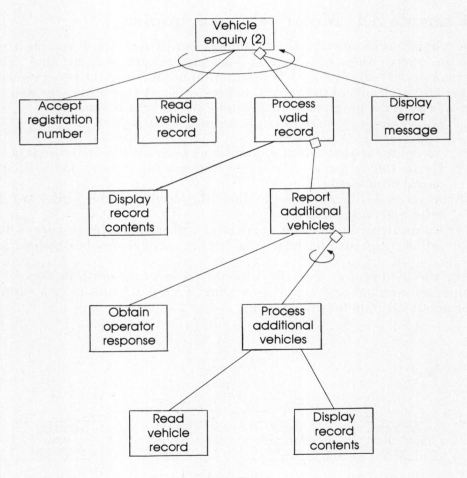

Figure 3.8

Example 3.2: Motor vehicle enquiries (continued)

The situation described in Example 3.1 is extended to cover the case in which a vehicle registration record, if retrieved successfully, may contain registration numbers of other vehicles belonging to the owner of the vehicle in the original enquiry. If this is the case, the terminal operator is to be given the option to display the details of these additional vehicles.

This will involve the addition of further processing modules:

(5) Following a successful retrieval of a vehicle's record, if the vehicle's owner has other vehicles registered in his or her name, the terminal operator must be asked whether those details are to be displayed.
(6) For each additional vehicle to be displayed (if any) there will need to be:
(a)   retrieval of the vehicle's record; and
(b)   display of the record details.

Figure 3.8 shows an amended structure diagram to reflect these additions.

The algorithm to implement the extended version of the program shown in Figure 3.8 would be:

```
global data
     VEHICLE : record
Motor Vehicle Enquiries (2)
     local data
          REGISTRATION _ NUMBER : character
begin
     while operator is logged on
          accept REGISTRATION _ NUMBER
          retrieve vehicle record from file
          if record is successfully read
               do Process Valid Record
          else
               display error message
          end-if
     end-while
end

Process Valid Record
     begin
          display record contents
          if owner has additional registered vehicles
               ask operator if further details are required
               if operator requests further details
                    while there are vehicles to report
                         retrieve vehicle record from file
                         display record contents
                    end-while
               end-if
          end-if
     end
```

Note that in this algorithm, the operations 'Retrieve vehicle record from file' and 'Display record contents' each appear in two places. Suspecting that these may each involve subsequent duplication of coding, we may have the foresight to place these operations in modules of their own and replace the current statements respectively by:

> **do** Retrieve Vehicle Record(READ _OK)
> **do** Display Record Contents

where READ _OK would be a boolean variable indicating whether or not the read was successful.

Example 3.3: Factory payroll

Before drawing a structure diagram for the payroll example used previously in this chapter, consider one modification to the algorithm given:

> As module 3, 'Read employee's history record', is to display the employee's name on the terminal for operator confirmation, it would be preferable if this operation were performed as a subordinate of module 2.

A tentative structure diagram for the problem is shown in Figure 3.9.

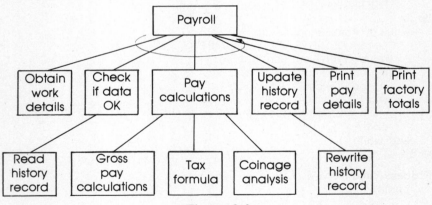

Figure 3.9

Further consideration of the diagram in Figure 3.9 reveals a weakness: there appears to be no mechanism for preventing the algorithm from proceeding to the pay calculations if the data entered via the terminal is incorrect. A better structure for the initial procedure in the algorithm is that shown in Figure 3.10. There the operator can be requested to supply an employee's details as often as is needed until the correct data is obtained.

To avoid making the overall structure diagram too complex, a separate diagram may be drawn for any portion of the problem. Hence, Figure 3.10 would be an appendix to the main diagram.

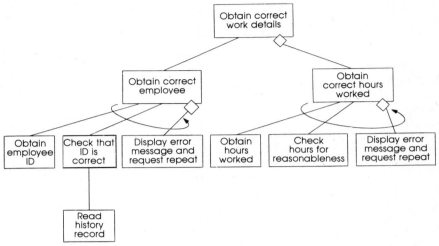

Figure 3.10

One last requirement remains to be specified before an algorithm can be constructed, and that is an answer to the question: how does the procedure terminate? Let us assume that the termination of processing occurs when the terminal operator inputs a response to the prompt for a further employee's details which indicates that no more employees remain to be processed. This could be by a blank response or a predetermined dummy employee ID as a response to the request for the next employee, for example, 99999 or −1.

This will mean that the performance of all subsequent modules will be conditional upon the operator not entering the end-of-data signal in response to the employee ID prompt.

This is now a serial processing environment and will benefit from a 'priming read' as described in Chapter 1. Figure 3.11 shows the final structure diagram for the solution of the problem.

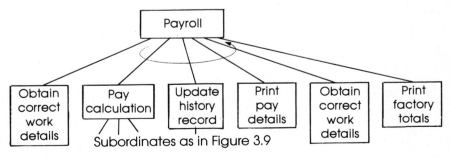

Figure 3.11

Note that the module 'Obtain correct work details' needs no elaboration on its subordinates as these are shown in an appendix as illustrated in Figure 3.10.

3.7   Skeleton pseudocode

An algorithm may now be constructed, in skeleton form (or pseudocode) to implement a solution to the problem:

```
global data
    SCREEN_DETAILS              :  record of
        EMPLOYEE_ID_SCN         :  character
        HOURS_WORKED (5)        :  integer array
        HOURLY_RATE             :  real

    EMPLOYEE                    :  record of
        EMPLOYEE_ID_REC,
        EMPLOYEE_NAME           :  character
        TOTAL_GROSS,
        TOTAL_TAX,
        TOTAL_NET               :  real

    PAY_DETAILS                 :  record of
        GROSS,
        TAX,
        NET                     :  real

    FACTORY_TOTALS             :  record of
        FACTORY_GROSS,
        FACTORY_TAX,
        FACTORY_NET             :  real

    NUMBER_OF_HOURS      :  integer, value = 5

Payroll
    local data
        END_OF_DATA         . :  boolean

begin
    END_OF_DATA = false
    do Accept Work Details (END_OF_DATA)
    while END_OF_DATA = false
        do Pay Calculation
        do Update History Record
        do Print Pay Details
        do Accept Work Details (END_OF_DATA)
    end-while
    do Print Factory Totals
    stop
end
```

Accept Work Details (END_OF_DATA)
    local data
        END_OF_DATA : boolean

    begin
        do Obtain Correct Employee (END_OF_DATA)
        if END_OF_DATA = false
            accept HOURS_WORKED from operator
            accept HOURLY_RATE from operator
        end-if

Obtain Correct Employee (END_OF_DATA)
    local data
        END_OF_DATA, VALID_ID : boolean

    begin
        VALID_ID = false
        while VALID_ID = false
           and END_OF_DATA = false
               accept EMPLOYEE_ID_SCN from operator
               if end-of-data signal is entered
                   END_OF_DATA = true
               else
                   read EMPLOYEE from file
                      using EMPLOYEE_ID_SCN as a key
                   if record is read successfully
                      VALID_ID = true
                   else
                     Ask operator to re-enter the ID number
                   end-if
               end-if
        end-while
    end

Pay Calculation
    local data
        TOTAL_HOURS, INDEX : integer
    begin
        TOTAL_HOURS = 0
        INDEX = 1
        while INDEX not > NUMBER_OF_HOURS
            TOTAL_HOURS = TOTAL_HOURS + HOURS_WORKED(INDEX)
            INDEX = INDEX + 1
        end-while
        GROSS = TOTAL_HOURS * HOURLY_RATE
        do Tax Formula (GROSS, TAX) ... not specified here
        NET = GROSS − TAX
        FACTORY_GROSS = FACTORY_GROSS + GROSS
        FACTORY_TAX = FACTORY_TAX + TAX
        FACTORY_NET = FACTORY_NET + NET
    end

Update History Record
begin
      TOTAL_GROSS = TOTAL_GROSS + GROSS
      TOTAL_TAX = TOTAL_TAX + TAX
      TOTAL_NET = TOTAL_NET + NET
      rewrite EMPLOYEE to file
end

Print Pay Details
begin
      print EMPLOYEE_ID, EMPLOYEE_NAME, GROSS, TAX, NET
end

Print Factory Totals
begin
      print FACTORY_GROSS, FACTORY_TAX, FACTORY_NET
end

3.8 Managing versus working

As we progress from the top to the bottom of the hierarchical structure of a program, we should expect to see a change in the nature of the instructions contained in the modules. The higher level modules should contain mostly 'managerial' instructions, that is, decision-making and directions to subordinates. As we move down the hierarchy, gradually more and more 'working' instructions begin to creep into the modules in the nature of calculations, movement of data, and so on. Avoid introducing working instructions too early in the hierarchy of any program. Certainly the first-level and possibly the second-level modules within a program should consist only of **do, while** and **if** statements, as shown, for example, in Figure 3.12.

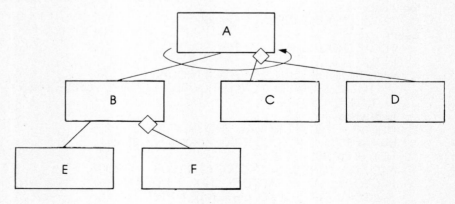

Figure 3.12

A (1st level)
    while Condition
        do B
        if Condition
            do C
        else
            do D
        end-if
    end-while
    stop

B (2nd level—as for C and D)
    do E
        .
        .   } Perhaps some minor work done
        .
    if Condition
        do F
    end-if

E (lower levels)
    .
    .
    .   } mostly working instructions
    .
    .

F
    .
    .
    .
    .

In this context, we should also avoid placing large groups of working instructions in a decision-making framework. It is much cleaner to remove the workers and place them in a module of their own, for example:

```
if Condition
    statement
       .
       .
       .
       . (group A)
       .
       .
       .
    statement
else
    statement
       .
       .
       . (group B)
       .
       .
       .
    statement
end-if
    Poor structure
```

```
if Condition
    do A
else
    do B
end-if


A
    statement
       .
       .
       .  (group A)
       .
       .


B
    statement
       .
       .
       .  (group B)
       .


    Better structure
```

3.9   Decision-making structure

A structure diagram gives a programmer an opportunity to review the decision-making structure of a program and to rearrange it, if necessary, before its implementation in code.

Two areas need to be considered in examining the control structure of any program:

(1) Aim to eliminate repetitive evaluations of any one condition, as shown, for example, in Figure 3.13. Here, Condition X is tested in three separate sections of the program. In Figure 3.14, it is tested only once.

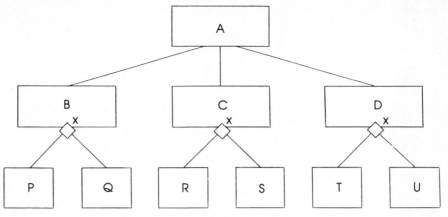

Figure 3.13 *Poor central structure*

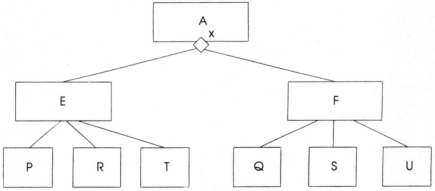

Figure 3.14 *Better control structure*

Note that the same working modules P, Q, R, S, T and U are required in each case; all that differs is the managerial control structure. In practical terms, the difference lies between the following strategies:

Strategy 1 (Poor)

Calculate Pay
    do Compute Gross
    do Compute Allowance
    do Compute Bonus

Compute Gross
    if permanent employee
        do Compute Gross for Permanent Staff
    else
        do Compute Gross for Temporary Staff
    end-if

Compute Allowance
>**if** permanent employee
>>**do** Compute Allowance for Permanent Staff
>
>**else**
>>**do** Compute Allowance for Temporary Staff
>
>**end-if**

Compute Bonus
>**if** permanent employee
>>**do** Compute Bonus for Permanent Staff
>
>**else**
>>**do** Compute Bonus for Temporary Staff
>
>**end-if**

Strategy 2 (Better)

Calculate Pay
>**if** permanent employee
>>**do** Compute Permanent Employee Pay
>
>**else**
>>**do** Compute Temporary Employee Pay
>
>**end-if**

Compute Permanent Employee Pay
>**do** Compute Gross for Permanent Staff
>**do** Compute Allowance for Permanent Staff
>**do** Compute Bonus for Permanent Staff

Compute Temporary Employee Pay
>**do** Compute Gross for Temporary Staff
>**do** Compute Allowance for Temporary Staff
>**do** Compute Bonus for Temporary Staff

In this example the nature and method of operation of the six compute modules are unaffected by the choice of either strategy. What is achieved is a neater and more maintainable control structure because of the centralization of the testing mechanism.

(2) Ensure that all processing which depends on the result of a decision is subordinate to the module in which that decision is made; see, for example, Figure 3.15.

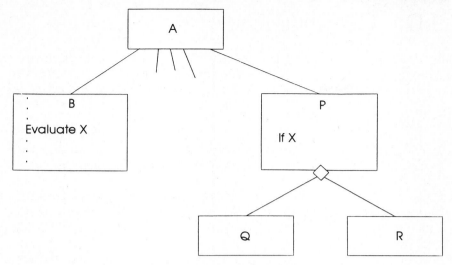

Figure 3.15 *Poor control structure*

In Figure 3.15, Condition X is evaluated in module B but the result of that evaluation is later tested in module P which may be far removed in the program from the source of the decision. Hence, a maintenance programmer amending B may fail to see the implication of some change which is made to the evaluation of Condition X and, conversely, a programmer looking at module P may fail to understand how the condition being tested was originally evaluated. In Figure 3.16, the results of the decision based on the evaluation of Condition X are made subordinate to the module (B) in which the evaluation is made and consequently can be seen related together.

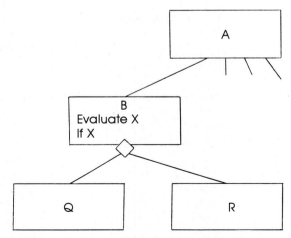

Figure 3.16 *Better control structure*

3.10 Conclusion

Given that one of the most important criteria in the assessment of any program is that of its module structure, it is extremely important to spend time in the program design stage to ensure that this criterion is met.

The steps involved are:

(1) Decompose the problem, working from the top down, into a hierarchy of modules or procedures each of which performs a single task.
(2) Draw a structure diagram which represents the hierarchy from top to bottom and indicates the sequence of operations from left to right.
(3) Indicate iteration and decision constructs within the diagram using appropriate symbols.
(4) Appraise the decision-making and control structure and redraft the hierarchy if required.
(5) Translate the structure diagram into pseudocode by a direct correspondence of pseudocode control mechanisms with those depicted in the structure diagram.

Remember that the whole procedure is iterative. Do not expect to arrive at the appropriate algorithm structure on your first attempt. Be continuously prepared to recast the hierarchy or the sequence of operations as the algorithm develops and be prepared to regroup or subdivide functions where a more effective structure would result.

3.11 Review questions

(1) An organization wants a program written to enable it to obtain selective listings of various categories of its employees. An Employee File contains a record for each employee consisting of the employee's name, classification code and annual salary.

The program is to request a classification code from an operator at a terminal. It is then to read serially through the Employee File and print a report listing all of the employees with that code. At the end of the report, the program is to print the total annual salary of the employees selected. The report is to print up to 50 employees per page, each page numbered and suitably headed (including the selected classification code).

After printing the report, the program is to return to the terminal operator and request another code for a further report. This procedure is to continue until a code of zero is input by the operator.

Draw a structure diagram for this program and write the pseudocode from which the program could be coded.

(2) An organization has a customer transaction file for which each record contains:

- customer ID number;
- current balance;
- date of last payment;
- amount of last payment.

This is a serial (sequential) file and the last record is a dummy record with an ID number of 999999.

Another file contains static information on customers:

- customer ID number;
- name and address;
- flag to indicate VIP customer.

This file is indexed on customer ID number and is accessible randomly.

A program is required to read serially through the transaction file and print reminder notices for all customers whose current balance is in excess of $500 and whose last payment was less than 10% of the current outstanding balance (e.g., one whose current balance is $700 and whose last payment was only $65). The name and address for the reminder notice is obtained by using the ID number from the transaction file to access the customer's record on the static file. If the customer is a VIP, however, no reminder notice is to be sent.

Write a pseudocode algorithm from which this program could be written.

(3) The following is a description of the computer-based checkout procedure used by a certain supermarket.

The checkout clerk enters the product code of a customer's purchase and the program uses that code as a key to retrieve directly the appropriate record from the Product File. If no such record can be found, the clerk is notified of the error and is expected to key in the code again, correctly.

If a product record is retrieved successfully, the price is displayed to the clerk and is added to the customer's total charge. In addition, the quantity-on-hand field in the product record is decremented by 1 and the product record is re-written to the Product File.

This procedure is repeated until the clerk enters a product code of zero, causing the customer's total charge to be displayed. The operator is then prompted to input the cash tendered in payment by the customer. If this is less than the purchase charge, the program displays an error message and asks the clerk to re-enter another amount otherwise the program displays the change due to the customer.

Draw a structure diagram and write the pseudocode from which this program could be coded.

4 Module design

4.1 Introduction

We have examined the means for specifying the procedure performed by individual program modules and their subsequent grouping to develop a program as an entity. This chapter is devoted to a consideration of the functions carried out by modules and the means by which they may communicate with each other.

4.2 Inter-module communication

Given that each module of a program will perform a function, the results of which will affect some or all of the other modules within the program, there must be some means by which those results may be made known to the other interested modules. There are basically two methods of module-to-module communications:

(1) communication by data items; and
(2) communication by status items.

Consider the case, discussed in Chapter 2, Example 2.5, of a module designed to check the validity of a calendar date. To communicate on a two-way basis with that module, two items must be specified:

(1) the data area holding the date to be validated; and
(2) some means of indicating whether or not the date was found to be valid.

Items used thus for communicating between various parts of a program are referred to as 'parameters' or 'arguments'.
   Parameters may have one of three functions:

(1) They may serve to pass information to a performed, or subordinate, module which may be referred to as a 'subroutine'.
(2) They may pass information back from a subroutine to its performer, or caller.
(3) They may fulfill a two-way role and contain information which is passed to the subroutine, amended in some fashion and then passed back again to the caller.

Hence, in the date validation subroutine, the date would be passed to the performed validation module and the OK/not-OK answer passed back to the calling module.
   Such communication parameters may be incorporated into a structure chart by the use of two symbols:

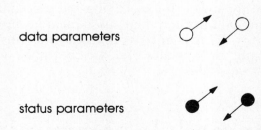

data parameters

status parameters

A structure chart incorporating the date validation procedure as part of its operations is shown in Figure 4.1

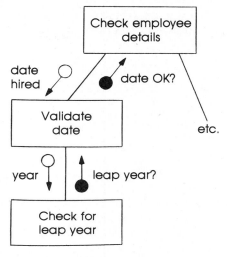

Figure 4.1

The chart indicates that the subroutine was to be used to check the validity of the date on which the employee was hired. It, in turn, calls a subroutine to which it passes the year and receives an indication of whether or not it is a leap year.

When designing algorithms and, ultimately, when writing programs, avoid using data parameters to also indicate status. In the example above, it would be possible for the subroutine to replace the date to be checked with a value of, say, zero if the date was found to be invalid. Subsequently, on return from the validation subroutine, the calling module could examine the content of the date parameter and, if a zero value was found, take this to indicate that the date was not valid.

Avoid this procedure! If a parameter is a data item by nature, let it remain a data item. Do not confuse the reader of your program by using it for another purpose entirely. In addition to the possibility of confusing the reader with, say, a date set to zero, there is the more urgent danger that if the program is amended at some later time, the amending programmer will be unaware that the date may have been set to a zero value and may rely on the original contents still being present in that item.

A status parameter should ideally contain only one of two possible values, True or False. Some programming languages reserve a separate class of variables, called logical or Boolean variables, especially for this purpose. Where such a feature is not included in the syntax of a language, the programmer should endeavour to set aside a number of variables expressly to be used as status parameters and to create two constants which represent respectively the logical value of True and False, for example: True may be the value of 1 or 'T' or 'Y' (for Yes) and False may be 0 or 'F' or 'N' (for No). The actual values used should be assigned to variables called TRUE and FALSE (or similar), and it is these symbolic names which will become the subject of instructions, not the specific values, that is:

if Date-OK = TRUE
   do . . . procedure . . .

not

if Date-OK = 1 (or 'T' etc.)
   do . . . procedure . . .

As an aside, it should be noted that there are two parameters returned from every performance of a module which is to read a record from a file and, in many cases, one which is to accept input from a screen. The more obvious of these is the data item sought; the other is a status variable which indicates whether or not the input operation was successful, that is, whether the record was unable to be read because of an end-of-file condition being reached or an invalid key (one for which no record exists on the file) being supplied to the read operation or the screen operator giving a null response to a prompt for data.

Hence, we should expect automatically to depict such an operation as shown in Figure 4.2.

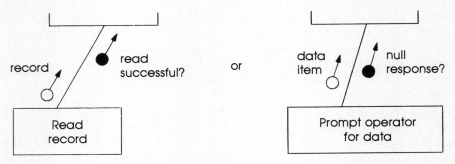

Figure 4.2

4.3   Module strength or cohesion

Module strength or cohesion is a measure of the extent to which the statements in a particular module belong together. When asked for a reason why a group of statements appears in a single module, there are several possible justifications which could be advanced, for example:

(1) The statements are all necessary to perform one particular task within the overall program structure.

(2) The statements encompass a variety of small unrelated tasks but, as these must be performed at the same time, for convenience they have all been included in a single module.

(3) The statements perform two or more related tasks which are always performed together and therefore have been placed in the same module.

These are all reasons for the inclusion of a number of statements in a single program module. The reasons become weaker, however, as we move from (1) to (3).

The prime reason for the existence of any module in a program should be that it performs a single logical task. The date validation procedure already discussed falls into this category. It emphasizes the separation of tasks by creating a subroutine to check for the occurrence of a leap year.

An example of the cohesion referred to as type (2) is the collection of tasks which one often needs to execute at the beginning of a program's operation, for example, linking data to specific files, setting counters and totals to initial values, heading pages ready for output and so on. Such actions are often placed together in an 'initialization procedure' and have no real connection with one another than that they all must be performed at that point of the program's execution.

Consider, as a further example, the case of a program which is written to run at the end of each month and print statements of overdue accounts for customers. Because it is run monthly, each run necessitates the aging of customers' debts by one period, that is, current debts become 30 days outstanding, 30 days become 60 days, and so on. Because of this, it may be tempting to include the aging procedure in the same module as the reading of the customer's record, an example of type (3) cohesion.

The problem arises here when circumstances change and the program has to be run more often than once a month. The maintenance programmer is now faced with two choices. The aging process may be removed and placed in a separate module which is executed only in the end-of-month run, as shown in Figure 4.3.

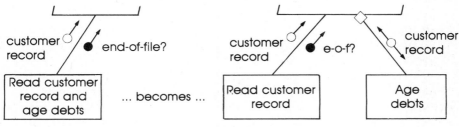

Figure 4.3

Alternatively, the single module may be retained as before and a status item passed to it which indicates whether or not the debts are to be aged this run, as shown in Figure 4.4.

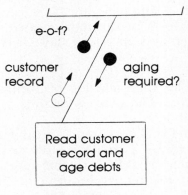

Figure 4.4

Of these two alternatives, the first (Figure 4.3) is preferred. Be very wary of passing status parameters downwards. This is an admission that the subordinate module performs more than one task (otherwise the status item would not be required) and that it would be better organized by being split into separate modules each with its own function.

4.4   Module coupling

Coupling is a measure of the interdependence between sections of a program or between a section of procedural code and one or more data items.

Consider the following example.

As part of its overall operations, a certain program is required to perform the following operations:

- Read records from a file.
- Validate certain data items in each record according to criteria for acceptance, one such item being a product ID number which is checked against valid product numbers held in a table; the table also holds the name of the product associated with each ID number.
- Print either an error message (in the case of an invalid record) or a report line containing the contents of each valid record with product ID numbers accompanied by their associated product name.

The structure diagram, in part, for the program would appear as shown in Figure 4.5.

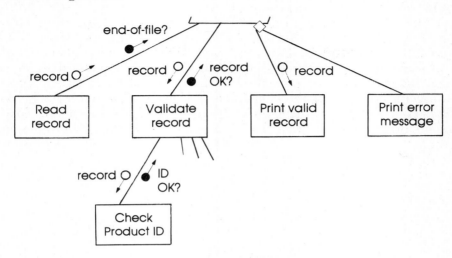

Figure 4.5

The programmer, when designing the algorithm (and later when writing the code) for the validate record procedure, specifies the procedure for checking the product ID number against those in the table as follows:

```
global data
    RECORD                      :  record
        (contents include :-)
        PRODUCT_ID_REC    :  character

Check Product ID Number(ID_FOUND)
    local data
        PRODUCT_ID(50)     :  character array
        TABLE_INDEX        :  integer
        ID_FOUND           :  boolean


    begin
        TABLE_INDEX = 1
        ID_FOUND = false
        while ID_FOUND = false
            and TABLE_INDEX not > 50
                if PRODUCT_ID_REC = PRODUCT_ID(TABLE_INDEX)
                    ID_FOUND = true
                else
                    TABLE_INDEX = TABLE_INDEX + 1
                end-if
        end-while
    end
```

Later in the program, when about to specify the procedure for the 'Print Valid Record' module, the programmer realizes that there is again the requirement to match the product ID number against its counterpart in the table in order to obtain the product name which also resides in the table. It is at this point that the programmer realizes that this task has already been accomplished in the Check Product ID Number module. On leaving that module, after locating the product referred to in the record being processed, the table subscript TABLE_INDEX was left holding the number of the element in the table at which a match was found. Given that nothing else in the program has since disturbed the contents of TABLE_INDEX, its value may be used to extract the name of the product associated with the ID number. Hence, the programmer specifies:

Print Valid Record

   .
   .
   .

   place PRODUCT_NAME (TABLE_INDEX) in line to print

   .
   .
   .

These procedures, although containing no errors of logic, have placed many restrictions on the future maintainability of that program because of several instances of coupling:

(1) Although there is no hint of it in the structure chart above, the Print Valid Record module is coupled with the Check Product ID Number module via the subscript variable TABLE_INDEX. If a subsequent amendment to the program causes the value in TABLE_INDEX to change between leaving Check Product ID Number and entering Print Valid Record, then that latter module will no longer print the correct name for any given product.

    One remedy for this would be to pass the position in the table at which the product ID was found as a formal parameter returned from the Check Product ID Number module. By making it a specified parameter and indicating it as such on the structure chart, there is less chance that a subsequent maintenance programmer will fail to recognize its significance. The passing of this parameter could be achieved by leaving TABLE_INDEX unaltered until Print Valid Record had executed or, better still, by placing the position indicated by TABLE_INDEX in a separate variable and thus releasing TABLE_INDEX for other purposes if required. The structure chart would then appear as that in Figure 4.6.

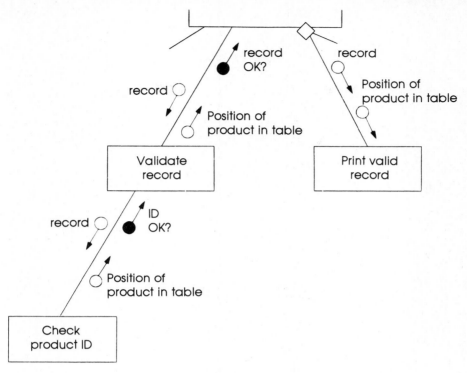

Figure 4.6

The suggested solution to this problem has introduced a further element of coupling! The operation of the Print Valid Record module now depends on the fact that Check Product ID Number uses a table as its means of validating the products. The range of products may expand to the point at which an internally stored table would be too large to tolerate in the program. The product validation may then be done via an access to a disk file to attempt to retrieve a record for the product ID number to be validated, the success or otherwise of that operation indicating whether or not the product is legitimate. In such a case, the table subscript passed as a parameter is now meaningless.

A better solution would be to pass the product name itself as the formal parameter rather than merely an indirect reference to it. This would achieve the objective of removing the necessity for the Print Valid Record module having once again to search for the product in order to know its name, and it would also make the operation of that module totally independent of whatever method the validation module needed to ascertain the validity of the product ID number.

The structure chart is now as shown in Figure 4.7.

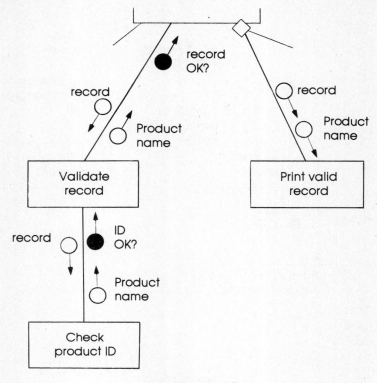

Figure 4.7

Note: The question of what the Product Name parameter contains if the validation module finds the product invalid will be considered later in this chapter.

(2) The original solution and the suggested amendments so far still suffer from a further coupling. The Check Product ID Number module is written to validate the product ID number in the record read from the file referred to in the original specification.

It is conceivable that future enhancements to the program may require a product ID number from a different source to be subjected to the same validation procedure. As it currently stands, the Check Product ID Number routine would be unable to perform the second, or subsequent, check because the statement

```
     .
     .
     .
if PRODUCT_ID_REC = PRODUCT_ID(TABLE_INDEX)
     .
     .
     .
```

restricts the procedure to operate only on the specified product ID.

A better solution would have been to pass the product ID number to be validated as a separate independent parameter to that module, for example:

```
        .
        .
        .
do Check Product ID Number(PRODUCT_ID_REC, ID_FOUND)
        .
        .
        .

Check Product ID Number(PRODUCT_TO_CHECK, ID_FOUND)
    local data
        PRODUCT_ID(50)          :  character array
        PRODUCT_TO_CHECK        :  character
        TABLE_INDEX             :  integer
        ID_FOUND                :  boolean
        TABLE_SIZE              :  integer, value = 50
    begin
        TABLE_INDEX = 1
        ID_FOUND = false
        while ID_FOUND = false
            and TABLE_INDEX not > TABLE_SIZE
                if PRODUCT_TO_CHECK = PRODUCT_ID(TABLE_INDEX)
                    ID_FOUND = true
                else
                    TABLE_INDEX = TABLE_INDEX + 1
                end-if
        end-while
    end
```

The structure chart, finally, appears as that shown in Figure 4.8.

One of the aims, then, in the design of any program module is to uncouple it from as much of its surroundings as possible. This is done by:

(1) passing as much of its required data as is possible by means of independent formal parameters rather than by designing the module to operate on data which is merely 'lying around for general use'; and

(2) writing the module as a self-contained unit which accepts any given parameters, operates on them without reliance on the functions of other sections of the program, and passes the results of its operation back to its caller again via a formal independent parameter.

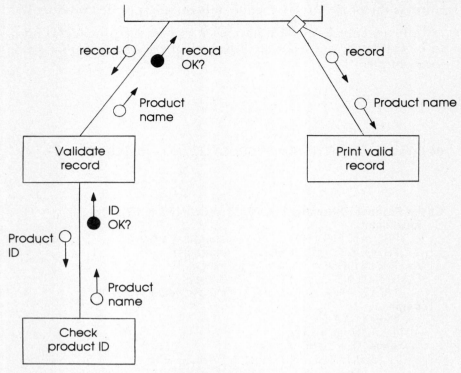

Figure 4.8

This procedure enables the function of any program module to be specified without reference to the manner in which the function is actually effected. For example, for the validation module we have been examining, a mini-specification may be written as:

Module name: Check Product ID Number
Function: To ascertain whether or not a given product ID number is a legitimate code
Input parameter: PRODUCT_TO_CHECK
                       Contains product ID number to be validated
Output parameters: ID_FOUND
                       Contains a status of True if the product ID is valid, otherwise contains a status of False
                       PRODUCT_NAME
                       Contains the name associated with a valid product ID, otherwise . . .

Notes:
(1) This specification is all one needs to make use of that module, despite no clue being given on how the module operates.

(2) A decision must be made at this point (and inserted in the specification) on what the contents of PRODUCT_NAME will be in the case of an invalid product; for example, contents may be blank, all asterisks, the words 'INVALID PRODUCT', and so on. Some definite content, however, *must* be specified.

4.5   Information hiding

One of the major concepts of software engineering is that of 'hidden intelligence' or 'information hiding'. It implies an approach to program design exemplified by the points considered in the previous section. Essentially, it states that the important feature of any program module is *what* it does not *how* it does it. Modules should be defined in terms of the function they perform and the means by which the rest of the program communicates with them, that is, their parameters. This procedure then leaves the programmer implementing the module free to choose whatever method of operation is thought best. Indeed, in the interests of efficiency or practicality (as seen previously in the case of the product ID validation), the procedure of the algorithm may be drastically changed from time to time. As long as the performed function and the communication parameters remain the same, however, there is no need for the rest of the program to be aware of any changes in procedure.

This concept imposes two restrictions on the programmer:

(1) The task module must not depend on the operation of any other section of the program.

The module performing any task must be entirely self-contained and must not rely on any feature of the program's environment outside itself, that is, any other procedural module or data which is not declared explicitly as part of the module specification.

For example, if the product ID validation module was obliged to fill PRODUCT_NAME with blanks in the case of an invalid product, it would be wrong of it to take no action at all in such a case merely because the programmer noticed that the operation of another part of the program happened to blank-fill PRODUCT_NAME before executing the validation module. The argument that PRODUCT_NAME will therefore contain blanks in the case of an invalid product simply because the validation module has not then put anything else in that data item is destroyed as soon as that other program operation, which has no connection with the validation procedure, has its mode of operation changed for some reason and no longer blank-fills PRODUCT_NAME.

(2) The task module must not have any side effects on any other section
of the program.

This restriction applies particularly to the use of data items other
than those referred to as explicit parameters of the task module. For
example, a module may be required to perform certain calculations
which necessitate the storage of temporary results during the
evaluation process. It would be wrong for that module to use data
items which, although they had no particular connection with the
current task, were not being used for any other purpose at that point
of the program's execution. In such a case, the calculation module
should create temporary storage areas for its own use. The additional
amount of memory utilization in such cases is usually trivial and the
problems avoided may be considerable.

4.6   Local and global data

To facilitate the concepts of module independence and information
hiding, it is advantageous for program modules to be able to lay
exclusive claim to certain data areas in a program. This means that they
may feel free to use these areas for whatever purpose is required without
any concern for effects on the remainder of the program and, conversely,
they need have no concern that other program modules are corrupting
data which belongs solely to that task. For this reason, as much data as is
feasible should be passed as parameters to task modules, operated on in
the modules' data areas and returned again as parameters.

Certain data, however, will fall outside this category. Either because
of its universal requirement for use by all sections of a program or
because of its volume, certain data may have to be regarded as globally
accessible by all sections of the procedural code. Records read from files
and large arrays, or tables of data will almost certainly fall into the
category of global data.

Some programming languages have syntax facilities for the
declaration of local and global data items, for example, FORTRAN, PL/
1, Pascal. Others, however, have no such formal facility and rely on the
discipline of the programmer to enforce such a standard, for example,
BASIC, COBOL.

Whether done by syntax or self-discipline, however, a programmer
should consciously seek to divide all data items in a program into two
categories:

(1) global items which may be accessed and altered by any portion of the
program code; and
(2) local items which are essentially the property of one task module and
which may only be used either as an input and/or output parameter
for that module or by the module itself as a repository of temporary
calculations.

Unless otherwise stated explicitly in the specification for any module, it is presumed that the data items provided as input parameters do not have their contents corrupted during the course of the module's operation.

4.7 Parameter checking

A perennial problem concerning the transfer of parameter data to and from processing modules is that of validation, that is, checking for correctness/reasonableness. In some instances, the nature of the module itself will detect erroneous input. For example, in a procedure to check the validity of a calendar date or the existence of a code in a table, it will be the nature of the task to detect a date or code which is invalid. Even such procedures, however, may require an initial check to ensure that the data presented for validation is of a correct type; for example, is the calendar date a numeric value? What would be the effect on the algorithm if it were asked to validate a date of ABCD1984? If the assumption by the module that the date was entirely numeric would cause the program to abort because of incorrect data type, it is essential that this check be made before proceeding to examine the date any further.

If a module were to compute the square root of a given number, it would seem to be essential that the parameter was checked to ensure that it was not negative.

Apart from such cases as those mentioned, a program module must often take on trust the parameter data passed to it. To do otherwise would result in excessive rechecking of data and consequent loss of efficiency. For example, a module required to compute the days' duration between two calendar dates may have to rely on the fact that the program has previously subjected both of those dates to a validation procedure and would only have executed the duration calculation provided that both of the dates had been found to be correct.

Despite the 'defensive programming' warning that all parts of the program should be mutually suspicious of one another and should, as far as is practicable, check their own input for validity, common sense must prevail, and the following guidelines are offered:

(1) A module must always validate its input against any condition which would cause program termination. Possible candidates here are non-numeric values in numeric data items, negative arguments to square root functions, and so on.
(2) Subject to (1), a module need not validate any input parameter which has been validated previously within the program (or by an earlier program) provided that the reliance on that earlier validation is explicitly stated as part of the specification for the module concerned.

Hence, the mini-specification for a module may appear as:

Module name:	Calculate duration.
Function:	To calculate the days' duration, in a positive or negative direction, between two given calendar dates.
Input parameter:	START_DATE and END_DATE are the boundaries of the duration to be calculated. Both dates are presumed to be of the format DDMMYYYY, to be not before 1/1/0000 and to have been previously checked for validity. Failure of these criteria will result in unpredictable results.
Output parameter:	DURATION Contains a signed integer representing the days' duration between the two given dates.

4.8   Conclusion

A program is best constructed as a collection of task-oriented modules which operate as independently of one another as possible. Each module must be defined in terms of what it does and how it communicates with any other section of the program which wants to make use of its services. The method by which it performs its function is best unknown to the remainder of the program, and it should operate as far as practicable on data which is local to itself.

Programs which are developed in this fashion are easy to check and easy to maintain.

Modules thus constructed may be placed in module libraries and may be incorporated in many different programs, this ability being the ultimate test of a module's independence from the rest of its surroundings.

4.9   Review questions

(1) A program is required to read the file of accepted records produced by question 6 Chapter 2 and produce a payroll listing for the employees. The input records will be in the format described for question 6 Chapter 2 and will end with a standard end-of-file sentinel. The output listing is to contain employee name, gross pay, tax and net pay and totals of gross, tax and net must be printed at the end of the listing.

The following rules apply to the calculation of pay:

- Gross Pay is calculated as the employee's hourly rate of pay multiplied by Payable Hours.
- Payable Hours is calculated as follows:
  For Monday through Friday the first 8 hours are to be paid at the normal rate. Each hour worked beyond 8 is to count as an hour and a half for pay purposes. On Saturday and Sunday, each hour worked up to and including 8 hours is to count as two hours for pay purposes and each hour beyond 8 is to count as three hours.
- Tax is to be calculated on Gross Pay as follows:
  The first $100   —   no tax
  The next $200   —   taxed at 15%
  The next $300   —   taxed at 25%
  The rest   —   taxed at 40%
- Net Pay = Gross Pay − Tax

The payroll listing is to be printed with no more than 50 lines per page, each page to be suitably headed and pages to be consecutively numbered.

You are required to construct a structure diagram for this program and to write a pseudocode algorithm from which the program could be coded.

(2) One of the simpler methods of predicting the number of units of stock to be sold in a future period is commonly called a 'weighted moving average'. This technique assigns weightings to the sales of a number of past periods and calculates the predicted sales of the next period by obtaining the sum of the products of each of the past periods' sales and its weighting and then dividing that sum by the sum of the weightings. The resulting quotient is the forecast sales for the next period. For example:

Period	Units sold	Weighting	Product of Units * Weighting
last month	400	5	2000
2 months ago	475	4	1900
3 months ago	500	2	1000
4 months ago	470	1	470
Sums		12	5370

Forecast for next month: 5370 / 12 = 448 units

An organization uses a weighted moving average to forecast its sales each month. A stock master file holds a record for each product containing the product code and description and the number of units sold in each of a period of four months (as shown in the example above). At the end of each month, a transaction file is used to update the master file. The transaction file contains one record for each product sold during the month just ended. Each record consists of the product code and the number of units sold during the month.

Both the master and transaction files are in ascending order of product code and end with a standard end-of-file sentinel. Product codes are numeric and fall within the range 1000 to 5000.

The updating program is required to match each transaction record with its corresponding master record (i.e., the record with the same product code). There may be some master records with no matching transactions, indicating that there have been no sales of that product for that month.

The procedure for handling each master record is as follows:

(i) move each of the four units sold fields along by one month, discarding the prior '4 months ago' value;

(ii) replace the 'last month' units sold by the value in the matching transaction or by zero if there was no matching transaction;

(iii) print a line on the stock forecast report containing the product code, description and the forecast sales for the next month using the method of calculation and the weightings shown in the example above.

Page changes and headings on the stock forecast report may be ignored for the purpose of this exercise and you may assume that all transaction records will have a matching master record.

(3) The following is a description of an order entry procedure.

The program is to prompt the terminal operator for the customer's account number. The operator will key in an account number which is then to be used to retrieve the customer's record from the Customer File held on disk. If no such customer record exists on the file, the program is to display a suitable error message and return to prompt the operator for another account number. If a customer record is successfully retrieved, the customer's name and address is to be displayed on the screen and the operator is to be asked to confirm that this is the correct customer. If the operator does not confirm that this customer is the one required, the program is to return to prompt the operator for another account number.

If the confirmation is successful, the program is to prompt for a series of line items which will constitute the order. Each line item will require a prompt for a product number. On acceptance of a number, the program will use that number to retrieve the associated product from the Product File held on disk. If no such product exists, the program is to return to prompt for another product number. If a product record is successfully retrieved, its description is to be displayed and the operator prompted for the quantity to be ordered. A response of zero or a negative value as the quantity is to be taken as an indication that the product is not that which was required and the program is to return to prompt for another product number. A positive quantity is to cause the program to multiply that quantity by the cost of the product, an item in the product record, and the total is to be displayed on the screen.

This procedure for accepting line items is to continue until the operator replies with a blank product number. At that point, the program is to display the total of the order and write the customer's details and those of all line items ordered (until now, temporarily held in a table) to the Order File.

The program is to continue prompting for customer numbers and associated orders until the operator replies with a blank customer number.

Draw a structure diagram and write the pseudocode from which this program could be written.

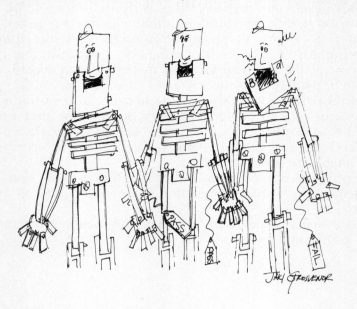

5 Programming standards

5.1 Introduction

The need for standards

Programming standards are needed to provide a degree of predictability in programs of a common type, written in a common language or written for a common computer installation.

Standards contribute to:

(1) ease of program design;
(2) ease of program maintenance; and
(3) efficiency of computer resource utilization.

Each of these considerations will be examined in some detail.

5.2 Criteria for program assessment

When embarking on the writing of a program, there are many criteria facing the programmer, for example:

- correctness of the solution;
- cleverness of the algorithm;
- minimum time taken to write the code;
- maximum speed of program execution;
- minimum use of memory space; and
- ease of comprehensibility and subsequent maintenance.

Many of these criteria are at odds with one another and the pursuit of one will necessarily be at the cost of others. Before giving attention to each of these individual criteria, the programmer must realize that, except in extremely rare situations, it is impossible to satisfy them all in any one program. Therefore, a programmer must establish a clear set of priorities which are always followed unless there is a reason for deviation in some specific set of circumstances.

Correctness of solution

It has been so often said that 'any program which works correctly is a good one and any program which doesn't is a bad one'; most people have come to believe this piece of nonsense.

The true test of most programs is their ability to serve their user over an extended period of time, perhaps three to ten years. During this time they will typically be amended many times to reflect changes in the user's requirements. A program which works correctly as initially written but, because of the programmer's poor technique, is either unable to be modified or is enormously difficult to modify is *not* a good program.

Conversely, a program which contains a 'bug' (or error) which produces incorrect results but which is written in such a clear style as to enable the source of the error to be quickly identified and corrected and which also enables the program to be successfully modified over a period of time is *not* a bad program.

Adopting correctness of solution as the preeminent goal in programming is a mistake. Concentration on clarity of structure and style will produce a better program and will achieve correctness of solution as a by-product.

Cleverness of the algorithm

There is a hackneyed principle in programming called KISS—Keep It Simple, Stupid. Unless there is some overriding need to the contrary, the best algorithm to use in the solution of any problem is one which will be apparent to another reader of the program, and indeed to its author when returning to the program after some time has elapsed.

If a need for, say, maximizing program speed or minimizing memory usage requires the abandonment of a simple solution in favor of one which is more efficient but somewhat difficult to follow, the programmer must include enough documentation in the program (by way of comments, etc.) to enable the solution to be understood at a later time.

Minimum coding time

Most programmers are familiar with the so-called 'quick and dirty' program, one which is written in a tearing hurry to serve a once-only need and which will then be discarded, thus removing the necessity for clarity of structure and style.

Those same programmers will know that the once-only program is then not discarded after use 'just in case it is needed again sometime'. It becomes part of an organization's software library and is almost certain to be modified later to meet a different set of circumstances. The maintenance programmer (who may be the original author) will rue the decision which resulted in such a monstrosity.

There really is no such thing as a one-shot-only program. Resist the temptation of quick and dirty coding. Write all programs as though they were to be maintained by programmers other than their author over a long period. The additional coding time will usually be minimal and is more than likely to be recouped in reduced testing time to ensure that the program operates correctly.

Maximum speed of execution

The vast majority of programs are not so time-critical in their execution that they warrant sacrificing simplicity of algorithm and clarity of structure to achieve additional speed. Normal efficiency standards, discussed below, should weed out gross wastage of execution time.

If the KISS principle is abandoned in favor of a procedure which, although obscure, saves time during execution, there should be enough documentation prepared by the programmer to enable subsequent program maintenance.

Minimum use of memory space

Precisely the same argument for the maximum speed of execution applies in this case. Normal efficiency standards should prevent gross wastage of memory. If special techniques are used in exceptional circumstances, the programmer must ensure that the procedures are well documented.

Comprehensibility and ease of maintenance

In the absence of any conflicting requirements, this factor should be regarded as the overriding criterion in program design. Given the length of time over which a program is used, the number of modifications typically needed to enable it to meet changing requirements and the number of different programmers likely to be involved in effecting those changes (or 'patches'), it is essential that the author of the program follows clearly defined standards aimed at producing clarity of structure and style.

This should achieve the two goals of:

(1) enabling the program initially to be written, tested and placed in production in the shortest possible time; and
(2) enabling subsequent 'generations' of programmers to read the program code, understand it readily and amend it without difficulty.

5.3 Standards for program design

(1) *Use standard algorithms*: Without wishing to cramp the initiative of any programmer, it will be far better if individuals or groups in an organization adopt standard approaches to common situations.

There are standard algorithms for table searching, file updating, sorting, and so on, which are available by reference to published works. Use of these common techniques will free maintenance programmers from having to be familiar with many other methods of tackling the same procedure.

(2) *Use standard structure patterns*: Adhere to the precepts of module design discussed in Chapter 4, and consistently construct programs in the same pattern. Use a mainline, or driving module to control the overall execution of a program. Use invoked subroutines to perform the individual tasks constituting the program's operations. Where programming languages have a variety of possible module entities, use only one as a standard; for example, in COBOL use sections not paragraphs as the module entity.

Never invoke a program segment as a subroutine module in some instances and use it as a section of code to be sequentially 'fallen through' in others.

The term 'subroutine' here is used to describe the concept of a module which is invoked from a distant point in the program (typically by an instruction such as CALL, GOSUB, PERFORM, etc.), executes and then returns program control to the instruction following its invocation. The pseudocode operation **do** has been used in this book to cover this concept.

(3) *Use standard control mechanisms*: When, as is often the case, a program module is to be repeated many possible times depending on the occurrence of a nominated condition, adopt a consistent procedure to handle the status items which control the iteration of the procedure; a recommended style is, for example:

```
Condition−x=False
while Condition−x=False
   statements
   .
   .
   .
end-while
```

Unless the controlling condition is explicitly set to its false status immediately before embarking on the loop, there is a danger that an earlier performance of the loop may have left the condition set to its TRUE status and hence any following **while** will ignore the loop as the controlling condition is already true.

(4) *Use the subroutine invocation, or procedure call, as the normal method of sequence control, not the branch instruction*:

As already emphasized in earlier chapters, indiscriminate use of branch instructions (typically a 'GO TO' instruction) causes poor program structure. The programmer should seek out and use whatever syntax constructs the current language provides to enable program control via

```
while          — loops
if/else  ⎫
case     ⎬    — conditional tests
do       ⎭
               — subroutine invocation
```

which are the pseudocode operations used to construct the program algorithm before its coding in the target language.

Branch instructions of the GO TO type should only be used in extraordinary situations or where needed to implement one of these constructs owing to the absence of a suitable programming language facility.

5.4   Standards for program maintenance

Defining data items

(1) Where the syntax of the language permits, use meaningful names, for example:

```
GROSS_PAY
STOCK_ON_HAND
TOTAL_MALES_UNDER_18_YEARS
```

Otherwise, provide a data dictionary as comments, for example:

```
REM G: GROSS PAY
REM S: STOCK ON HAND
REM T1: TOTAL MALES UNDER 18 YEARS
```

Take pains to ensure that the data names are *really* meaningful. The name SALES_TAX, for example, could mean the amount of the tax, the percentage tax to be levied, a factor to be multiplied by the cost of an item of goods, and so on. Make the name quite explicit, for example:

```
SALES_TAX_VALUE
SALES_TAX_PERCENTAGE
SALES_TAX_FACTOR
```

etc.

Unless the language used restricts data names to only a few characters, do not use abbreviations, that is:

```
Use GROSS_WEEKLY_PAY
not GRWKPAY
```

```
Use PAGE_NUMBER
not PGENO
```

(2) Define related data items together in a group and provide a comment if this would be helpful, for example:

```
COMMENT: PAY CALCULATION ITEMS
    HOURS_WORKED
    HOURLY_RATE
    GROSS_PAY
    TAX_AMOUNT
    NET_PAY
```

For clarity, separate each such group from its neighbors by a few blank lines.

(3) Never rely on data items having a specific initial content other than that which your program explicitly assigns to them.

Some implementations of some languages initialize data items to, say, zero or blanks. This should never be relied on. If, for example, a counter or a total must start with an initial value of zero, ensure that a program instruction puts that value in the data item. Never presume that such an item automatically starts at zero.

(4) Preserve the distinction between data items and status indicators.

As already mentioned, some languages have a special class of 'logical' or 'Boolean' variables to be used to represent status items. Those languages which do not have this facility must use ordinary data items to perform the task of status indicators. Use two such items, for example, TRUE (value, say, 1) and FALSE (value, say, 0) to set and test the contents of these indicators and do not use data items to perform both the task of holding data at some times and at others indicating the status of a condition.

(5) Preserve the distinction between local and global data items.

To facilitate module independence, inter-module coupling may be reduced by providing each program module with its own parameter data items to communicate with the other segments of the program. These items are local in the sense that they may only be used for the purposes of their owner modules and for two-way communication with those modules.

Data which is freely available for any portion of the program to access, for example, a record read from a file, a table of reference material, and so on, may be regarded as global. Many languages have no means of formally differentiating between these two types of data and it becomes a matter for the programmer to implement by means of a discipline in the code.

Procedural code (instructions)

(1) Write one instruction per line.
(2) Separate program modules or related groups of instructions by a few blank lines to enhance comprehensibility.

(3) Indent related instructions in loops and conditional statements where the syntax of the language permits, for example:

```
FOR N = 1 TO 10
    A = B + C(N)
    P = Q*R(N)
    X = Y/Z(N)
NEXT N

IF A = B
    MOVE X TO Y
    ADD P TO Q
ELSE
    MOVE D TO E
    ADD J TO K.

BEGIN
    A:=B;
    P:=Q*R;
    X:=Y−Z
END
```

(4) Do not use constants (or literal values) in the procedural code.

Consider the following program statements (the programming language is immaterial):

```
COMPUTE GROSS_PAY = HOURS_WORKED * 14.75

IF EMPLOYEE_TYPE = 6
    PERFORM SPECIAL_CALCULATION

IF DATA_OK=FALSE
    DISPLAY 'LAST RECORD READ WAS INVALID'.
```

In the first example, we may draw the inference that the factor 14.75 is most likely the hourly rate of pay of the employee (i.e., $14.75) and is hence used here in calculating the employee's gross wage. When the hourly rates change, as they are bound to do, the maintenance programmer must spend a considerable amount of time in locating the places (because there may be several pay calculations to cover several types of employees) where these pay rates have been used and amend each of the values. If one is missed, that class of employees will not receive their pay rise!

In the second example, two problems arise. The first is that it is not at all clear what a 'type 6' employee is. The second problem is that if whatever type of employee this is testing for has his or her category changed from 6 to some other value, the maintenance programmer is faced with the same search-and-amend task as in the first example.

In the third example, it is possible that the error message may need to be shortened, to say, 'INVALID RECORD' at some future time. Again, the search-and-amend is needed.

The solution to each of these problems lies in defining the constant as a data item with a mnemonic name and using that name in the procedural code, for example:

```
HOURLY_RATE                    ... VALUE 14.75
CASUAL_EMPLOYEE_CODE           ... VALUE 6
ERROR_MESSAGE                  ... VALUE 'LAST
                                   RECORD READ WAS INVALID'
```

and then

```
COMPUTE  GROSS_PAY
   = HOURS_WORKED * HOURLY_RATE
IF EMPLOYEE_TYPE
   = CASUAL_EMPLOYEE_CODE
       PERFORM SPECIAL_CALCULATION
IF DATA_OK = FALSE
   DISPLAY ERROR_MESSAGE
```

If any of the literal values change, irrespective of the number of times which they are used in the procedural code, there is only one amendment needed to the program, that is, the altering of the VALUE assigned to the symbolic name.

(5) Construct the program from a number of small, independent, functionally oriented modules.

This tends to be a reinforcement of the precepts expounded in this and earlier chapters. Each program module should conform to the following criteria:

(a)   It should have a meaningful name (e.g., COMPUTE_TAX) where the syntax of the language permits, otherwise it should have a comment statement to indicate its function.

(b)   Unless its purpose is plainly apparent from its instructions, it should contain a few comment lines explaining its purpose within the program.

(c)   Where appropriate, it should have local data items assigned to it for its own use and for communication with modules which make use of its function.

(d)   It should carry out a single function.

(e)   It should consist of relatively few instructions, say a maximum of 50 lines of code.

5.5 Standards for efficiency

(1) Where the syntax of a language permits several types of data items to be defined (e.g., binary, packed decimal, character), ensure that the most suitable data format is used when programming mathematical calculations. This will normally imply the use of binary variables. This point is particularly applicable to languages such as COBOL and PL/1 where computations may use character variables at a consequent cost to program efficiency. Languages such as BASIC, FORTRAN and Pascal will permit numeric variables to be held only in binary format.

(2) Avoid repeated operations on subscripted variables; for example, rather than coding:

```
if item (N) > zero
    add Item (N) to Total
    multiply Result by Item (N)
    subtract Item (N) from Answer
end-if
```

it would be far more efficient to write:

```
Temporary Item=Item (N)
if Temporary Item > 0
    add Temporary Item to Total
    multiply Result by Temporary Item
    subtract Temporary Item from Answer
end-if
```

Evaluation of subscripts is an onerous task for the program at run-time. In the second example above, only one evaluation is needed, compared with four in the first example, to achieve the same result.

(3) Use efficient testing procedures. Two points are worth noting when using testing procedures:

(a) When testing for a range of possible values, do *not* repeat unnecessary tests, for example do not write:

```
if Item=value-1
    statement(s)
end-if
```

```
if Item=value-2
    statement(s)
end-if
```

```
if Item=value-3
    statement(s)
end-if
```

This will cause the item being examined to be subjected to *every* test. Instead, write:

```
if Item=value-1
    statement(s)
else
    if Item=value-2
        statement(s)
    else
        if Item=value-3
            statement(s)
        end-if
    end-if
end-if
```

The use of **else** as a connector between all of these tests will ensure that as soon as one value has been successfully recognized, no further tests will be carried out.

(b)   When testing for a range of possible values, test for them in their order of probability of occurrence, that is, from the most likely down to the least likely. Hence, if a program was required to check the type of each employee before a pay calculation and the distribution of employees was:

Type 1	10%
Type 2	16%
Type 3	54%
Type 4	20%

the most efficient testing order would be:

```
case of employee type:
    3: statement(s)
    4: statement(s)
    2: statement(s)
    1: statement(s)
end-case
```

(4)   No loop should contain statements which do not vary as the loop progresses.

For example, we may need to place the result of a calculation in each item of an array. The coding could take the form:

```
N=1
while N ≤ 50
    ITEM (N)=A*B/C+D−E
    N=N+1
end-while
```

In this example, the expression A*B/C+D−E is calculated 50 times, presumably each time giving an identical result, in order to place the result in each of the 50 occurrences of the item. A much more efficient solution would be:

```
X=A*B/C+D−E
N=1
while N ≤ 50
    ITEM (N)=X
    N=N+1
end-while
```

In this example, the arithmetic expression needs to be evaluated once only.

(5) Owing to the practice of 'paging' or 'program segmentation' whereby a program is read into memory to be executed in a series of 'pages' or 'segments' or 'overlays', it is often advantageous to place program modules which are related in their function physically adjacent to one another in the coded program. If module A calls for the performance of modules B, C and D as part of its execution, it will be advantageous if A, B, C and D are all in the program segment currently in memory. This is only achievable if those modules follow one another in the program code.

For this same reason, that is, to minimize the number of disk file accesses needed to read segments of a program into memory as it is executed, it is preferable to group often-used modules together at the top of the program code and to relegate once-only or exception procedures to the bottom of the code.

Further considerations related to program efficiency are usually dependent upon the specific characteristics of one particular language or model of computer. The programmer should be aware, however, of the impact on efficiency which the use or avoidance of certain procedures causes. Determination of these factors will normally require diligent perusal of the language or computer manuals.

5.6   System standards

While arguably falling more within the province of system design, there are standards which the programmer should adhere to when implementing a group of programs comprising a system. These standards relate to the interface between the user's environment and the computer system, that is, the input and output of data.

(1) *Screen procedures*: The following guidelines will ensure that the user of a computer system will have as easy a task as possible when entering data under program control:

(a)   All programs in a system should use identical procedures to call and to exit from programs (or functions). The calling of programs will normally be via a menu of choices from which the user selects a desired operation. One available choice should always be to exit from the menu without making a selection of any operation. This can be standardized by the use of a function key on the keyboard or by the selection of a menu choice which takes the user back to the operation from which this menu was called. If a function key is used, it should be the same function key for all programs. If a menu choice is used, it should be the same choice number or code for all programs, that is, choice 0 or 1.

(b)   Responses to common questions should be treated in the same way by all programs. Dates should be requested by programs in a common format, for example, DD/MM/YY. Questions requiring a YES/NO response should expect a common manner of reply from the user, for example, Y or N and should indicate this to the user as part of the prompt for the question; for example:

IS A RECEIPT REQUIRED? (Y/N) [   ]

In such a case, the program should ensure that either a Y or N is the reply and should not accept any other response as valid.

(c)   Where input is to be keyed by the user from data on a form (e.g., an order, invoice, etc.), ensure that the sequence of data on the screen is the same as that on the form. The user should not be obliged to move back and forth through the form in order to answer prompts on the screen.

(d)   Indicate the size of the answer required when issuing a prompt on the screen. This may be done by painting an inverse video box in which to key the response, by displaying a pair of brackets between which the response must fit or by displaying an equivalent number of underscore characters to the size of the expected response. Failure to do this may result in the user entering more characters than the program has allowed in its input data item.

(e)   Minimize the volume of data required to be entered by the user. Whenever possible display a number of choices and corresponding identifiers and have the user key only the identifier for the item chosen.

(2) *Printed output*:
- (a) Ensure that all printed reports have a specific name printed at the top of each page, an identification code for unambiguous reference in the case of enquiries from a user and the date on which they were produced, for example:

FR67   STOCK LISTING (at 15/7/90)   Page 17

- (b) Ensure that all pages are consecutively numbered.

- (c) The final page of a report should terminate with a line similar to

*** END OF REPORT ***

This enables computer operators and users to check reports for completeness and ensure that part of one report has not been attached to the start of the next.

This is only a basic set of standards to be followed in the interaction between user and program. Their implementation will, however, make a significant improvement in user satisfaction when operating a system comprising many programs written, perhaps, by many programmers.

5.7   Conclusion

Standards are often seen by programmers as a limitation on their ingenuity or inventiveness. Following a set of standards, however, is the only means of producing programs of consistent design structure and clarity.

A programmer should aim to develop a set of personal standards and an installation should adopt a realistic set of standards which are sufficiently concise to be understood and remembered by the programmers without descending to trivial levels which, by annoying programmers, result in the rejection not only of them but also of the more important standards.

5.8   Review questions

(1) The following procedure was found in a program. Explain what it does and replace it with a more understandable algorithm.

```
Fix Table
    local data
        ITEM(100)  : integer array
        N          : integer, value = 100
        J          : integer
    begin
        J = 1
        while J not > N
            ITEM(J) = J / (N + 1)
            J = J + 1
        end-while
    end
```

(2) The following algorithm is badly written. You are required to determine what it is doing and rewrite it according to acceptable standards.

```
Task Four
    local data
            ITEM(100)         : integer array
            INDEX1,INDEX2 : integer

            PERSON : record of
                NAME      : character
                CODE(10) : integer array
    begin
            INDEX1 = 1
    Clear
            ITEM(INDEX1) = 0
            INDEX1 = INDEX1 + 1
            if INDEX1 < 101
                go to Clear
            else
                go to Read
    Read
            input PERSON from file
            if end-of-file is reached
                stop
            else
                INDEX1 = 1
                go to Check
    Check
            if CODE(INDEX1) = 0
                go to Next
            else
                INDEX2 = 1
                go to Look
```

```
Look
    if CODE(INDEX1) = ITEM(INDEX2)
        go to Next
    else
        if ITEM(INDEX2) = 0
            ITEM(INDEX2) = CODE(INDEX1)
            go to Next
        else
            if INDEX2 = 100
                stop
            else
                INDEX2 = INDEX2 + 1
                go to Look
Next
    if INDEX1 = 10
        go to Read
    else
        INDEX1 = INDEX1 + 1
        go to Check
end
```

6 Program documentation

6.1 Introduction

The provision of documentation is one of the most neglected areas of the programming discipline and is also one of the greatest points of separation between the amateur and professional programmer. The amateur programmer usually writes programs which only he or she needs to understand, operate and maintain. The professional programmer is writing programs for others to use and maintain over a long time. Because the provision of the necessary documentation to support a program is not seen as a challenge or intellectual exercise (and because it is almost invariably left until after the program has been developed and is then seen as delaying the new program), it is seldom done or done properly. It should be one of the fundamental principles of programmer management that no program is allowed to be used without having been provided with sufficient documentation.

6.2   Who needs documentation?

There are three groups of people who need to refer to program documentation and their requirements are all somewhat different.

Programmers

Once having been written, programs are used in their operating environment for a period which may span ten or more years. During this time they will be subject to many alterations or enhancements to reflect the changing requirements of their users. This task is referred to as 'program maintenance' and is carried out by 'maintenance programmers'. It is not uncommon to find that most organizations spend much more than 50% of their programming effort in this area. This means that the average programmer is spending well over half of his or her time working with programs which were most likely written by other programmers who may no longer be around to be consulted on the details of their code. Unless the programs were initially well written and adequately documented, maintenance programming is an extremely unattractive pastime!

Operators

Amateur programmers run their own programs; professionals usually do not. In a situation in which programs are run by an organization's computer center on data which is collected, batched and run in periodic cycles, there will be a group of computer operators whose task is to manage the physical environment of the computer equipment. It is essential that these operators are aware of the task carried out by any program and any likely interaction between the program and the operator at run-time (i.e., during the program's execution).

Users

The user is the person or section of an organization for whom a program is run and who relies on its output for the continuance of their functions. Like the programmer, the user may never see the programs actually run, this task being managed by the operators. Users must understand what input they are required to provide for the program, the nature of the processing carried out by the program and the output which they will receive. They need to be aware of any restrictions on the nature and content of the input and any errors which may be reported on the output. They do not need to know the precise means by which the data is processed except to understand any limitations which may affect subsequent amendments to the program's task.

In an interactive operating environment or one which uses microcomputers, the roles of user and operator are combined. A clerk accepting orders over a telephone and entering their details immediately into a computer system via a terminal needs the documentation required both to initiate and manage the program's operation and to understand the input-processing-output cycle.

6.3   Documentation for programmers

The documentation required to enable a programmer to maintain a program over its life span may be divided into two categories.

Internal documentation

This covers the aspects of programs which are embodied in the syntax of the programming language. The important points, already covered in the previous chapters, are:

- meaningful names used to describe data items and procedures;
- comments relating to the function of the program as a whole and of the modules comprising the program;
- clarity of style and format: one instruction per line, indentation of related groups of instructions, blank lines separating modules; and
- use of symbolic names instead of constants, or literals, in the procedural code.

External documentation

This category covers the supporting documentation which should be maintained in a manual or folder accompanying any program. It is essential that as changes are made to a program, its external documentation is updated at the same time. Out-of-date documentation can be misleading to a maintenance programmer and result in a lot of time being wasted. There has been emphasis recently on the inclusion of as much as possible of any program's documentation in the source program itself.

External documentation should include:

- A current listing of the source program, that is, the program as written by the programmer, including any memory maps, cross-references, and so on, that are able to be obtained from the compilation process.

- The program specification, that is, the document defining the purpose and mode of operation of the program.
- A structure diagram depicting the hierarchical organization of the modules currently comprising the program.
- An explanation of any formulae or complex calculations in the program.
- A specification of the data being processed, that is, data accepted from or displayed on a screen, items in reports, external files processed, including the format of record structures and fields within those records, all data being described in terms of its size, format, type and structure.
- Where applicable, the format of screens used to interact with users and of printed reports.
- The test data used to validate the operation of the program.
- Any special directions of importance to programmers subsequently amending or enhancing the program; for example, restrictions on the sizes of tables, and so on.

6.4   Documentation for operators

Persons operating programs do not need to know precisely how the programs work. They need to know the points at which their actions and the program interrelate, that is, their interface with the program.

Such documentation is usually contained in an operating instructions document and should cover:

- the command(s) necessary to load the program into memory from secondary storage (e.g., disk or tape) and to start its operation;
- the names of all external files accessed by the program;
- the format of all messages which the program may display to the operator during its execution, describing the text of the message; the situation causing the message to be displayed and any action to be taken by the operator as a result of the message;
- any options in the program's operation which require operator action to trigger at run-time (e.g., a special end-of-month run, etc.);
- a brief description of the program's function so that the operator can obtain a feeling for whether or not the program is behaving correctly;
- any technical details relating to the equipment being used (e.g., a minimum amount of memory space required for execution, a minimum number of peripherals or file storage capacity).

6.5   Documentation for users

As in the case of operators, users are concerned more with how they interact with the program and what the program does for them than with the technicalities of how the program goes about its tasks.

All programs or collections of programs comprising a composite system should have a user's manual. This document follows much the same path as that of the operating instructions except that the user will not normally be as concerned with equipment technicalities as will the operator.

The user's manual should cover:

- a detailed description of the function performed by the program;
- the means by which the user supplies data to the program to be processed, covering the format and content of the data together with any restrictions on values included, and so on;
- a detailed description, preferably with examples, of any output produced by the program for the user;
- details of any error messages or exception reports which the program may produce, explaining precisely their impact on the users and any subsequent action required on their part;
- details of any options able to be exercised by the user, including the implications of each option and the means of selecting each option; and
- any restrictions on subsequent amendments or enhancements to the program, to enable the user to obtain a realistic appraisal of the prospective usage of the program.

As with any technical report, the user's manual should be clearly presented, simply explained and indexed to facilitate its use by its target audience which will usually consist of non-technical staff who may have only a rudimentary understanding of the nature of a computer system.

6.6   Documentation for interactive systems

As stated earlier, a large proportion of contemporary data processing systems requires on-line interaction between program and user via terminals. The documentation required in such systems is a combination of that for operators and users. Care must be taken that the technical aspects of the system are kept separate from the operational aspects to allow users to follow their routine procedure without becoming embedded in a morass of detail.

6.7   Conclusion

The lack of sufficient documentation at all levels plagues most computer installations. The production of documentation must be seen as a task as necessary and important as the writing of program code. It is a function of professional programming management to ensure that no system is allowed to become operational without having a sufficient volume of appropriate documentation, and to ensure that the documentation is continually updated as the system itself changes to meet the altered requirements of its users.

6.8   Review questions

(1) An organization is located in a multi-story building and requires a computer system to maintain its internal telephone directory. Each employee will have an entry in the directory containing:

Entry contents	Example
Employee name	Brown, Charles
Extension number	3445
Department and section	Accounts—Credit control
Floor and office number	3rd floor—Room 23

The organization's switchboard operator needs to be able to update the directory by entering details of new employees, deleting entries for employees who leave and changing entries for employees who move their location. In addition, an enquiry function would be needed to enable the details of a particular employee to be retrieved and displayed and the directory would need to be printed periodically.

You are required to:

(a) Write the specifications for the programs which would be needed to implement this application;

(b) Design the screen formats for the operations of the system, assuming that all interaction with the system will be via a terminal;

(c) Write a user's manual which could be given to a new switchboard operator to enable him or her to use the system.

7 Program testing/debugging

7.1 Introduction

Although many authors attempt to draw a distinction between *testing* and *debugging* a program, in practical terms they amount to the same thing. Consequently, the term *testing* is used to cover this procedure.

> *Testing is the process of executing a program with the deliberate intent of finding errors.*

114

This definition is important because it specifies a state of mind on the part of the person performing the test. It is akin to the engineering practice of testing a mechanism or structure not only to verify that it can perform its designed task under ideal conditions but also to determine the point (if any) at which it fails.

7.2 Testing in its correct perspective

Diligent and exhaustive testing is no substitute for careful design. The time taken to test a program to satisfaction will be in proportion (with an inverse ratio) to the time taken in designing the program before its coding. Days spent in design will save weeks in testing.

The elegance of design of any program will directly affect both the ease of testing the program and the incidence of errors detected. Errors will not be referred to as 'bugs' because gracing them with a euphemism makes it easier for us as programmers to ignore the fact that they are *errors*. They are faults in the execution of a program which have been induced by the programmer through poor design or incorrect logic.

Most errors are the result of incorrect control functions in programs rather than incorrect computation or data manipulation. The latter types of error are usually the easiest to detect and correct; the former often go undetected and remain in programs after they have been approved to run in a production (or 'live') environment. Control functions are those which regulate the sequence in which tasks are performed, the selection of appropriate processing modules for a given situation, the number of times a loop is executed, and so on.

7.3 When to test?

Program testing is a continuous procedure. The first test of a program should be in advance of any coding. Once the algorithm has been expressed in pseudocode, it should be subjected to a desk-check. This is a procedure which should be applied to each module of the algorithm and involves selecting sample values of test data for the inputs to the module and processing them precisely as directed by the algorithm to determine whether or not they produce the desired output. This presupposes that the correct result was initially calculated independently of the written algorithm.

Such desk-checking is ideally done by a person other than the author of the algorithm. This could be another programmer, or if the pseudocode has been well written, the user of the program. Presumably the user is in the best position to know whether the results produced by an algorithm are what he or she would have required.

Once convinced that the algorithm is correct, the programmer proceeds to code it in a programming language. The next stage of testing occurs when the coding has been freed from syntax errors and is in a format which allows it to be executed. It may then be tested module by module or as a complete entity.

7.4   Desk-checking

The procedure of desk-checking is illustrated by this example:

(1) *The problem definition*: A factory pays its employees each week on the basis of a data record prepared for each employee. This record contains:

Employee Name, Hours Worked, Hourly Pay Rate

It is the factory policy to pay time-and-a-half for hours worked beyond 40 in any week. Taxation is to be calculated at 20 percent of any wage greater than $200 for a week and nil otherwise. The program is to print each employee's name, gross pay, tax and net pay.

(2) *The pseudocode written by the programmer*:

```
Calculate Wages
    local data
        EMPLOYEE      : record of
            NAME      : character
            HOURS     : integer
            RATE      : real

        PAYABLE_HOURS            : integer
        GROSS_PAY,TAX,NET_PAY    : real

    begin
        read EMPLOYEE

        while end-of-file is not reached
            if HOURS ≤ 40
                PAYABLE_HOURS=HOURS
            else
                PAYABLE_HOURS=40+(HOURS−40)*3/2
            end-if
```

```
        GROSS_PAY=HOURS*RATE
        if GROSS_PAY is not < 200
            TAX=GROSS_PAY*20/100
        end-if
        NET_PAY=GROSS_PAY-TAX
        print NAME, GROSS_PAY, TAX, NET_PAY
        read EMPLOYEE
    end-while
    stop
end
```

(3) *Test data*: This table shows the data to be used to test the program and the expected results in each case.

Test data			Expected results		
Name	Hours	Rate	Gross	Tax	Net
ADAMS	35	5.00	175.00	0.00	175.00
BAKER	40	5.00	200.00	0.00	200.00
CAIRNS	44	5.00	230.00	6.00	224.00
DONALD	20	6.00	120.00	0.00	120.00

(4) *The check table*: The procedure used to check the operation of the program is to allocate an area on a working pad for each data name used by the program and to follow the program instructions, doing precisely what they indicate, *not* what you 'think' should be done in each case. It is important to start each data area with an initial value which is unknown. Unless a program initializes an area by a specific operation, its contents are likely to be unpredictable. The following table illustrates the testing of the program above with the test data shown:

Test	Name	Hours	Rate	Payable hours	Gross	Tax	Net pay
Start	?	?	?	?	?	?	?
1	ADAMS	35	5.00	35	175.00	?	(175.00–?)
2	BAKER	40	5.00	40	200.00	40.00	160.00
3	CAIRNS	44	5.00	46	220.00	44.00	176.00
4	DONALD	20	6.00	20	120.00	44.00	76.00

The program has, so far, not produced a single correct result! In working through its operation, the programmer should have discovered the following faults:

(a) Because the first employee had no tax calculated, the initial contents of TAX is unpredictable and hence the first value of NET_PAY is unpredictable in such a case.

(b) In the case of overtime (hours exceeding 40), the PAYABLE_HOURS are being correctly calculated, although unnecessarily in the case of exactly 40 hours, but the program is using HOURS not PAYABLE_HOURS in its calculation of GROSS_PAY.

(c) If the GROSS_PAY is exactly $200.00 it should not be taxed; however, the program only exempts incomes less than $200.00.

(d) If the gross pay exceeds $200.00 the whole gross pay is taxed instead of only the excess over $200.00.

(e) If an income is less than $200.00 there is no tax calculation performed. This will leave undisturbed the existing contents of TAX which will then be imposed on the employee with the non-taxable income.

Having discovered these faults in the algorithm logic, the programmer should correct the erroneous instructions and retest the program with the same test data. This procedure would be repeated until the program executes successfully on all test data.

It is important that the programmer does not proceed to the coding phase until the pseudocode algorithm has been verified.

Exercise

Rewrite the algorithm above and prove that it works by application of the test-data using a desk-check table.

7.5   Data-driven versus logic-driven testing

Data-driven testing refers to the principle of regarding the program, or any segment of it, as a 'black box' and ensuring that it gives a correct output for all input data. This approach regards the algorithm as relatively unimportant provided that it executes correctly for the range of data that it is required to process.

The advantages of data-driven testing are:

• It requires empirical testing of an algorithm with real data rather than the forming of an opinion about the correctness of an algorithm by examining its construction.

• It can be done by a user of the program as an alternative to a programmer.

- It provides documentary evidence, by way of printed or displayed output, that an algorithm works correctly.

  Its disadvantages are:

- The programmer may omit to supply test data which would have uncovered a flaw in the algorithm.
- 'Correct' results may sometimes be the consequence of compensating errors within an algorithm, errors which may cease to compensate one another as a result of a subsequent change in the operating environment.

Logic-driven testing relies on an examination of the algorithm of the program, or any segment of it, with the aim of detecting any flaw in its procedure.
  The advantages of logic-driven testing are:

- A thorough walkthrough of the logic using desk-check procedures should uncover any weakness in the processing procedure; these weaknesses are often detected as a by-product of processing data which is itself handled correctly but indicates to the programmer doing the testing that a somewhat different choice of data would not have been handled correctly.
- If the testing is done by a programmer other than the author, suggestions may be made concerning the improvement of the structure, style or efficiency of the algorithm.

  Its disadvantages are:

- Test data may be chosen to fit the algorithm and its author may either deliberately or subconsciously avoid causing an error.
- It requires a programmer to effect the test; a user cannot be relied upon to have sufficient knowledge of the programming language.
- A programmer, whether the original author or another, may bring to the testing procedure the same preconceptions about the operation of the coded instructions as were brought to the coding operation; for example, the programmer who wrote the instruction

```
IF SEX _CODE IS NOT='M'
OR SEX _CODE IS NOT='F'
    PERFORM ERROR _ROUTINE
```

will be just as convinced of the correctness of this test during the checking of the program as during its coding and will be at a loss to explain later on why the program rejects *all* SEX _CODEs (including M and F!)

7.6   Selection of test data

The design of test data for any program is an extremely important task. Test data should be designed from the program specification, not from the program algorithm or the code itself. Although programmers may construct test data to satisfy themselves that the program executes correctly, the primary responsibility for the formulation of test data and the expected result lies with the user of the program, that is, the person or organization requesting the program to be written.

Remember, the purpose of testing a program is to verify that:

- The program does what it is supposed to do.
- The program does *not* do anything which it is *not* supposed to do.

Consider the problem of testing a program to read three positive integers and print them in ascending sequence. Using A, B and C to represent any three different integers where A is the smallest and C the largest, the test data should include the following patterns:

```
A, B, C
A, C, B
B, A, C
B, C, A
C, A, B
C, B, A
A, A, B
A, B, A
B, A, A
A, A, A
```

In addition to these patterns, the test cases should include:

- cases where one, two and all numbers are zero;
- cases where some or all of the data is invalid; for example, negative values, non-integer numbers, non-numeric items (e.g., 4B3); and
- cases where the number of data items is too few or too many.

Approximately twenty test cases would have to be submitted to even a trivial program to ensure that:

(1) it handles correct data correctly;
(2) it does not treat correct data incorrectly;
(3) it does not treat incorrect data as though it were correct.

It will also be apparent that the testing of programs consisting of hundreds or thousands of instructions to perform a complex function is an extremely creative and intellectually challenging task.

Test data should exercise every path of logic within a program and ideally it should exercise every combination of paths. In a program containing nine decision points, there would be 2^9 possible logic paths taking 512 separate combinations of test data. If the program was designed as three modules each containing three decisions, however, the testing could be reduced as $2^3 + 2^3 + 2^3 = 24$ combinations of test data to test each of the paths in each of the modules, plus a few additional cases to test the communication between the modules.

This is a powerful argument for designing programs as a collection of modules rather than as single monolithic structures.

It is well to remember that it is variety rather than volume which is the requirement of test data. Unless a program is being tested specifically for its ability to handle a certain number of transactions in a given time or its ability to accumulate totals from a series of identical transaction types, there is no merit in providing multiple occurrences of identical data items. In the above example, if the program could handle the pattern A, B, C for one set of data, it could handle that pattern for any number of such sets and further A, B, C test patterns would prove nothing at all. In selecting test data, one must provide a sufficient variety of test data to exercise all paths of a program's logic and all combinations of occurrences which the program must be able to handle.

In a production environment, a set of test data should be created, preserved and maintained for each program. Any time a modification is made to a program, however minor the patch, the program must be retested on the entire test data set to ensure that the correct results are still produced.

This use of specially designed test data is usually preferable to the testing of programs on 'live' data. The use of live data, that is, data which has been taken from the actual system in which the program is to operate has a certain attraction in the process of program testing. Live data contains real instances of the types of input which the program must process rather than data merely contrived for the testing procedure alone. However, it is highly likely that whatever subset of live data is used in the test, it will not contain all of the combinations of conditions which the programmer needs to test. It is also unlikely that boundary, or threshold situations will be present in a random sample of live data. For example, if tax is to be calculated on gross pays over, say, $200, then the program should test that specific $200 value to make sure that the program has dealt with it correctly. The program may have been written to tax incomes of '$200 and over' instead of 'over $200'. If a very large volume of live data is selected as test data in the hope that it will include as many variations of conditions as possible, the volume of the output from the test will be so large as to preclude the programmer from examining it in sufficient detail to detect subtle errors.

7.7   Testing procedure

The correct execution of a program implies:

- the correct execution of each component module;
- the correct communication of data between modules; and
- the correct sequence of execution of the modules.

The testing of a program is then reduced to verifying these three conditions.

This verification may be done by a variety of methods, all of which are variations on a theme often referred to as tracing. Tracing must be applied to the data processed by a program and the control, or execution path of the program. It will involve communicating to the programmer the point at which the program is currently executing and the values contained in selected variables at that time. The crucial points at which to insert traces in a program are usually the entry and exit to each module.

The information required by the programmer may be printed or displayed on a terminal and may be produced by an instruction (a PRINT, TYPE, DISPLAY, etc) inserted by the programmer for that purpose or by means of a software tool such as an interactive debugging aid which allows the programmer to specify one or more statements at which the program is required to halt for interrogation of the contents of data areas.

In a true-to-life example of a payroll calculation such as that quoted in the earlier example to this chapter, the control structure may be similar to:

global data
```
    EMPLOYEE  :  record of
        NAME  :  character
       HOURS  :  integer
        RATE  :  real
```

Calculate Wages
   local data
```
        PAYABLE_HOURS              :  integer
        GROSS_PAY,TAX,NET_PAY      :  real
        END_OF_FILE                :  boolean
```

```
begin
    do Read Employee(END_OF_FILE)
    while END_OF_FILE = false
        do Compute Payable Hours(PAYABLE_HOURS)
        do Compute Gross Pay(PAYABLE_HOURS, GROSS_PAY)
        do Compute Tax(GROSS_PAY, TAX)
        do Compute Net Pay(GROSS_PAY, TAX, NET_PAY)
        do Print Pay Details (GROSS_PAY, TAX, NET_PAY)
        do Read Employee(END_OF_FILE)
    end-while
    stop
end
```

It should be possible to place in each of these modules tracing procedures which indicate the flow of program control and the intermediate results progressively calculated by the program instructions. Maintaining the errors which existed in the given example, the algorithms for each module (after inserting typical tracing statements) would be:

```
Read Employee(END_OF_FILE)
    local data
        END_OF_FILE  :  boolean

    begin
        print 'READ EMPLOYEE'
        read EMPLOYEE
        if end-of-file is encountered
            END_OF_FILE = true
        else
            END_OF_FILE = false
        end-if
        print 'NAME = 'NAME
        print 'HOURS = 'HOURS
        print 'RATE = 'RATE
    end

Compute Payable Hours(PAYABLE_HOURS)
    local data
        PAYABLE_HOURS  :  integer

    begin
        print 'COMPUTE PAYABLE HOURS'
        if HOURS not > 40
            PAYABLE_HOURS = HOURS
        else
            PAYABLE_HOURS = 40 + (HOURS − 40) * 3 / 2
        end-if
        print 'PAYABLE HOURS = 'PAYABLE_HOURS
    end
```

Compute Gross Pay(PAYABLE_HOURS, GROSS_PAY)
   local data
      GROSS_PAY, PAYABLE_HOURS : real

   begin
      print 'COMPUTE GROSS'
      GROSS_PAY = HOURS * RATE
      PRINT 'GROSS PAY = 'GROSS_PAY
   end

Compute Tax(GROSS_PAY, TAX)
   local data
      GROSS_PAY,TAX : real

   begin
      print 'COMPUTE TAX'
      if GROSS_PAY not < 200
         TAX = GROSS_PAY * 20 / 100
      end-if
      print 'TAX = 'TAX
   end

Compute Net Pay(GROSS_PAY, TAX, NET_PAY)
   local data
      GROSS_PAY, TAX, NET_PAY : real

   begin
      print 'COMPUTE NET'
      NET_PAY = GROSS_PAY − TAX
      print 'NET PAY = 'NET_PAY
   end

Print Pay Details(GROSS_PAY, TAX, NET_PAY)
   local data
      GROSS_PAY, TAX, NET_PAY : real

   begin
      print NAME, GROSS_PAY, TAX, NET_PAY
   end

(Given that the purpose of this last module is to print the contents of all associated variables, it is hardly necessary to insert additional tracing instructions.)

The tracing output from the processing of, say, the third and fourth test records as shown below should, when compared to the expected results already calculated, point out the existence of several errors in the program:

```
READ EMPLOYEE                    (3rd record)
NAME=CAIRNS
HOURS=44
RATE=5.00
```

```
COMPUTE PAYABLE HOURS
PAYABLE HOURS=46              (correct)
COMPUTE GROSS
GROSS PAY=220.00             (46 hours @ $5.00 = $230)
COMPUTE TAX
TAX=44.00                    (tax should be $6.00)
COMPUTE NET
NET PAY=176.00               (consistent with gross pay and tax)
READ EMPLOYEE                (4th record)
NAME=DONALD
HOURS=20
RATE=6.00
COMPUTE PAYABLE HOURS
PAYABLE HOURS=20             (correct)
COMPUTE GROSS
GROSS PAY=120.00             (correct)
COMPUTE TAX
TAX=44.00                    (tax should be zero)
COMPUTE NET
NET PAY=76.00                (consistent with gross pay and tax)
```

From the trace output the programmer can ascertain that some modules work correctly each time (e.g., COMPUTE PAYABLE HOURS), some work incorrectly sometimes (e.g., COMPUTE GROSS PAY and COMPUTE TAX), and others give incorrect results but results which are consistent with the data which they have had to operate on (e.g., COMPUTE NET PAY and, presumably, the printing of the pay details).

Without this display of intermediate results, the programmer would merely see that the final pay results produced were incorrect for the data input but would not know where the incorrect processing was occurring.

7.8   Interactive debugging

The procedure described in Section 7.7 made use of the standard syntax of the chosen programming language to output items of data which will enable the run-time operations of the program to be traced. This procedure would be necessary in a situation in which the programmer was obliged to test the program in an off-line manner, that is, by placing it in a job queue and collecting the output some time later.

Most current programming environments permit the programmer to test a program on-line, that is, to run the program while the programmer may monitor its operations on a screen. In such a case, the procedure in Section 7.7 will still work with the output directed to the screen rather than to a printer. The benefit of on-line, or interactive testing is that the trace facilities may be inserted in a section suspected of error and may then be removed and inserted elsewhere if the first test failed to detect the error. This process may be repeated as often as is necessary until the source of any error is eventually tracked down.

The ease with which such insertion and removal of traces within a program may be effected depends on the type of language chosen. For an interpreted language such as BASIC, statements may be inserted and removed extremely easily between successive runs on test data. For compiled languages such as most implementations of COBOL, however, this insertion and removal must be accompanied each time by the laborious process of recompiling and linking the object code. This distinction between interpretive and compiled languages is discussed in Chapter 15. To eliminate this tedium, many languages are provided with a software tool typically referred to as an interactive debugger.

An interactive debugger enables a programmer at run-time to select one or more break points in a program being tested. When the program reaches a break point it will halt its execution and signal its position to the programmer at a terminal. The programmer may then examine the contents of any of the data items used within the program, change those contents if desired and resume operation of the program. These break points may be set and removed as the program executes without the need to recompile. Data items are interrogated by the programmer quoting their symbolic name, for example, TOTAL, rather than having to know their actual memory address. This will normally necessitate the programmer indicating to the compiler at compile time the intention to use the debugger. This indication ensures that the compiler generates whatever code and tables may be needed for the debugging activity to take place at run-time.

7.9   Progressive testing (top-down versus bottom-up)

For a large program, it may not be necessary for the programmer to wait until the entire program has been coded to begin testing. Modules which have not been coded may be replaced by 'stubs' which enable the call to the module to be executed but do not perform all or any of the module's functions.

In the payroll program above, for example, it is likely that the coding of the taxation calculation would be delayed until all other sections of the program are operating correctly. (The actual method of calculating tax is obviously not as trivial as that in the example!) In such a case, the Compute Tax module could be coded to always return to a value of, say $10 and the rest of the program could be tested independently of that procedure.

The procedure of developing the higher level control modules and testing their operation in advance of the lower level 'nuts and bolts' procedures is referred to as top-down development. Such a procedure allows the programmer to insert progressively more coding, testing each new segment as it is introduced and enabling any errors discovered to be localized and corrected with minimum disruption to the remainder of the program which had previously operated correctly.

In practice, top-down development is often mixed with a certain amount of bottom-up implementation. In some systems, the operation of a low-level procedure within certain restraints, for example, a time limit or a memory usage limit, is critical to the functioning of the program as a whole. In such a case the low-level module(s) may be coded in advance of the main program structure and independently tested to ensure that they operate within their design criteria. This requires the critical modules to be surrounded by a 'test harness' of sufficient code to provide them with typical operating input and to evaluate their output.

The taxation calculation procedure in our example could be developed in such a manner by executing it in conjunction with a simple-minded module which provided it with an artificial gross pay that started at a certain value and was incremented after each calculation until a prescribed limit was reached.

7.10   Testing strategy

There are several guidelines worth following when testing programs:

(1) For each set of test data used, ensure that the expected results are pre-calculated.
(2) Do not swamp a program with such a deluge of test data that the results will be too voluminous to check in detail. Often small errors can go undetected in a mass of output.
(3) Thoroughly inspect the results from each test run. Do not assume that something which was correct in the previous run will automatically remain correct. Often the fixing of one error will upset another output which was previously valid.
(4) Test data must cover the invalid and unexpected as well as the valid and expected. Remember that testing is a procedure of trying to find errors in a program.
(5) Ensure that test data is designed by somebody other than the author of the program which it is testing.
(6) In the initial stages of program testing, test one feature at a time. Attempting to test everything in a single run will not initially help to determine which parts of a program work correctly and which do not.
(7) Watch for side-effects errors, that is, ensure that a program segment not only performs its own function correctly but that it does not interfere with another module by, for example, corrupting data which will not be used until a later stage of the program.

7.11   Program walkthroughs

Much attention has been given in recent years to the pros and cons of having one or several other programmers examine in detail the code produced by any programmer. The advantages of such 'walkthroughs' are:

- The reviewing panel has no preconceptions about what the code should do and hence may detect errors which fell in a 'blind spot' of the author of the program.
- The reviewing panel may be able to make suggestions to improve the structure, style or efficiency of the code.
- The reviewing panelists may learn something from the code reviewed.

On the other hand, criticism must be constructive. Despite the urging toward egoless programming, most programmers still have difficulty in divorcing themselves from their product and in accepting that criticism of their code is not directed against them.

7.12   Common sources of error in programs

Mistakes made by programmers tend to be of the same nature independent of the programming language used. The following list is a selection of points to check when debugging programs in any language:

(1) Make sure that all constants and variables are explicitly assigned initial values and not assumed to have been initialized by the compiler.
(2) In languages allowing for implicit definition of variable names (e.g., BASIC and FORTRAN) check for misspelling of data names (e.g., MISTAKE = MISTEAK + 1).
(3) Check for variables shared between program modules—one module leaving a temporary value in a data area which is then corrupted by another module before being retrieved by the original procedure.
(4) Check that status variables (flags/switches) are cleared immediately prior to their use.
(5) Make sure that subscripts do not direct the program beyond the bounds of an array. Many compilers do not generate object code which checks the validity of subscripts at run-time. Some languages allow array indexes to have meaningful zero values; others have a minimum index value of 1.

(6) Ensure that the control of loops is correctly implemented and that they correctly handle first, intermediate and last iterations. Check also for a zero-iteration loop, that is, a condition requiring no executions of the loop.

(7) Check that tests are handled correctly and that all test cases are handled explicitly; for example, a test for a variable to contain a value from 1 to 3 may test explicitly for 1 and 2 and erroneously assume that anything else must be 3.

(8) Check for compound negative conditions to be expressed correctly, for example, a test to ensure that SEX contains only either 'M' or 'F' and expressed as:

```
IF SEX NOT='M' OR NOT='F'
THEN execute error routine
```

will reject every value of SEX including 'M' and 'F'. The test should have been expressed as:

```
IF SEX NOT='M' AND NOT='F'
THEN execute error routine.
```

It is better to avoid compound negative conditions altogether, for example,

```
IF SEX='M' OR SEX='F'
    no action
ELSE
    execute error routine
```

or alternatively,

```
IF SEX NOT='M'
    IF SEX NOT='F'
        execute error routine
```

This latter example may be preferred to compounding the tests by the use of AND in cases where the IF instruction has no provision for a 'no action' statement.

7.13 System testing

In a working environment, a data processing application may involve anything between five to a hundred programs, all of which must interact to provide a service to the user. Testing in such an environment involves not only testing each individual program but also testing the flow of data through the system as a whole. Essentially this is only a larger version of the procedure used in testing a single program because we are still testing a number of modules (in this case each is a program), the sequence in which they operate and the communication of data between them.

The main problems arising in system testing are:

(1) *Misunderstandings of the functions of programs*: Program B presumes that program A has performed certain operations on data passed between them, when program A has not performed them at all or has performed something else or something in addition. This can be guarded against only by ensuring that the program specifications are spelled out in detail before the coding starts and that programs adopt a healthy mutual suspicion of one another during execution. This latter point implies that, at least during the testing phase, each program performs as much validation as is practical on any data which it inherits from other programs. This principle is a more global application of that referred to in Chapter 3 when considering parameter checking between program modules.

(2) *Inconsistent descriptions of data*: Data will be passed from program to program by being transferred as parameters specified as part of a calling procedure or by being written to a file on an external peripheral by one program and read by others. In both of these mechanisms it is possible for one program to contain a data description which differs from the description contained in others. This difference may be in the size or type of data items concerned. This is best overcome by having a single definition of any major data item held once only within the system. This description may then be included in the source code of any program using that data. The inclusion may be effected by means of a copy facility which may be part of the syntax of the programming language used or may be done via a text editor. It also has the obvious benefit that any alteration to the format of the data items needs to be done in one place only, although it will usually then involve a recompilation of all programs using that data.

(3) *Availability of test data*: A significant problem in the testing of multi-program systems is that programs are not necessarily written in the sequence in which they will execute during the operation of the finished system. Hence, a programmer wishing to test a program well down the execution sequence is often tempted to wait until all the preliminary programs have been tested in order to obtain test data which has been passed through the system. Such a strategy is usually untenable in a large system. In effect, all parts of it need to be tested in parallel. This necessitates the creation of test files in advance of the programs which will ultimately produce them in the

natural operation of the system. If this cannot be done easily by means of, say, a text editor, the system designer should commission the development of a software tool which operates as a test file loader. Such programs are easily written and the time spent on their development is repaid many times over. Unless the creation of adequate test data is made as painless as possible, programmers and users will tend to supply meagre test material which, because it does not exercise programs sufficiently, may allow errors to go undetected into the production system.

(4) *Multiple versions of programs*: As programs are compiled, tested, modified, recompiled, retested, and so on, there is an ever-present danger that several versions of any one program may exist in the program library. It is essential that care is taken in performing a librarian function to manage this procedure. This function may be carried out by the programmers themselves, by a person appointed as a librarian or by a software-automated process. However it is done, it must be done with as much attention to detail and documentation as the development of the system itself; otherwise the running of a previous version of a program which has subsequently been modified to correct certain errors will result in those errors once again being introduced into the system.

In addition to the problems associated with the system-testing phase of the initial implementation of an application, there is the ongoing problem of the testing of modifications to the system during its lifetime. Modifications during the maintenance phase of a system are implemented to fix existing errors in programs, to alter the operation of certain functions or to enhance the capabilities of the system.

Changes brought about in this way will require the updating of user, operations and system documentation and will necessitate the following of a planned schedule of procedures to ensure that all parties concerned are aware of the nature and scope of the modifications and the time scale for their implementation. Modifications such as these are normally a joint effort supervised by a working team comprising users, programmers/analysts and operations staff and will require access to test data on the same basis as the procedure for system implementation. For this reason, test data should not be discarded after implementation or subsequent modifications. An ongoing file of test data should be accumulated to enable the trial of any change to illustrate conclusively that not only has that change worked correctly but that it has not negated something that should not have been altered at all. A 'test harness' may be constructed of operating instructions, test files and file comparison programs to demonstrate that system changes have occured correctly and that results which should not have changed have in fact not changed.

7.14   Conclusion

The importance of methodical and exhaustive testing of programs cannot be overemphasized. The time taken and pain suffered during this phase of program development will be in inverse proportion to the care with which the algorithm was designed and the code written, that is, there should be more emphasis placed on 'antibugging' than 'debugging'. Attention to elegance in program structure and style will prevent errors from being introduced into the program at coding time, and mastery of these techniques must be regarded as more important than spending large amounts of time in searching for errors in programs as a result of poor initial programming.

7.15   Review questions

(1) An algorithm was required to count the length of the longest string of sequential numbers in a series of positive integers in which no value was repeated and which ended with a value of 999. The 999 was not to be regarded as a candidate in calculating the requried string length.

For example, for the data:

14, 36, 2, 9, 18, 37, 22, 46, 81, 999

the result should be calculated as 4 (the string 2, 9, 18, 37)

The following algorithm was designed to solve the problem:

```
Longest Run
    local data
        RUN, LONGEST_RUN,
        NUMBER, PREVIOUS_NUMBER : integer
    begin
        RUN = 0
        LONGEST_RUN = 0
        input NUMBER
        PREVIOUS_NUMBER = NUMBER
        while NUMBER not = 999
            if NUMBER > PREVIOUS_NUMBER
                RUN = RUN + 1
            else
                if RUN > LONGEST_RUN
                    LONGEST_RUN = RUN
                end-if
                RUN = 1
```

```
      end-if
      PREVIOUS_NUMBER = NUMBER
      input NUMBER
   end-while
      output LONGEST_RUN
end
```

After coding and executing the algorithm, it was found to work correctly for some sets of test data but not for others.

Explain the circumstance(s) in which the algorithm will not give the correct answer and show the amendment(s) needed to the algorithm to correct the error(s).

(2) A program has been written to compare the items in two arrays and to output the items in Array A which have matching items in Array B and, in such a case, the number of times the item in Array A appears in Array B. Each item in Array A appears once only, those in Array B may appear many times.

For example, for the data visible in the arrays shown below, the expected output would be:

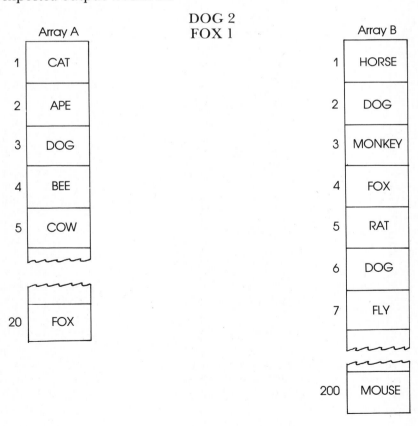

DOG 2
FOX 1

134   Chapter 7

The programmer designed the program using the pseudocode shown below and coded the program from that algorithm.

```
Compare Arrays
    local data
        ARRAY_A (20), ARRAY_B (200) : character array
        INDEX_A, INDEX_B, COUNTER : integer
        SIZE_A                      : integer, value = 20
        SIZE_B                      : integer, value = 200
    begin
        COUNTER = 0
        INDEX_A = 1
        while INDEX_A < SIZE_A
            INDEX_B = 1
            while INDEX_B < SIZE_B
                if ARRAY_A (INDEX_A) = ARRAY_B (INDEX_B)
                    COUNTER = COUNTER + 1
                end-if
                INDEX_B = INDEX_B + 1
            end-while
            if COUNTER > 0
                output ITEM_B (INDEX_B), COUNTER
            end-if
            INDEX_A = INDEX_A + 1
        end-while
    end
```

The program is found to give correct answers in some cases but not in others.

You are required to:

(i) Explain in what circumstances the program would give the correct answer.
(ii) Make the necessary correction(s) to the algorithm to ensure that it works correctly for all cases.

(3) A program segment has the task of checking a product code in a sales record against a table of 40 such codes and their associated descriptions. The items are held in the table in ascending order of product code.

The aim of the processing is to return to the calling module the description associated with the code in the record or to set an error indicator to signal that the code could not be located in the table.

For example, for the part of the table shown below, a code of 10 should return a description of 'Refrigerator' and a code of 14 should be reported as an error:

Code	Description
.	.
.	.
7	Microwave Oven
10	Refrigerator
16	Convection Heater
.	.
.	.

The following algorithm was designed by a programmer and then coded. State, with reasons, whether this algorithm will give correct results. You should comment on any other aspects of the algorithm which you consider less than satisfactory. You may assume that the sales record and the table are defined as global data items.

```
Match Code(FOUND_OK, DESCRIPTION)
    local data
        INDEX        : integer
        FOUND_OK     : boolean
        DESCRIPTION : character
    begin
        FOUND_OK = false
        INDEX = 1
        while INDEX < 40
            and FOUND_OK = false
                if RECORD_CODE = TABLE_CODE(INDEX)
                    FOUND_OK = true
                end-if
                INDEX = INDEX + 1
        end-while
        DESCRIPTION = TABLE_DESCRIPTION(INDEX)
    end
```

(4) Consider the payroll exercise described in question 1 in Chapter 4.
    Draw up a set of test data which would be suitable for ensuring that the program worked correctly.

8 File organization and processing

8.1 Introduction

The traditional means of storing data on external media has been by the use of files. Although there is a growing movement towards a database approach to data storage, the majority of commercial computer-based applications involve the processing of files.

It is not the function of this book to provide an exhaustive treament of the principles of file design. However, given that the majority of programs are written to process files, a programmer must have an understanding of the types of file organization commonly encountered and the types of operations which each permits.

8.2 The hierarchy of data

As explained briefly in Chapter 2, a file is an hierarchical data structure consisting of records which, in turn, are composed of fields. It is customary for all of the records in a given file to relate to the same entity or activity within the operations of the using organization. Hence, one would typically expect to encounter a customer file with a record for each customer, a personnel file with a record for each employee, a student enrolment file with a record for each student or an invoice file with a record for each invoice outstanding.

The records on a file may be termed logical or physical records:

(1) *Logical records*: A logical record is the complete set of data relating to one entity on the file, i.e., one customer, one employee, one student, one invoice. This is the unit of data dealt with at a programming level. A read operation on a file will make one logical record available to the programmer.
(2) *Physical records*: A physical record is the unit of data accessed in one physical operation on the hardware storage medium. The operation of physically reading from or writing to a magnetic disk or tape is extremely time-consuming in terms of relative computer speeds. On an equivalent scale, data which the CPU could process in several minutes would take several months to retrieve from its storage medium.

   Therefore, in the interest of efficiency, logical records are usually packed on their storage medium in such a way that several are read into or written from memory in one physical operation. These units in which they are packed are usually referred to as blocks on magnetic tape or buckets on disk.

   The packing and unpacking of logical records into and from physical records is a function of library routines incorporated in a program at compile time or called up during run time and does not have to be managed by the programmer. Most programming languages will be careful to define a read operation as 'making available the next logical record' rather than as executing a hardware operation on the storage medium. A logical record is provided to the program on the demand of a read instruction, or its equivalent, and the physical supply of these records is managed by the program holding physical records in an internal buffer area and releasing them as required.

Records are divided into fields, each of which represents one item of data relating to the entity represented by the record. Hence, a customer record might contain an account number, name, address, credit rating, balance currently outstanding, and so on. Each of these fields may be a single item or may itself be a group of sub-fields. The address field would contain separate sections for street, suburb, state and postcode. Ideally, a programming language should provide the programmer with a means of describing this hierarchy to the program and allocating a name and description to each field and sub-field. A typical description would be:

```
CUSTOMER
    ACCOUNT_NUMBER : character (6)
    NAME                 : character (30)
    ADDRESS
        STREET           : character (30)
        SUBURB           : character (20)
        STATE            : charactrer (15)
        POST_CODE        : character (5)
    CREDIT_RATING        : integer
    BALANCE_OWING        : real
```

A notational convention would be needed within the programming language to convey the hierarchical groupings indicated by the indentation convention used above. A means would also be needed to indicate to the program the size of each of the fields and, thereby, the total size of the record itself. The values in brackets serve that purpose in the example above.

8.3   File organization

The organization of a file refers to the manner in which the records are arranged on the storage medium. The type of organization used for any file determines the way in which it can be processed and the type of access available to its records.

The types of organization most commonly encountered are:

serial
indexed
relative
hashed

Each of these will be looked at in terms of their implications on programming strategy.

8.4   Serial organization

A serial file is one in which records may be accessed only in the order in which they are physically held on their storage medium. Some storage media provide only serial access to their records, examples being punched cards, punched paper tape and magnetic tape. Disk files will normally permit serial access to their records but are also capable of providing direct access if required.

A program has no means of locating a record in a serial file other than by commencing to read at its beginning and progressing through each record as it is read until the desired record is found. Serial files are mostly used for storing transaction data prior to using these transactions to update a related master file.

When the records on a serial file are arranged in a particular sequence, that is, in ascending or descending order of one or more key fields, the file is usually referred to as a 'sequential' file. It is important to note, however, that the terms 'serial' and 'sequential' are not necessarily synonymous.

The processes peculiar to serial files are dealt with in some detail in Chapter 9.

8.5 Indexed organization

The storage of files on direct access media, such as disks, permits records to be accessed in a variety of ways. A commonly used method is that of maintaining one or more indexes to the records and permiting a program to access records either serially, sequentially or directly.

Serial access is usually permitted by allowing a program to access the records in physical sequence on the file. As explained below, this may not necessarily imply that the records are then presented to the program in any particular logical sequence.

Records held in an indexed file may appear to a processing program to be in sequence while being held either partly in sequence or in random order on the file itself. This sequence is achieved by constructing indexes on one or more key fields within each record.

The index holds the keys of the records and the position of the associated record on the file. A program which needs to access the records in key sequence reads serially through the index and retrieves the records from the positions indicated. It is then largely immaterial whether or not the records are physically in key sequence. The benefit of an index sequential file is that records may be processed sequentially or directly. As described below, sequential access may be achieved by reading records in their physical sequence, with occasional diversions to locate records which have overflowed from their 'home' position, or by reading sequentially through an index and retrieving records from random physical placements but in order of their key values.

Some file housekeeping systems do attempt to maintain the records physically in key sequence. Usually, several records are held in an area referred to as a block (or sometimes a 'bucket') and the key of the last record in that block is noted in the index. In such a system, the index would appear as:

Block number	Highest key
1	57
2	86
3	149
4	205
5	261

Index of highest keys

In such a system it is presumed that all records with keys not greater than 57 are resident in block 1, those not greater than 86 and in block 2, etc. This presents an accessing program with two problems. The first problem is not knowing whether or not a desired record is on the file by merely referring to the index. In the above example, a program attempting to read a record with a key value of 92 would determine from the index that, if such a record was on file, it would be in block 3. The program would then need to read the contents of block 3 into memory and search through it to determine whether or not record 92 existed.

The second problem concerned with such a file is that of block overflow. In the above example, if a series of new records were to be added to the file, with each record having a key value between 149 and 205, they would all be directed to block 4. If the space available in block 4 was insufficient to accommodate any or all of these records, those unable to reside in block 4 would need to be placed elsewhere. The overflow so caused would typically be dealt with by the same techniques as discussed in Section 11.5 as applying to tables, that is, by storing the overflow in a nearby vacant block, by maintaining a chain of pointers or by setting aside a specific overflow area on the file.

To avoid the problem associated with attempting to keep records in physical sequence, many file maintenance systems use an approach which is usually still referred to as indexed sequential but was sometimes titled indexed random. The records themselves are stored in contiguous positions on the storage device in the order in which they were created, that is, potentially a random sequence as far as their key values are concerned. Their sequence is achieved by holding all key values in an index (not merely the highest key value as was the case in the previous method) and maintaining that index in sequence.

The index entry for each record contains the key value and the position of the record in the file. It will be evident that the problems associated with keeping the index up-to-date, as new records are added to the file and existing ones deleted, are similar to those described for maintaining records themselves in sequence.

What is required to contain the index is a data structure which enables sequence to be maintained without the necessity to move large quantities of data, in this case record key values and positions, whenever items are added or deleted. The structure usually chosen for such a task is a tree. Trees are described in Chapter 12. The variant most often used for file indexes is that of a B-tree. By constructing such a balanced tree with each node containing several index entries, it is possible to access any record in an indexed file by extremely few index references, as shown below:

Number of records in file	Number of index entries per node	Number of index accesses needed
1,000	8	4
100,000	12	5
1,000,000	20	5

Whatever method of indexing is chosen for a file housekeeping system, it is common to find a prohibition on duplicate keys. This is not universally the case, but usually each record in an indexed file will be required to have a unique key value.

Some file systems permit the use of multiple, or alternate, keys. In such systems a record may be indexed on several keys and retrieved by whichever is the most convenient for a processing program. An employee file, for example, may have records indexed by ID number, name and department. While it is common to find that one of these keys, for example, the ID number, must be nominated as the primary key and must not have duplicated values on the file, the secondary keys will usually be permitted to have duplicates. In such a case, a program retrieving a record by a secondary key may need to have additional information in order to be able to choose between several records with that same key value.

8.6   Relative organization

A relative file is one in which records are accessed by their position within the file rather than via a key. For example, consider the case of a company selling one thousand separate products, each of which has a product code from 1 to 1000. This would present an ideal situation for a product file with relative organization. Each product record would be stored in a position on the file which corresponded to its product code. Thus, the record for product 379 would be stored in and retrieved from record position 379.

Consider a slightly different case where the one thousand products have codes between 1000 and 1999. Here, an extremely simple formula can be used to calculate the position of a record on the file from its product code:

Position = Code − 999

However, consider a further case where the one thousand products have codes which range between 10001 and 20999. This range has been chosen by the company because some of the digits in each code are able to indicate the type of product, the warehouse in which it is stored, and so on. There is now no obvious connection between the code of a product and its position, still from 1 to 1000, on the file. In order to store any product record in a nominated record position (and be able to find it and retrieve it when required) a formula is needed to operate on a code within the range of 10001 to 20999 and produce a number in the range of 1 to 1000. Such a formula is referred to as a hashing function and the procedure involved is described in the next section.

8.7   Hashed organization

A hash-addressed file is one for which the position of a record is determined by applying a formula, called a hashing function, to the key of the record to produce its address. The procedure involved is similar to that described in Chapter 11 for the handling of hash-addressed arrays. There are a variety of hashing methods used to generate file addresses from record keys but their common aim is that of generating a unique address from each record key. Failing that, and such a unique address generation is usually impossible, their aim is to produce as few collisions as possible. A collision occurs when more keys generate the same address than the number of records which may be stored in that address.

Note that for a file, unlike an array, it may be acceptable for a number of records to generate the same file address. This generated address may be the number of a block, or bucket on the file in which a number of logical records may be stored. In such a case, collisions only become a problem when they attempt to place more records in that bucket than will fit. In such a case, the records which overflow will be stored in an alternative bucket, the address of which is determined by a method similar to those described in Section 11.5.

8.8   File sorting

A common requirement for a wide variety of data processing environments is the need to be able to access data in a particular sequence. A product file may need to be processed in stock number sequence, an employee file may need to be in employee number, or name (or both) sequence. The dual problems are those of arranging the data in the required sequence to start with and then maintaining the sequence as data is added to or deleted from the data set.

The concept of sorted data is an abstraction. What we really mean by 'sorted' is the ability to access the data in a desired sequence. To a large extent, whether or not the data is physically held in that sequence is immaterial.

The two generic methods of achieving sequenced data are:

(1) sequence by sorting into physical order;
(2) sequence by indexing.

The concept of processing records in a given sequence by the use of indexes has been discussed earlier in this chapter. The following sections deal with the principles involved in the placement of records in physical sequence.

8.9   Sequence by physical placement

Where data is kept on a medium which permits only serial access, such as magnetic tape, there is no alternative to achieving a desired sequence other than to physically arrange the records in that order on the medium.

The physical sorting of records involves the examination of each record on a file and the comparison of the value in one or more key fields with the values in the key (s) of the other records. Where multiple keys are involved it will usually be more efficient to assemble the keys in one consecutive character string in which the key components appear in their order of importance in the sort. For example, if records relating to sales of goods need to be sorted into order of product code within area code within state code, it will be advantageous to construct a composite key of the format

STATE	AREA	PRODUCT
3 characters	2 characters	6 characters

and to regard the composite field as a single key of, in the example above, eleven characters.

This composite key may appear in the record itself or may be constructed in a working area within the sorting program.

Physical sorting methods may involve the manipulation of the entire records (record sorting) or of the keys only (key sorting).

8.10   Record sorting

Record sorting procedures involve taking the unsorted records and breaking them up into sorted strings and then merging these strings together until a complete sorted file results.

Consider the case of a file consisting of thousands of records, each of several hundred characters. It is obviously impossible, due to space constraints, to read more than a handful of these records into memory at a time. This group of records could be sorted into the required order and written to an ouput device. By this means, a large number of sorted strings of records, each only a few records long, could be obtained and then gradually merged until a single string of sorted records resulted.

Obviously, the more records contained in the sorted strings, the fewer such strings will exist and hence the merging operation will be faster. One means of obtaining sorted strings containing as many records as possible is the tournament sort.

A tournament sort takes a number of records and 'plays them off' against each other as is done in a tennis tournament. Pairs of records are compared at a time and, in the case of an ascending order sort, the record with the lower key wins. This winner progresses to the next round of the tournament where the procedure is repeated. The whole process is repeated until a winner of the whole tournament is obtained. That record is written to an output file and is replaced in the tournament by the next record from the unsorted file and the tournament is replayed to obtain another winner which is, in turn, written to the output file, and so on. In this way a sorted string can be obtained on the output file from the records being played through the tournament. The following trivial example will illustrate the procedure so far:

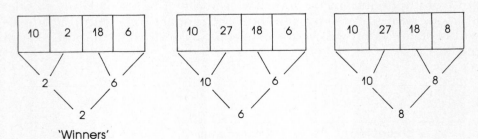

'Winners'

The output file currently has a string of three records (keys 2,6,8) and will continue to grow until a record is read from the input (unsorted) file which has a key lower than that last written to the output file. In the above example, if the next input record had a key value of 1 and that key was allowed to be chosen as the winner of the tournament, the ascending string of output records would be broken. To prevent this, any input key, which is less than the last output key, is marked (with an * in the following example) and does not take part in the tournament. This continues until all keys in the tournament are so marked.

Continuing with the previous example:

Next input key	Tournament 'players'				Winning key	Output string
1	10	27	18	1*	10	2,6,8,10
46	46	27	18	1*	18	2,6,8,10,18
12	46	27	12*	1*	27	2,6,8,10,18,27
30	46	30	12*	1*	30	2,6,8,10,18,27,30
28	46	28*	12*	1*	46	2,6,8,10,18,27,30,46
35	35*	28*	12*	1*	Start new output string	

When this situation arises, the markers are cleared from the tournament records and the procedure progresses to write another output string to a different file. A minimum of two such output files is needed although more may be used.

If two such files are used, alternate strings are written to each file. Hence, one file will hold string 1, string 3, string 5, etc., while the other holds string 2, string 4, string 6, etc., as in the following example:

Output file A:

    2,6,8,10,18,27,30,46,   7,13,21,39,52
    └──────────────────┘   └──────────┘
          string 1   string 3

Output file B:

    1,5,12,23,28,35,   4,11,26,33,49
    └─────────────┘   └──────────┘
        string 2   string 4

These files are now progressively merged using two other work files until a single sequenced string is obtained:

1st Pass:
Input —

File A	2,6,8,10,18,27,30,46,7,13,21,39,52
File B	1,5,12,23,28,35,4,11,26,33,49
File C	empty
File D	empty

Output —

File A	empty
File B	empty
File C	1,2,5,6,8,10,12,18,23,27,28,30,35,46
	(strings 1 and 2 merged)
File D	4,7,11,13,21,26,33,39,49,52
	(strings 3 and 4 merged)

2nd Pass:
Input is the output of 1st pass, that is, files C and D.

Output —

File A	1,2,4,5,6,7,8,10,11,12,13,18,21,23,26,27,28,30,33,35,39,46,49,52
File B	empty
File C	empty
File D	empty

At this point, all records have been merged into a single, sorted file. This technique is known as an N-way merge where N is the number of files being merged together during each pass. In the above example, $N = 2$ and hence we have a 2-way merge. In such a task, the number of files required is $2N$ (4 in the above example) and the number of passes required is $\log_N S$ where S is the number of strings (*not* the number of records) and N is the size of the merge (as stated above). Hence, in the example, the number of passes is $\log_2 4$, that is, 2.

It is apparent that this type of sorting procedure must involve a large amount of input/output time by the computer as the records are read and written and reread and rewritten repeatedly. However, all input/output is serial in nature and may be achieved by reading and writing large blocks containing several records rather than one record at a time. Many contemporary file sorting packages still use merge sorting as their basic technique.

8.11   Key sorting

Key sorting, or tag sorting, is a means of obtaining a physically sorted file without the repetitive and time-consuming input/output operations required by record sorting. Key sorting, however, will only work on direct access files. In a key sort, the unsorted file is scanned, record by record, and from each record a 'tag' is constructed containing the sort key(s) and the position of the record on the file.

In the example used in Section 8.10, had the records been stored on a direct access file, the tags constructed would have been:

Key value	Record position
10	1
2	2
18	3
6	4
27	5
8	6
1	7
46	8

Tags prior to sorting

etc.

The tags are then sorted into key sequence. Using only those shown in the above diagram, the sorted tags would be:

Key value	Record position
1	7
2	2
6	4
8	6
10	1
18	3
27	5
46	8

Tags after sorting

The records are now retrieved in this sorted order and written to an output file. Note that this retrieval, while in key sequence as required by the sort, is in random sequence of record position and hence records may only be retrieved one at a time rather than in blocks as was the case with a record sort. In a tag sort, the records themselves need to be read twice (once to construct the tags and again after the tags have been sorted) and written once.

8.12   Conclusion

The vast majority of commercial programming is involved with the processing of files. It is essential that a programmer understand the common types of file organization and the processing methods which each permits.

Many data processing situations require a program to be able to access records on a file in key sequence. For a transaction file, the most effective approach may be to physically sort the records into the desired sequence. For a master or reference file subject to continuous amendment in the nature of additions and deletions, it will normally be more efficient to facilitate direct access and to provide sequential processing by choosing an indexed organization. It is unlikely that a contemporary programming language will require the programmer to write algorithms to either sort records or manipulate indexes; however, it is desirable that the programmer understand the processes which occur behind the scenes to support these common operations.

8.13   Review questions

(1) A serial file contains information on stock items held within a total of 15 warehouses operated by a certain organization. Each record consists of:

Item Code
Item Description
For each of a maximum of 6 warehouses:
    Warehouse Code Number (1 . . .15)
    Quantity of stock at that warehouse

For example:

P4732
Piston Ring
3, 475
5, 1000
8, 500
10, 2500

The file is held in ascending order of Item Code. The organization wants printed reports listing, for each warehouse, the stock items held in that warehouse and their quantity on hand. These reports are to be in ascending sequence of Item Description.

You are required to describe a processing strategy to produce the reports from the stock file.

(2) An examination is conducted among high school students throughout Australia. The number of participants is unpredictable from year to year but is always in the order of 30,000. Results are received from around the country and entered on a serial file in no particular order. Each student record contains the following data:

Student Name : (30 characters)
State Code   : 1 through 6
Exam Mark   : 0 through 100

The examining authority wishes you to produce a report from the file with the following format:

EXAMINATION PERFORMANCE REPORT

STATE CODE	STUDENT NAME	EXAM MARK	VARIATIONS AGAINST	
			STATE AVERAGE	NATIONAL AVERAGE
1	Adams	60	+3	−2
	Barnes	53	−4	−9
	Bennett	72	+15	+10

The report is to be in order of Student Name within State and the calculation of state and national averages is your responsibility. It is anticipated that further reports in order of student within state could be required and it is hoped that your approach to producing the above report will take account of such a future demand.

Explain a strategy for producing the report from the initial serial results file.

(3) A certain college has 16000 students enrolled in a variety of courses and subjects. In all, there are 25 courses and 750 subjects, each course and subject having its own 5-character identifying code. Each student has an ID number of 7 digits, the first two representing the year in which the student was first enrolled. A student is enrolled in only one course and may be enrolled in up to 10 subjects at any one time.

For each student, the college wishes to keep a record containing the student's name, ID number, address, sex, date of birth, course enrolled in and subjects enrolled in.

The college wishes to be able to perform the following operations on the student records:

- directly access any student by using either their surname or ID number,
- obtain the following listings in either surname or ID number sequence depending on an operator's choice:
  — all students
  — all male or all female students
  — all students in a particular course
  — all students in a particular subject.

You are required to described the file(s) needed to implement the student records application in terms of:

organization
access methods
record content

to enable the required information to be obtained. You should state the processing strategy needed to permit each of the operations described above.

9 Serial file processing

9.1 Introduction

The nature and organization of serial files have been discussed in Chapter 8. Three areas associated with processing serial files will be examined in this chapter:

(1) processing single input files;
(2) updating master files; and
(3) producing printed reports with control breaks.

Much of this approach to file processing is somewhat dated at present as it belongs to batch-processed systems which concentrate on a validate-sort-update-report cycle. Although very few such systems are being currently developed, there are sufficient examples of them remaining in service to warrant some consideration of their associated techniques.

9.2   Processing input files

The first task associated with the processing of an input file will normally involve the reading and processing of a file header record. Such a record may have an identifier or period indicator which may have to be validated and found to be correct as a prerequisite to proceeding with the following records.

The processing of the body of the file should follow the 'priming read' logic introduced in Chapter 1. This involves the reading of the first record before entering the main processing loop and thereafter reading each successive record as the last operation within the loop.

A serial file may typically end with a file trailer record which contains one or more record counts and/or balancing totals which serve as a check on the accuracy of preceding file processing, for example, the total number of all customers' records on a file together with an accumulated total of their outstanding balances. These values in the file trailer record would be compared with similar totals accumulated independently by the program reading the file. Any discrepancies would be reported for follow-up action. The skeleton structure of such a program would be as shown in Figure 9.1.

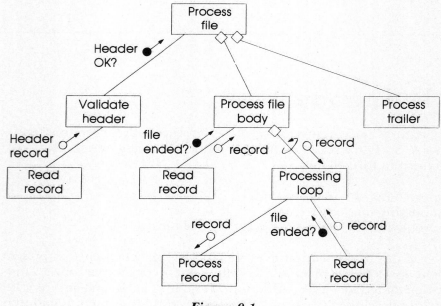

Figure 9.1

The resulting algorithm would be (in general terms):

```
global data
    RECORD : record

Process File
    .
    .
    begin
        do Validate File Header (HEADER_OK)
        if HEADER_OK = true
            do Process File Body
            do Process File Trailer
        end-if
        stop
    end

Process File Body
    .
    .
    begin
        do Read Record (END_OF_FILE)
        while END_OF_FILE = false
            do Processing Loop
        end-while
    end

Processing Loop
    begin
        do Process Record
        do Read Record (END_OF_FILE)
    end
```

To avoid the multiplicity of separate modules which this approach creates, a more concise algorithm may be expressed by amalgamating the control logic into a single module, for example:

```
global data
    RECORD : record

Process File
    .
    .
    begin
        do Validate Header (HEADER_OK)
        if HEADER_OK = true
            do Read Record (END_OF_FILE)
            while END_OF_FILE = false
                do Process Record
                do Read Record (END_OF_FILE)
            end-while
            do Process File Trailer
        end-if
        stop
    end
```

In general, the structure of the algorithm processing a serial file should correspond with the structure of the file itself. The structure of the file for the example above is shown in Figure 9.2.

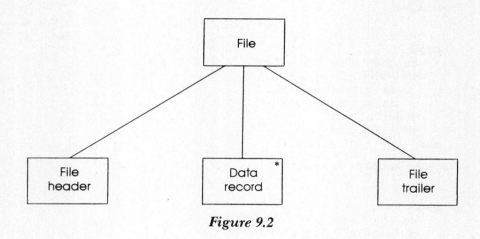

Figure 9.2

The asterisk (*) is used here to indicate the repetition of this element in the structure. A diamond (◇) will be used later to indicate a choice between several possible alternatives or the possible existence of an optional record. The structure of the algorithm was essentially as shown in Figure 9.3.

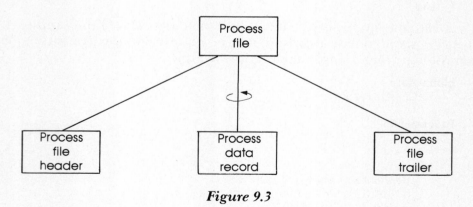

Figure 9.3

If this approach is adhered to, there should be one module of the program which controls all of the processing for an associated record. If that record is repeated in the file, its processing module would be built into a loop in the program.

A more complex case arises when the file contains records in groups, each group possibly consisting of a variable number of varying types of records. Consider the following example:

A file contains records relating to customers of a certain organization together with any invoices outstanding for those customers and possibly special delivery in instructions for goods sent to them and special credit arrangements for discount or extended payment terms. The set of records for any one customer will comprise:

Name and Address Record — always present
Invoice Record — as many (could be zero) present as there are outstanding invoices for this customer
Aged Balance Record — always present
Delivery Instructions Record — optional
Special Credit Arrangements Record — optional

In addition, the overall file itself contains a file header and file trailer record.

The structure of the file may be represented as in Figure 9.4.

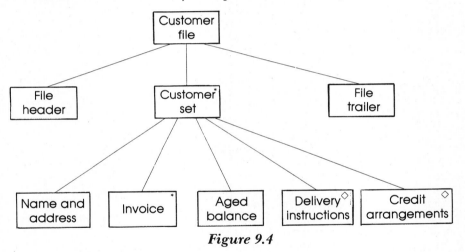

Figure 9.4

Based on the structure of the data, the structure of the algorithm should essentially be as in Figure 9.5.

When combining this process with the principle of a priming read, it must be remembered that there are nested serial processing operations here. There is the serial processing of the customer sets within the file as a whole, and, within each set, the serial processing of a number of possible invoice records and of a number of possible optional records. All of these operations will need a priming read. A skeleton algorithm is set out below which presumes that the file structure is valid, that is, that no essential records are missing and no records are encountered other than those whose types are known. In reality, a programmer would need to check for breaches of both of those assumptions.

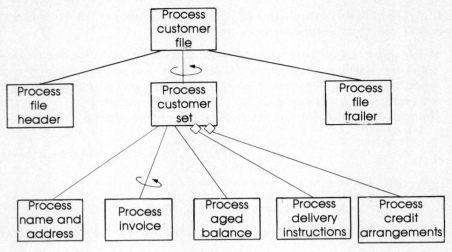

Figure 9.5

Process Customer File
.
.
.
    begin
        do Validate File Header
        if Header_OK = True
            do Read Record (Priming read for Customers)
            while Record_type not = File_Trailer
                do Process Name_and_Address Record
                do Read Record (Priming read for invoices)
                while Record_type not = Aged_Balance
                    do Process Invoice Record
                    do Read Record
                end-while
                do Process Aged_Balance_Record
                do Read Record (Priming read for optional records)
                while Record_type not = Name_and_Address
                          or File_Trailer
                    if Record_type = Delivery_Instructions
                        do Process Delivery Instructions Record
                    else
                      do Process Special Credit Arrangements Record
                  end-if
                  do Read Record
                end-while
            end-while
            do Process File Trailer Record
        end-if
        stop
    end

9.3   Structure clashes

The correspondence between data structure and program structure is one of the cornerstones of the Michael Jackson programming methodology. Hand-in-hand with this structure correspondence is the need to resolve structure clashes.

A structure clash occurs when the structure of the required output from a program does not agree with the structure of the input data. Basically the structure clash may be one of sequence or one of format. Each of these will be considered in turn:

(1) Sequence clashes

Consider the following problem:

The operating system for a certain computer creates a logging record each time a program starts or terminates. The record contains the program identifier, an indicator as to whether this is the start or finish ('S' or 'F') and a time stamp indicating the hour, minute and second at which the event occured. The records are written to a serial file held on disk. A typical sequence of such records would be:

Program ID	S/F flag	Time HHMMSS
PR1	S	090000
PR2	S	090230
PR3	S	090546
PR2	F	091509
PR4	S	092031
PR1	F	092700

At the end of each day a report is required stating the number of programs run during the day, the duration of the longest-running program and the average time taken for all programs to run.

The difficulty in this situation is that the input data is time-related and the required output is job-related.

One simple solution to this problem would be to sort the input file into Program ID sequence. This will cause the start and finish events for each program to be positioned adjacent to each other and hence each pair of successive read operations on the file will provide the complete data for one program.

The records will now be input as:

Program ID	S/F Flag	Time HHMMSS
PR1	S	090000
PR1	F	092700
PR2	S	090230
PR2	F	091509
PR3	S	090546
PR3	F	093100
PR4	S	092031
PR4	F	092925

From this point it is a simple procedure to read each pair of start and finish times, calculate the elapsed duration of each program, detect the program with the longest duration, and so on.

However, it may have been possible to produce the required ouput without having to spend the time and use the resources needed for the sorting of the input file. It may have been known, for example, that because of a characteristic of the operating system producing the input data, no more than 20 programs would ever be running concurrently. In such a case, an internal table could be constructed of the format:

	Program ID	Start Time
1		
2		
3		
.		
19		
20		

At no time, given the 20-program constraint could the reporting program have read from the input file more than 20 start times before it encountered a finish time. As soon as finish time is read, it is matched with its corresponding start time in the table (by matching their respective Program IDs) and its duration can be computed. That entry can now be removed from the table to make room for another start time, and so on.

This technique is often referred to as program inversion. The functions of the reporting program are inverted around the operations of filling and emptying the interim table. The input file becomes a means of filling the table and its emptying provides the information required to produce the report.

(2) Format clashes

Consider a further problem:

A program is required to read a series of 80-character records containing English text and to typeset the text in a column, the width of which will be supplied at run time by the operator of the program. The input text is a continuous character stream and words may be broken across record boundaries, for example:

```
Record 1: Once upon a time  .......................................  a lar
Record 2: ge house  .......................................  the small bo
Record 3: y ran away  .......................................  over the wall.
Record 4: The first  ...........................................  ever after
etc.
```

The output text is to be assembled for printing or screen display in a column of nominated width, lying between 40 and 120 characters at the discretion of the operator. Words are not to be broken or hyphenated at the end of a line. If there is not sufficient room for a whole word to fit on the current line, it is to be used to start the next line.

The input text file will terminate with an end-of-file sentinel which will follow the last data record.

The problem facing the programmer here is somewhat different from the previous example. The problem here is not one of sequence but rather one in which the input is structured as blocks of 80 characters (either or both ends of which may consist of part of a word) and the output is to consist of lines of indeterminate length and consisting only of entire words.

There is no direct correspondence between the unit of input, a block of 80 characters, and the unit of output, a line of 40 to 120 characters. If the operator chooses an output line size of the maximum of 120 characters, more than one input record will be needed to satisfy each output record. If the choice of output line is, say, 50 characters, each input record will furnish more than one output record. Therefore, a program strategy of read-record-write-record will not work.

The common element of data between the input and output records is the word. The input data consists of words (or parts of words) and the output data consists of words. Once again, program inversion provides the answer. The input data must be seen as a source of words and the output data as their destination. Hence, the central entity in the program becomes a word. The program may be broken into two halves. The first half has the task of constructing a word. The second half receives this word and, providing that there is room, inserts it in the output line. If there is not sufficient room the current line is printed/displayed and the word is used to commence the next line.

We have a further problem in handling the input data. Our job is to extract words from the 80-character input blocks but these blocks may not consist entirely of complete words. Once again, a read-record-separate-into-words strategy will not work. The common element of data between a word and an input block is a character. So, the input half of the program must be inverted and the input records seen as a source of characters and words as their destination. In this manner, the processing of the input 80-character blocks will consist of merely handing out the data one character at a time and reading a new block whenever the current store of 80 characters is exhausted. The word building procedure accepts these characters one at a time, oblivious of their source, and forms them into a word until a space character is received.

9.4   Updating serial master files

The most common form of updating carried out on serial files is the technique known as father/son updating. Transactions are applied against a master file and a new generation of the file produced. Customarily, at least three generations of the master file, together with the corresponding transaction files, are retained as a security measure in case of data loss or corruption.

   The underlying principles of this procedure are:

• The master file records are in sequence (usually ascending) on a key field (or fields).
• The transaction file records have been sorted into the same key sequence as the master file (the primary sort key).
• There may be zero, one or several transactions for any master record.
• Transactions fall into three broad categories: amendments to existing master records, deletions of existing master records and insertions of new master records.
• In the case of several transactions for any one master record, they are sequenced on a secondary key which is usually the transaction type or the date on which the transaction occured.
• Transactions are applied against the master records on the basis of attempting to match their respective primary sequence keys (e.g., customer number, product code, car registration number, etc.).
• When each file ends, its record key has placed in it a 'padded' value equal to the largest possible content (e.g., 999999) which the field could hold, and a match between master and transaction records of this key value signifies the end of the procedure.
• It is customary for the transaction file to contain a file generation number in its file header record, this number being required to match that in the file header record of the master file to ensure that the transactions are updating the correct edition (generation) of the master file.

A summary of the actions required is set out in Table 9.1.

Table 9.1

Transaction type	Matching master record found	No matching master record found
Amendment	Action A	Action B
Deletion	Action C	Action B
Insertion	Action D	Action E

Actions:

A: Amend the master record with the data contained in the transaction.
B: Reject the transaction as an error because it purports to relate to a non-existent master record.
C: Flag the master record as deleted and do not write it to the updated file.
D: Reject the transaction as an error because it is attempting to insert a duplicated master record.
E: Create a new record ready to be written to the updated master file.

Below is an algorithm for a standard serial file update:

```
global data
    INPUT_MASTER_RECORD    : record
    OUTPUT_MASTER_RECORD : record
    TRANSACTION_RECORD     : record


File Update
    local data
        OK_TO_PROCEED : boolean
    begin
        do Update Initialization (OK_TO_PROCEED)
        if OK_TO_PROCEED = true
            END_OF_JOB = false
            do Read Master
            do Update Procedure
            do Update Finalization
        end-if
        stop
    end
```

Update Initialization (OK_TO_PROCEED)
    local data
        OK_TO_PROCEED : boolean
    begin
        do Read Master   } Read respective file header records
        do Read Transaction
        if MASTER_EOF = false
        and TRANS_EOF = false
        and file generation numbers match
            OK_TO_PROCEED = true
            increment file generation number
            write file header record to new master file
        else
            OK_TO_PROCEED = false
        end-if
    end

Read Master
    begin
        read INPUT_MASTER_RECORD
        if end-of-file is encountered
            place 'padded' key value in the key fields of both
           INPUT_MASTER_RECORD and
           OUTPUT_MASTER_RECORD
        else
            copy the INPUT_MASTER_RECORD
           to the OUTPUT_MASTER_RECORD
        (Note: This will not destroy the copy of the record in the
        input buffer.)
        end-if
    end

Read Transaction
    begin
        read TRANSACTION_RECORD
        if end-of-file is encountered
            place the 'padded' key value in the key field
           of the TRANSACTION_RECORD
        end-if
    end

Update Procedure
    local data
        END_OF_JOB, DELETE_RECORD, CREATE_RECORD : boolean
    begin
        END_OF_JOB = false
        while END_OF_JOB = false
            do Read Transaction
            while key field of OUTPUT_MASTER_RECORD
           < key field of TRANSACTION_RECORD
                do Master Key Low (DELETE_RECORD, CREATE_RECORD)

```
        end-while
        if key field of OUTPUT_MASTER_RECORD
          > key field of TRANSACTION_RECORD
            do Master Key High (CREATE_RECORD)
        else
            (i.e. keys are equal)
            if key field of TRANSACTION_RECORD = 'padded' value
            END_OF_JOB = true
            else
                do Master Key Match (DELETE_RECORD)
            end-if
        end-if
    end-while
end

Master Key Match (DELETE_RECORD)
    local data
        DELETE_RECORD : boolean
    begin
        if transaction type = Deletion (Action C)
            DELETE_RECORD = true
        else
            DELETE_RECORD = false
            if transaction type = Insertion
                report transaction as an error (Action D)
            else (i.e. transaction type = amendment)
                update OUTPUT_MASTER_RECORD with the data
                 in TRANSACTION_RECORD (Action A)
            end-if
        end-if
    end

Master Key High (CREATE_RECORD)
    local data
        CREATE_RECORD : boolean
    begin
        if transaction type is not = Insertion
            report transaction as an error (Action B)
            CREATE_RECORD = false
        else
            CREATE_RECORD = true
            create a new record in OUTPUT_MASTER_RECORD
             from the data in TRANSACTION_RECORD
```

(Note: This will obliterate the copy of the latest master record read from the input file; however, another copy of that record is still retained in the *input* master record area.)

```
        end-if
    end
```

Master Key Low (DELETE_RECORD, CREATE_RECORD)
    local data
        DELETE_RECORD, CREATE_RECORD : boolean
    begin
        if DELETE_RECORD = True
            DELETE_RECORD = False
        else
            write OUTPUT_MASTER_RECORD to the new master file
        end-if
        if CREATE_RECORD = True
            CREATE_RECORD = False
            copy INPUT_MASTER_RECORD to
             OUTPUT_MASTER_RECORD
        else
            do Read Master
        end-if
    end

Update Finalization
    begin
        (Note: At this point the file trailer records for both the master and transaction files should ɹe in their respective buffer areas.)
        carry out any reconciliation procedures appropriate for the data within the trailer records
        write a trailer record to the new master file
    end

Note: This algorithm presumes that multiple transactions for any master record will have been sorted into the sequence : Insertion, Amendment, Deletion.

9.5   Printed reports with control breaks

Reports are often printed requiring certain totaling procedures to be carried out each time a 'control' field changes value. A sales report, for example, may relate to many sales representatives working in many districts in each of several states. Totals of goods sold, and so on, may be required for each sales representative in each district in each state together with a grand total for the report as a whole, for example:

```
State: VICTORIA
    Districts: GIPPSLAND
                BROWN               2000
                JONES               4000
                SMITH               3000          9000

            WIMMERA
                HUNT                4000
                JONES               6000         10000        19000

State: QUEENSLAND
    Districts: GOLD COAST
                ROSE                5000
                WHITE               7000         12000

            CAPRICORNIA
                GREEN               2000
                ROSE                4000          6000        18000
                                                                .
                                                                .
                                                                .


        GRAND TOTAL                                          200000
```

The production of such a report would presume that the sales records were sorted on a three-part key of State Code (Highest) — District Code — Sales Representative Code (Lowest). Whenever there is a change of value between the sort keys of successive input records (i.e., a 'control break') a total must be printed for the entity whose value has changed and totals for all entities subordinate to the changed key. In the above example, the printing requirements are:

Change of:	Totals to print:
Sales Representative Code	Sales Representative
District Code	Sales Representative District
State Code	Sales Representative District State

A skeleton algorithm for a general case involving a three-level control structure is given below. The reader should be able to extrapolate from that to a case involving more (or fewer) control breaks. This is a further instance of serial (sequential) file processing and hence the priming read principle applies again.

Where the algorithm refers to a change of one of the components of the key, it means the detection of a different value in that component of the key of the latest record read from that component of the control key set up from some preceding record.

global data
    Report record
    Control Key
    Report Totals at 3 levels
    Grand Total

Print Report
    clear totals to zero at all control levels
    read Record
    place record key (i.e. all 3 components) in Control Key
    while End-of-file is not reached
        if highest key component has changed value
            do Lowest Level Change
            do Middle Level Change
            do Highest Level Change
        else
            if middle key component has changed value
                do Lowest Level Change
                do Middle Level Change
            else
                if lowest key component has changed value
                    do Lowest Level Change
                end-if
            end-if
        end-if
        accumulate lowest level total(s) for current record
        read Record
    end-while
    do Lowest Level Change   } These totals are required because
    do Middle Level Change   the end-of-file is reached.
    do Highest Level Change
    print Grand Total
    stop

Lowest Level Change
    print total(s) for lowest level entity
    add lowest level total(s) to middle level total(s)
    clear lowest level total(s) to zero
    place lowest level key value (in the latest record read) in lowest level
     of the Control Key.

Middle Level Change
    print total(s) for middle level entity
    add middle level total(s) to highest level total(s)
    clear middle level total(s) to zero
    place middle level key value (in the latest record read) in middle
     of the Control Key

Highest Level Change
    print total(s) for highest level entity
    add highest level total(s) to grand total
    clear highest level total(s) to zero
    place highest level key value (in the latest record read) in
     highest level of the Control Key

9.6   File buffering

Because of the vast disparity in speed between the processing done by the CPU and the relatively pedestrian input/output operations using peripherals, serial file processing will usually involve the multiple buffering of files. By this process a number of areas are set aside within the program's working space in memory, each area large enough to hold one block of data transferred to or from the file storage device.

The principle behind this is that the operating system can direct the peripheral to transfer a block of data into or from one buffer while the program is processing the records in another. In this manner the program can achieve simultaneity of processing and input/output. This is achievable because storage peripheral controllers have sufficient facilities to be able to effect autonomous transfers, that is, they are told by the operating system the address in memory into which or from which the block is to be transferred and they can effect the transfer of data without any further supervision by the operating system. An interrupt signal will be generated by the device when the transfer is completed to allow the operating system to take further appropriate action.

In an ideal situation, a program would therefore never need to suspend its operation pending a peripheral transfer as input data would be read into memory in advance of being needed and output data would be written while the next block was being constructed in memory.

The buffers allocated to any file may be as few as two (double buffering) or may comprise several operating as though they were in a ring (circular buffering). In this latter case a group of, say, five buffers would be operated on as though buffer 1 was on the right of buffer 5 and the sequence of use would be 1, 2, 3, 4, 5, 1, 2, 3 etc.

9.7   Conclusion

Serial file processing has historically constituted the majority of commercial data processing. Despite its disappearance in favor of on-line processing, it is worthwhile being familiar with the principles involved and having access to some of the most common algorithms employed.

Many of the principles involved are also carried across into other areas of programming, particularly the priming read concept, which is applicable to any series of similar operations.

9.8   Review questions

(1) An organization has a computer system relating to its sales and customer accounts functions. The following are specifications for two of the files comprising that system:

A.   File Name: SALES
Organization: Serial
Sequence: Ascending order of PRODUCT
Record Structure:

CUSTOMER	integer	Customer ID number
PRODUCT	integer	Product ID number
DATE	character	Date of sale
QUANTITY	integer	Number of items sold

B.   File Name: PRODUCTS
Organization: Indexed Sequential
Record Key: PRODUCT
Record Structure:

PRODUCT	integer	Product ID number
DESCRIPTION	character	Product name
PRICE	integer	Item selling price in cents

A report is required in the following format, with 50 detail lines per page:

	SALES LISTING		PAGE XXX
PRODUCT	DESCRIPTION	TOTAL QUANTITY	TOTAL VALUE
XXX	XX-----XX	XXX	XXX

where the columns will contain:

PRODUCT:	Product ID number
DESCRIPTION:	Product name
TOTAL QUANTITY:	Total number of items sold for that product
TOTAL VALUE:	The value in TOTAL QUANTITY multiplied by the PRICE for that product.

At the end of the report, a grand total is required for TOTAL VALUE.

You are required to write a pseudocode algorithm from which a program could be coded to read the records from the SALES file, access data as required from the PRODUCTS file and produce the SALES LISTING report.

(2) A college's student record system incorporates an enrollment file holding approximately 1000 records of the following format:

```
File Name:     ENROLLMENTS
Organization:  Serial
Sequence:      Random
Record Structure:
     STUDENT ID      integer     Student Number
     SUBJECT CODE    character   Code of unit in which
                                 student is enrolled.
     DATE            character   Date of enrollment.
```

A report is required listing the total number of students enrolled in each subject within the college. There will be no more than 40 such subjects. The format of the report is to be:

ENROLLMENT LISTING

SUBJECT CODE	ENROLLMENT COUNT
X_____X	XXX
X_____X	XXX
X_____X	XXX

where the columns will contain:

SUBJECT CODE	The code of each of the 40 possible subjects in which students have enrolled.
ENROLLMENT COUNT	The total number of students enrolled in that subject.

At the end of the report, a grand total is required for the Enrollment Count column.

You are required to:

(a) Explain the processing strategy for a program which would read the Enrollments file and produce the Enrollment Listing.

(b) Write a pseudocode algorithm from which the program described in part (a) could be coded.

(3) The census data taken on persons in a certain country has been recorded in a computer system on the following file:

```
File Name:     CENSUS
Organization:  Serial
Sequence:      Random
Record Structure:
     AGE    integer     Person's age last birthday
     STATE  integer     An identifier of the State
                        in which the person resides.
     SEX    character   'M' or 'F' male/female
```

You are required to:

Write a pseudocode algorithm to read the census data and accumulate totals of people by Sex within Age Group within State. Age Group is to be based on the person's Age, according to the following formula:

Age	Age-group
0-9	1
10-19	2
.	.
.	.
.	.
90-99	10
100 +	11

The State in each record will hold a value from 1 through 9.

10 Database structure

10.1 Introduction

While the traditional means of storing large volumes of commercial data has been by the use of files and records, there is a growing movement towards the use of database structures as an alternative.

Databases evolved in the early 1970s and originally were based on hierarchical or network models in which sets of records were connected in list structures and processed by the programmer navigating a path by means of a series of pointers.

Recent developments have centered around a relational model in which data is stored in a series of tables and manipulated by means of a relational algebra or calculus. The proliferation of languages such as dBASE has brought a requirement that programmers be able to organize data in tabular format and process it by means of non-procedural as well as procedural operations.

This chapter will cover the basic principles of normalizing data prior to the construction of relational databases and using relational operators to manipulate the data.

10.2   The relational model

The aims of database design are:

(1) To move away from application-centered system design towards entity-centered design.

Traditional system design constructed files around data processing activities such as customer billing and material acquisition. If a particular entity was involved in several activities, the data on that entity may have been held in each of the several activities' file systems. If a company was both a customer of ours and a supplier of materials, that company's details may have been held in the customer billing files and again in the stock purchasing files.

(2) To remove redundancy from the database.

In the above example, the company's address, phone number and other details may have been held in a number of separate records. By eliminating all but a single copy of this data, storage space is saved and the updating of data (e.g., a change of address) is localized to one entry.

(3) To provide data integrity.

By having only one copy of any item of data, such as the company's address as discussed above, there is no possiblity of having two items of data which should have the same value but do not. For example, the company's address could have been amended on one file but overlooked on the other.

A relational database is one in which the data is presented to the user as a series of tables, or relations. Each table consists of rows, sometimes referred to as tuples, and columns, sometimes referred to as attributes. In broad terms, the rows are somewhat equivalent to records in a file-based system and the columns equivalent to fields.

A Stock Item table might appear as:

Part Number	Description	Supplier Code	Quantity on hand
123	WHEELBARROW	A436	15
97	SCREWDRIVER	T107	200
346	LADDER	A436	6

STOCK ITEM

Rules for table construction:

(1) Columns must be non-repeating, that is, it would not be permissible to have provision for, say, three Supplier Codes for each stock item.
(2) Rows need not be in any particular sequence.
(3) No two rows may have identical contents.
(4) Some column or combination of columns must make each row unique, that is, there is the concept of a single or compound key.
(5) All columns in any given table must contain data which is functionally dependent on the key column or columns. Functional dependency implies that there is a direct rather than indirect relationship between two items. In the Stock Item table there is a direct relationship between part number 123 and its supplier A436. However, if part number 123 were a hardware item and *all* hardware items were supplied by supplier A436, the relationship would be only indirect.
(6) A column in one table may not be the key for that table but may contain a value which is all or part of the key to another table. Such a value is referred to as a foreign key. The supplier code in the Stock Item table would be such an item because it would be the key by which the supplier name and address would be accessed in another table.
(7) Every column in every row should contain a non-null value. (This is usually not strictly enforced by relational database products.) The presence of a null value in any column indicates that the column is an optional attribute in that relation.

10.3   A notation for data structure

In order to be able to define and describe data concisely, a notation has emerged and it, or one of its variants, has become a commonly accepted format for data definition. The symbols used are:

=	consists of,
+	and,
N{ .. }M	a repetition of item(s) of between at least N and no more than M occurrences,
–	underlined items are key field(s) which uniquely identify that entity.

Using this notation, a student record may be described:

```
Student = ID Number
        + Name
        + Home address
        + Course Code
        + 1 {Subject Code + Mark} 4
        + 0 {Term address} 1
```

This states that the data held on each student consists of an ID number, name, home address and course code, together with from one to four repetitions of a group consisting of a subject code and a mark, and the possibility of a term address. Each student is uniquely identified by the ID number. The repetition of an item from zero to one times indicates that the item is an optional field which may or may not be present in any instance of that group of data.

This notation will be used in describing data in this chapter.

10.4   Data normalization

Prior to the construction of relational tables, the data to be stored should be reduced to a format referred to as third normal form (3NF). This normalization of data is the means by which repeating values are removed and functional dependency is enforced in accordance with the rules described in 10.2.

The stages involved in normalizing data are:

(1) Remove all repeating items.
     The data is now in first normal form (1NF).
(2) Remove all items dependent on only part of a group key.
     The data is now in second normal form (2NF).
(3) Remove all items which depend on other non-key items or which are otherwise derivable. (3NF).

The following example should illustrate this procedure.

Example 10.1

The following data definition relates to a Purchase Order used by a particular company:

```
Purchase Order = Order Serial Number
                 + Date of Order
                 + Supplier Account Number
                 + Supplier Name
                 + Supplier Address
                 + 1 {Product Code
                       + Product Name
                       + Quantity Ordered
                       + Unit Price
                       + Extended Price} 20
                 + Total Order Cost
                 + 0 {Delivery Instructions} 1
```

Notes:

(1) Each supplier has a unique account number.
(2) Each product has a unique code and the unit price of each product depends only on that product code (that is, it does not differ from order to order or from supplier to supplier).
(3) Extended Price is the product of the quantity ordered and the unit price (that is, 10 @ $15.60 = $156.00).
(4) Delivery instructions, if present, are unique for that order.

Solution:

Step 1: Reduce the data structure to 1NF by removing the repeating items into relations of their own together with the key field of the relation from which they are removed. This leaves us with three relations:

```
Purchase Order = Order Serial Number
                 + Date of Order
                 + Supplier Account Number
                 + Supplier Name
                 + Supplier Address
                 + Total Order Cost

Order Item =     Order Serial Number
                 + Product Code
                 + Product Name
                 + Quantity Ordered
                 + Unit Price
                 + Extended Price

Order Delivery Instructions = Order Serial Number
                              + Delivery Instructions
```

1st Normal Form

Step 2: Reduce the data to 2NF by removing from any relation with a compound key (i.e., Order Item, in this example) any attribute which depends on only part of that key.

In this case, the Product Name and Unit Price depend only on the Product Code.

The data now appears as:

Purchase Order = Order Serial Number
+ Date of Order
+ Supplier Account Number
+ Supplier Name
+ Supplier Address
+ Total Order Cost

Order Item = Order Serial Number
+ Product Code
+ Quantity Ordered
+ Extended Price

Product = Product Code
+ Product Name
+ Unit Price

Order Delivery Instructions = Order Serial Number
+ Delivery Instructions

2nd Normal Form

Step 3: As a final stage, reduce the data to 3NF by removing from each relation any attribute which depends on another non-key attribute or which can be otherwise derived, for example by a calculation using other data items.

The final data appears as:

Purchase Order = Order Serial Number
+ Date of Order
+ Supplier Account Number

Supplier = Supplier Account Number
+ Supplier Name
+ Supplier Address

Order Item = Order Serial Number
+ Product Code
+ Quantity Ordered

Product = Product Code
+ Product Name
+ Unit Price

Order Delivery Instructions = Order Serial Number
+ Delivery Instructions

3rd Normal Form

In the above set of normalized relations, the Supplier Account Number in the Purchase Order and the Product Code in the Order Item are foreign keys. By means of these values, data is cross-linked between the relations.

The data from these purchase orders would now be held as a series of five tables:

Order Serial Number	Date of Order	Supplier Account Number
1436	10 APR 90	37402
1437	12 APR 90	43916
1438	15 APR 90	28361

PURCHASE ORDER

Supplier Account Number	Supplier Name	Supplier Address
28361	WILLIAMS	NEWCASTLE
30918	BENSON	ADELAIDE
37402	HUNTER	PERTH

SUPPLIER

Order Serial Number	Product Code	Quantity Ordered
1436	A372	4
1436	C048	26
1437	A409	18
1438	B613	5
1438	C048	30

ORDER ITEM

Product Code	Product Name	Unit Price
C048	WRENCH	14.90
A372	LADDER	146.80
B613	WHEELBARROW	97.00
A409	SCREWDRIVER	8.15

PRODUCT

Order Serial Number	Delivery Instructions
1437	Deliver between 9am and 4pm

ORDER DELIVERY INSTRUCTIONS

10.5   Relational operations

Given that the effect of normalizing data is to store it in a series of tables (relations) each of which contains columns (attributes) which are all functionally dependent, a procedure is required whereby related items of data may be combined or manipulated to construct larger entities or to provide answers to enquiries. For example, consider an enquiry:

"Which orders contain an item for a wrench?"

An examination of the Order Item table tells us which orders have ordered which products but the products are identified only by their code. It requires an examination of the Order Item and Product tables together to be able to determine which of the products ordered, if any, is a wrench. This procedure provides us with the answer to the enquiry:

Orders 1436 and 1438

Similarly, had the enquiry been:

"Which suppliers have we ordered wrenches from?",

we would need to examine together the two tables used for this first enquiry plus the Purchase Order and Supplier tables to be able to provide the answer:

Hunter and Williams

Relational databases provide non-procedural operations to effect this extraction of information by combining tables. The operations are non-procedural in the sense that the programmer is required only to state what the operation is to achieve, not how it is to be executed. Provided with a set of tables as described above, an algorithm could be expressed to carry out the searching and matching required to answer the sample enquiries. Relational model databases do not require such an algorithmic procedure. They provide the programmer with table-oriented operations referred to as either relational algebra or relational calculus. Using these operations enables the tabular data to be combined by stated criteria to produce a required result.

Each of these methods of table manipulation will be considered.

10.6   Relational algebra

Relational algebra provides us with a group of four fundamental operations on tables. Each operation will take one or two (but no more) tables as its input and provide a single table as its output. These operations are:

(1)   Restrict

A restrict operation produces a new table from an existing table by removing all rows except those which match the criterion or criteria for restriction.

Its format will approximate to:

```
NewTable = RESTRICT OldTable
           FOR criterion 1 (AND/OR) criterion 2 . . .
```

For example: Given an existing table:

Vehicle Number	Manufacturer	Year Manufactured
ABC - 123	FORD	1985
PQR - 789	TOYOTA	1980
DEF - 456	FORD	1989
MNO - 234	MAZDA	1984

TABLE 1

an operation:

```
TABLE2 = RESTRICT TABLE1
         FOR Manufacturer = FORD
```

would produce a resulting table:

Vehicle Number	Manufacturer	Year Manufactured
ABC - 123 DEF - 456	FORD FORD	1985 1989

TABLE 2

The contents of the original TABLE1 would remain unaltered.
Similarly, the operation:

```
TABLE3 = RESTRICT TABLE1
          FOR Manufacturer = FORD
          And Year Manufactured > 1987
```

would produce:

Vehicle Number	Manufacturer	Year Manufactured
DEF - 456	FORD	1989

TABLE 3

(2) Project
A project operation produces a new table from an existing table by removing all but the nominated columns.
   Its format will approximate to:

```
NewTable = PROJECT OldTable
           FOR column1, column2, ...
```

For example, using the previous tables,

```
TABLE4 = PROJECT TABLE1
          FOR Vehicle Number, Year Manufactured
```

would produce:

Vehicle Number	Year Manufactured
ABC - 123	1985
PQR - 789	1980
DEF - 456	1989
MNO - 234	1984

TABLE 4

(3) Append

An append operation creates a new table by adding the records of one existing table to the end of those of another existing table.

Its format will approximate to:

NewTable = APPEND OldTable1 TO OldTable2

For example, given the following table:

Vehicle Number	Year Manufactured
BCD - 345	1987
RST - 567	1989
VWX - 890	1986

TABLE 5

the command:

TABLE6 = APPEND TABLE5 TO TABLE4

would produce:

Vehicle Number	Year Manufactured
ABC - 123	1985
PQR - 789	1980
DEF - 456	1989
MNO - 234	1984
BCD - 345	1987
RST - 567	1989
VWX - 890	1986

TABLE 6

(4) Join

A join operation creates a new table from two other existing tables by forming a table with all of the columns from both of the joined tables and as many rows as meet one or more expressed criteria for the join.

Its format will approximate to:

```
NewTable = JOIN OldTable1 with OldTable2
           FOR criterion 1, criterion 2, . . .
```

Each of the criteria will specify a relationship between the contents of a column in the first table with those of a column in the second table. If columns in both tables have identical names, it will be necessary to indicate in which of the tables the column referred to is to be found.

For example, given the following table:

Vehicle Number	Driver Name	Driver Address
PQR - 789 VWX - 890 MNO - 234 ABC - 123	COOMBS CARTER FRASER SHARP	ROWVILLE MOORABBIN CANTERBURY ALBANY

TABLE 7

the command:

```
TABLE 8 = JOIN TABLE1 WITH TABLE7
          FOR TABLE1.Vehicle Number
          = TABLE7.Vehicle Number
```

would produce:

Vehicle Number	Manufacturer	Year Manufactured	Vehicle Number	Driver Name	Driver Address
ABC-123 PQR-789 MNO-234	FORD TOYOTA MAZDA	1985 1980 1984	ABC-123 PQR-789 MNO-234	SHARP COOMBS FRASER	ALBANY ROWEVILLE CANTERBURY

TABLE 8

Relational database products, such as dBASE, will have commands which will be variations or combinations of these operations. For example, some may enable the programmer to effect a restrict and a project or a join and a project in a single statement. However, it is essential that the programmer understands these fundamental table manipulations and is able to work with them individually, if needed.

10.7   Relational calculus

The standard in relational database operations is settling in favor of a relational calculus rather than a relational algebra. A relational calculus is a higher level of statements of table operations than needs to be carried out in a relational algebra. The programmer is freed from having to perform individual projects, restricts and joins and is able to use a higher form of expression of the information required.

A typical format, and one which is fast becoming an industry standard, is that used by SQL (Structured Query Language). The format of an enquiry is:

```
SELECT   column name(s)
FROM     table name(s)
WHERE    selection criteria (if any)
```

For example, using TABLE1 from the previous section, the command:

```
SELECT Vehicle Number, Year Manufactured
    FROM TABLE1
```

would produce the result:

```
ABC-123 1985
PQR-789 1980
DEF-456 1989
MNO-234 1984
```

A variation on this command:

```
SELECT Vehicle Number, Year Manufactured
FROM TABLE1
WHERE Manufacturer = FORD
AND Year Manufactured < 1987
```

would produce:

```
ABC-123 1985
```

Once again, using TABLE1 and TABLE7 from the previous section, the driver information relating to certain vehicles could be extracted by a command:

```
SELECT Vehicle Number, Driver Name
FROM TABLE1, TABLE7
WHERE TABLE1.Vehicle Number  =  TABLE2.Vehicle Number
AND Manufacturer  =  MAZDA
```

would produce:

```
MNO-234 Fraser
```

It will be apparent that this method of obtaining information from a set of relations, or tables, is much more concise that the equivalent set of restricts, projects and joins required by relational algebra. However, it must be kept in mind that, although the problem is more easily stated in relational calculus rather than in relational algebra, the behind-the-scenes workings required to produce the result are essentially the same. That is, the Select operation will still achieve its result by effecting a series of joins, projections and restrictions. A programmer must be wary of confusing the ease of stating the problem with the ease of obtaining an answer.

10.8   Conclusion

The importance of this chapter is to see that the traditional file-based approach to data storage is being replaced by a table-based methodology. Along with the change in data structure is coming a change in the means of manipulating the data. The algorithmic approach inherent in file-related operations is giving way to an algebra or calculus by which tables may be manipulated as entities rather than their contents accessed item-by-item.

10.9   Review questions

(1) The following data is held by a Motor Registration Office as the record for each vehicle in the Vehicle Registration File.

```
Vehicle = Registration Number
          + Make of car (e.g. Toyota)
          + Model of car (e.g. Corona)
          + Type of body (e.g. Sedan)
          + Horsepower
          + Weight of car
          + Engine number
          + Due date of next registration fee
          + Amount of registration fee
          + I{Owner Name
            + Owner address
            + Date of acquisition} N
```

Notes: Horsepower and weight will be the same for all vehicles which have the same make, model and type of body.

The details of owners will be present for all past owners of the vehicle.

The registration fee is calculated on the vehicle's weight and horsepower, the actual formula changing from time to time.

Many owners, particularly companies, own several vehicles.

You are required to show the above data in third normal form.

(2) An organization runs a variety of professional development courses for fee-paying registrants. Each course may be presented several times during any year and may have a different lecturer each time.

Set out below is the data held for each course:

```
Course Name
Course ID Code
Duration (in days)
Commencing date
Terminating date
Fee payable
Lecturer's name
Lecturer's fee
Venue
Maximum number of registrants
For each registrant:
    Name
    Address
    If sponsored by an employer:
        Employer's Name
        Employer's Address.
```

Notes: The fee payable by registrants and the duration of each course do not vary from one presentation of the course to another. The maximum number of registrants for any course depends on its venue.

The lecturer's fee. is negotiable and hence depends on the course and the lecturer concerned but not on the time at which the course is presented.

You are required to show the above data in third normal form.

(3) Set out below are tables of normalized data relating to a car rental operation.

VEHICLES

REG'N NO.	YEAR OF MANUFACTURE	MAKE	MODEL
BPD 146	1986	HOLDEN	SEDAN
CAL 203	1987	TOYOTA	4WD
BLF 000	1985	FORD	TRUCK

RATES

MODEL	DAILY CHARGE
SEDAN	$35
WAGON	$42
4WD	$45

HIRE AGREEMENTS

HIRER	REG'N NO.	NUMBER OF DAYS	DATE HIRED
HUNT	CAL 203	6	8/10/88
BOWMAN	BRM 149	4	15/10/88

Using the relational algebra constructs of APPEND, PROJECT, RESTRICT and JOIN, you are required to construct the following additional tables:

(i)   TABLE 1 containing the Registration Number and Model of all Toyota vehicles;
(ii)   TABLE 2 containing the Registration Number and Daily Charge of all vehicles;
(iii)   TABLE 3 containing the Hirer of all Holden vehicles for which the total hire charge will exceed $200.

(4) Using the tables provided for question 3 and the relational calculus construct of SELECT ... FROM ... WHERE ..., write queries which would produce:
(i)   the daily charge for the vehicle with the registration number CAL203, and
(ii)   the total hire charge due from hirer BOWMAN.

11 Array processing

11.1 Introduction

An array, or table, is a group of elements all of the same type and size and all having the same name. Any individual element is accessed by nominating its position within the array, for example, ITEM (10) or ITEM (POINTER).

The types of arrays which may be constructed and some consideration of the uses to which they might be put will be dealt with in this chapter, and algorithms will be provided for the operations most commonly performed on them.

11.2 Unordered linear arrays

A linear array, sometimes referred to as a linear list (as opposed to a linked list, see Chapter 12), is the simplest table structure able to be created and manipulated by a program. It consists of a contiguous series of data items, each able to hold one or more pieces of data. An unordered linear array is one in which the data items are held in no particular sequence. It is usually assumed that as many items as are currently stored in the array start at the first element and continue without gaps for as many elements of the table as are required.

Insertions/deletions

In an unordered linear table, additions to the table are inserted after the last element occupied. But how is that vacant element found? One method would be to examine the contents of each element in the table, starting with the first element, until one was found which contained no data, this being signaled by its contents containing some predetermined value which indicates its vacancy. A better method would be to maintain a pointer, the contents of which would always indicate the position of the first vacant element in the table. The concept of such a pointer is of importance in handling many data structures and will be referred to as a 'free pointer'. The free pointer must be incremented or decremented each time an item is added to or deleted from the table and is the prime means of determining when the table is full.

Deletions in such a table would normally be followed by some procedure to fill the gap in the table. This could be done by 'shifting up' the following elements but if a free pointer were maintained, this could be used to remove the last element currently held in the table and insert it in the gap caused by the deletion. This procedure is preferable as the shifting up operation would involve an average of $n/2$ movements of data, where n is the number of elements in the table.

Access to data in the table

In an unordered linear table, the only means of locating an item of data in the table is by a linear search. This involves the examination of each element of the table starting with the first, and proceeding until either:

(1) the required item is found;
(2) the data in the table is exhausted; or
(3) the physical end of the table is reached.

Hence, to locate an item which is in the table, the average number of elements which must be examined is $n/2$ (where n is the number of occupied elements in the table) and to detect the absence of an item from such a table will involve n examinations.

A typical algorithm to perform such a linear search would be:

```
Linear Search(ITEM_SOUGHT, ITEM_FOUND)
    local data
        TABLE_ITEM(100)              : character array
        INDEX, LAST_ITEM             : integer
        ITEM_SOUGHT                  : character
        ITEM_FOUND, SEARCH_DONE      : boolean
        TABLE_SIZE                   : integer, value = 100
    begin
        LAST_ITEM = TABLE_SIZE
        INDEX = 1
        SEARCH_DONE = false
        while SEARCH_DONE = false
            if ITEM_SOUGHT = TABLE_ITEM(INDEX)
                ITEM_FOUND = true
                SEARCH_DONE = true
            else
                if INDEX < LAST_ITEM
                    INDEX = INDEX + 1
                else
                    ITEM_FOUND = false
                    SEARCH_DONE = true
                end-if
            end-if
        end-while
    end
```

Notes:
(1) The status variable ITEM_FOUND will indicate the success or failure of the search on completion of the execution of the algorithm.
(2) An alternative approach would have been to set ITEM_FOUND to, say, False before starting the loop and then to alter its value to True only if the item sought was found. That is a weaker solution than explicitly setting the variable to True or False within the loop when one of the terminating conditions is encountered.
(3) A further alternative would have been to control the loop with two variables rather than one as shown, for example:

```
while ITEM_FOUND=False
    and INDEX ≤ LAST_ITEM
```

Again, it is preferable to control loops with a single variable to avoid the complications likely to arise in evaluating compound condition expressions (see Figure 11.1).

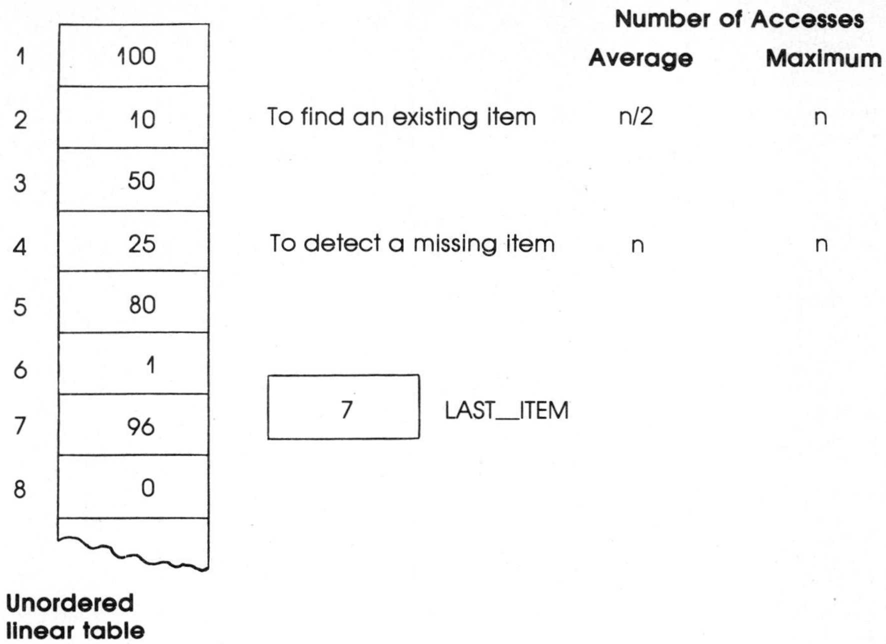
Number of Accesses
Average
Maximum
To find an existing item
n/2
n
To detect a missing item
n
n
1
100
2
10
3
50
4
25
5
80
6
1
7
96
8
0
7
LAST_ITEM
Unordered
linear table

Figure 11.1 *Linear search*

11.3 Ordered linear arrays

An ordered, or sequenced, linear array is one in which data items are held in a specific ascending or descending sequence.

(1) *Insertions/deletions*: In an ordered linear table it is essential that data items be maintained in sequence. Additions of new items will involve the shifting along of current items to make room for the insertion in the appropriate element. Deletions will similarly involve a shifting operation to fill the gap.

(2) *Access to data in the table*: Data in the table may be sought by a linear search as described above, but a much more efficient method is by means of a binary search.

A binary search is a technique whereby the area under consideration is continually halved until the item sought is found or its absence is detected. Unlike a linear search, it takes no longer in a binary search to detect the absence of an item than to detect its presence.

An algorithm for a binary search on an array in which data was held in ascending sequence would be:

```
Binary Search(ITEM_SOUGHT, ITEM_FOUND)
    local data
        TABLE_ITEM(500)                : character array
        HIGH, LOW, INDEX               : integer
        ITEM_SOUGHT                    : character
        ITEM_FOUND, SEARCH_DONE : boolean
        TABLE_SIZE                     : integer, value = 500
    begin
        LOW = 1
        HIGH = TABLE_SIZE
        SEARCH_DONE = false
        while SEARCH_DONE = false
            INDEX = (HIGH + LOW) / 2
            if ITEM_SOUGHT = TABLE_ITEM(INDEX)
                ITEM_FOUND = true
                SEARCH_DONE = true
            else
                if ITEM_SOUGHT < TABLE_ITEM(INDEX)
                    HIGH = INDEX − 1
                else
                    LOW = INDEX + 1
                end-if
            end-if
            if LOW > HIGH
                ITEM_FOUND = false
                SEARCH_DONE = true
            end-if
        end-while
    end
```

Using a binary search, the maximum number of elements which must be examined to detect the presence or absence of any item is given by $1 + \log_2 n$ where n is the number of elements in the table.

It should be noted that although a binary search is possible for an ordered table, a linear search will be faster if the table is small. The reason for this lies in the amount of computational overhead involved in a binary search compared with a simple subscript increment to accomplish a linear search.

11.4   Directly accessed arrays

The principle underlying the operation of a directly accessed table is that the location of any item within the table is indicated by the item itself. A simple example would be the case of 100 descriptions associated with 100 items having a code number ranging from 1 to 100. Hence, item 36 would be found in element 36 in the table, item 92 in element 92, and so on (see Figure 11.2).

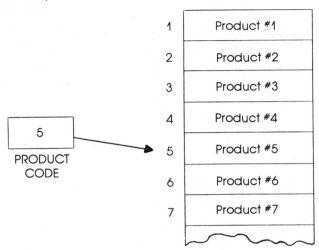

Figure 11.2 Directly accessed table

11.5   Hash-addressed arrays

The advantage of a directly accessed array was that no searching algorithm was needed to locate data held in the array. The disadvantage, however, was that the data stored needed to be such as to provide an exact correspondence between some attribute of the data (e.g., a product code) and the position in which it was stored. Such a correspondence does not often occur in practice.

It would be more common to find, for example, that an organization's range of 600 products had 5-digit identification codes spread more or less randomly between 1 and 99999 and perhaps even containing non-numeric characters. If it is still desirable to pursue speed of retrieval of data by a direct access technique rather than a searching technique, a process referred to as 'hashing' may be carried out on the key (i.e., the unique identifier) of the data item. Hashing is a procedure which computes a table address from a given key. Because the procedure is a numerical operation, the key must be expressed as a numeric quantity. This implies that any non-numeric characters within the key are reduced to numeric values by either ascribing an arbitrary value to each character (e.g., A=1, B=2 . . . Z=26, etc.) or by operating on the binary coded internal representation of the character as held in ASCII, EBCDIC, and so on.

The numeric key is then subjected to a procedure which computes from it a number within the range of 1 to the size of the array. This procedure is referred to as a 'hashing function' or 'mapping function'. A commonly used hashing function is one which uses a division technique and computes the table address from the remainder, for example:

(1) Divide the key of the item to be stored or retrieved by the largest prime number which is not greater than the number of elements in the table.
(2) Ignoring the quotient, add 1 to the remainder of the division to give the table address.

For example:

Size of table: 100 elements
Largest prime number $\leq$ 100: 97
Key of item to be processed: 30679
$$\frac{30679}{97} = \text{Quotient } 316$$
$$\text{Remainder } 27$$

Array address $= 27 + 1$
$= 28$
that is data item 30679 would be stored in the 28th element of the array.

The advantage of such a technique is that it is much faster than a searching operation. The obvious disadvantage is that there are likely to be a number of keys for which the hashing function produces identical array addresses. These are referred to as synonyms or collisions and must be handled by storing the collided items in elements other than those indicated by the hashing function.

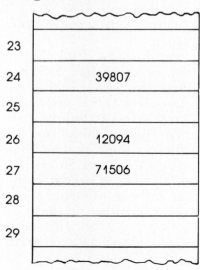

Figure 11.3

Consider a table which currently contains the items as seen in Figure 11.3. Three further items are to be placed in the table, all of them generating the same element address via the hashing function:

Key of item to be stored: 14796   20493   37108
COMPUTED ADDRESS: 23   23   23

Three typical approaches to the solution of storing the collided items are:

(1) Store the first item in its 'home' address and store the collisions in the next vacant table element located via a linear search. They would be subsequently retrieved by the same procedure (see Figure 11.4)

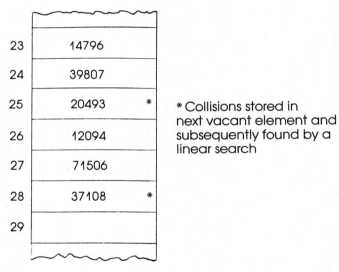

Figure 11.4

(2) Store the items as indicated in (1) but maintain a series of pointers to the collided items (see Figure 11.5). This method shortens the retrieval process by eliminating the necessity for the linear search as needed for method (1).

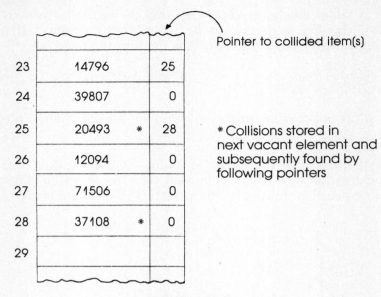

Figure 11.5

(3) Store the first item in its 'home' address and store collisions in a separate overflow table (see Figure 11.6). This method eliminates the problem which occurs with both of the previous methods, that is, that each collision stored in the main table occupies an element which another data item would be likely to compute as a 'home address and find it already occupied.

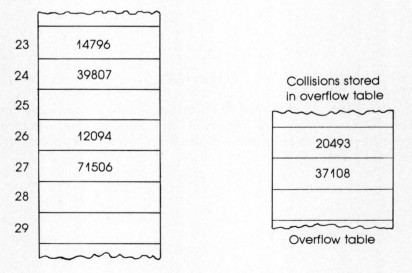

Figure 11.6

11.6   Indexed linear arrays

A compromise between a single linear table and a directly addressable table may be reached by the use of a directly addressable index to an unordered linear table. The following example should illustrate the technique.

Consider a case where a table of product descriptions, each of 40 characters, must be maintained by a program which must translate a three-digit numeric product code into its appropriate alphanumeric description. The three-digit code allows for 1000 possible values, but it is found that only 200 of these values are actually used and are randomly spread between zero and 999.

Three alternatives may be considered:

(1) A linear table of 200 elements each of 43 characters (the three-digit product code + the 40-character description).

   Storage requirements: $200 \times 43 = 8600$ characters

   Access time:
   (a)   If table is unordered, access is slow owing to the linear searching operation, but table insertions and deletions are simple.
   (b)   If table is ordered, access may be via a binary search which will take up to 8 table accesses + related computation overhead for each search, and table insertions and deletions are lengthy procedures.

(2) A directly addressable table may be constructed using either 1000 elements of 40 characters (= 40,000 characters of storage) and enabling each description to be retrieved by using its code as a subscript, or by using only 200 elements of 43 characters and employing a hash function for computing the address of each description together with a collision-handling procedure. Both of these methods are time-consuming.

(3) Two tables may be constructed:
   (a)   An index table of 1000 elements each of three digits (= 3000 characters of storage) — For each product code used between 0 and 999, the corresponding element in this index table would contain a pointer to its description held in the second table, that is, the subscript of the element in the second table which held the description relating to that code.
   (b)   An unordered linear table of 200 elements each of 40 characters (= 8000 characters of storage), each element holding one description.

The access to any description would therefore involve only two table accesses and no computation or searching procedure, the operation being:

(a)   Use the product code to directly access the index table and extract the subscript of the related description.

(b)   Use that subscript to directly access the second table and retrieve the appropriate description.

It can be seen that this third alternative provides an access time almost as fast as a single directly addressable table without paying a large penalty in storage space beyond that required by an unordered linear table and without the complexities of maintaining an ordered linear table (see Figure 11.7)

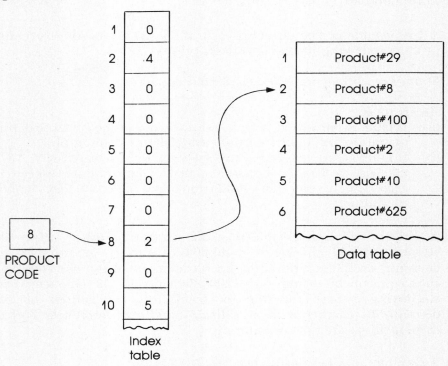

Figure 11.7 *Indexed array*

11.7   Multi-dimensional arrays

Most programming languages give the programmer the facility to construct arrays of more than one dimension. Thus, two-dimensional arrays may be thought of as having rows and columns. Three-dimensional arrays may be thought of as having pages, rows and columns, and so on. Remember that the pages, rows, columns are only a notional concept to aid the programmer. The array held in memory is still essentially a one-dimensional array. The physical arrangement of the array elements is referred to as 'mapping' and is effected in different ways for different languages, as, for example, in Figure 11.8.

When accessing elements in a multi-dimensional array, a separate subscript is required for each declared dimension. The subscripts must be nominated in the hierarchy required by the conventions of the programming language used.

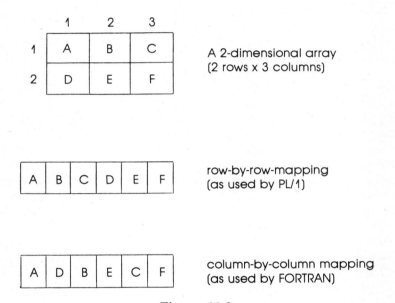

Figure 11.8

Hence, in a language which uses column-by-column mapping, the array in Figure 11.8 would be declared as:

ARRAY (3,2)

(i.e., 3 columns each of 2 rows). The element containing C would be accessed as element (3,1) and that containing D would be element (1,2).

Whatever the mapping convention, the quoted order of the subscripts when accessing an element in an array must be the same as the order used in the declaration, or creation, of the array.

11.8 Pseudo-ordered and self-organizing arrays

From the previous discussion it can be seen that there is a conflict which must be resolved between speed of access to data and ease of maintenance of the data held in an array. Unordered arrays provide for simple maintenance procedures (i.e., additions and deletions) but do not provide speedy access, being limited to linear searching. Ordered arrays provide rapid access via a binary search but make the maintenance of the sequence of the items a burden.

There is a further technique which provides a compromise in this area. A linear search is easy to implement but slow to execute on large arrays because the items sought may be located randomly throughout the array. An alternative approach is to sequence the data in order of frequency of access rather than according to the primary characteristic of the data itself (i.e., numeric or alphabetic sequence). This implies that the most often-sought data items are held toward the start of the array and those least often accessed toward the end. A linear search will now enable the most 'popular' data to be found rapidly by a procedure which does not require the computational overhead of a binary search.

A problem still remains, however, with the maintenance of the array. New items inserted in the table would seem to require a prediction about their future frequency of access in order to locate them appropriately. Similarly, deleted items would seem to still require the 'shifting along' procedure dictated by an ordered array. Another apparent problem is the changing access patterns to the data in the array. As items become more or less frequently accessed, they will need to move toward the front or back of the array, respectively.

These problems of maintenance can be overcome in a variety of ways, two of which are outlined below:

(1) *Dynamic reorganization*: When any item of data within the array is accessed, it is exchanged with the item immediately before it in the table. With this procedure, frequently accessed data will automatically shift toward the top of the array. displacing less frequently accessed data.

At any given instant, the positions of the data items in the array will be an accurate reflection of their current 'popularity'. With this operation, new items can be added to the array at the lowest position and will rise automatically to whatever level is appropriate to their access pattern. Deleted items may be flagged and removed when they eventually reach the bottom of the array.

The searching performance which this method of organization enables is only achieved at the cost of some additional housekeeping procedures (the swapping of adjacent items of data) for *every* access to the array. This method is used by some operating systems in managing memory space allocation to programs.

(2) *Periodic reorganization*: This procedure is essentially similar to dynamic reorganization in its aim to keep the most frequently accessed data at the head of the array. It differs from the former method in that the re-sequencing is done at prescribed intervals rather than every time data is accessed. Associated with each data item in the array is a counter which is incremented each time the data item is accessed. At the end of a period, which may be a month, a day or an hour, depending on the urgency of the task involved, the array is re-sequenced on the contents of the counters and the counters all returned to a value of zero.

This procedure provides an array of data which is never as up to date in access frequency sequence as that provided by dynamic reorganization but does not require the housekeeping overhead of that method.

11.9   Sorting

The evolution of computer sorting techniques parallels the evolution of computers. Sorting of data was possibly the first common point of contact between the original scientific uses of computers and their increasing involvement in commerce.

The considerable body of theory underlying the principles of sorting and the more esoteric procedures involved are left to the pursuit of the more interested student and this section will deal with sorting problems which may be encountered in common program applications and which may be worthwhile solving within a program rather than by having recourse to a manufacturer's standard sort utility.

11.10   Bubble sort

The 'bubble sort' is the simplest method of sorting the elements in an array. It relies on a series of compare-and-exchange operations performed on successive passes through an array until the items are in the required sequence.

On each pass through the array, each pair of adjacent elements is compared and their contents exchanged if they are not already in the desired sequence. This is repeated for as many passes through the array as are required to reach a situation where a complete pass may be made without any exchanges being necessary. On each successive pass, data items need be compared no further than the point at which the last exchange occurred in the earlier pass. Figure 11.9 should illustrate the procedure.

Element number:	1	2	3	4	5	6	7	8	9	10
Initial contents:	14	6	23	18	7	47	2	83	16	38
After first pass:	6	14	18	7	23	2	47	16	38	83
After second pass:	6	14	7	18	2	23	16	38	47	83
After third pass:	6	7	14	2	18	16	23	38	47	83
After fourth pass:	6	7	2	14	16	18	23	38	47	83
After fifth pass:	6	2	7	14	16	18	23	38	47	83
Final pass:	2	6	7	14	16	18	23	38	47	83

Figure 11.9

An algorithm for this procedure is as follows:

```
Bubble Sort
   local data
         TABLE_ITEM(10)        : integer array
         TARGET, LEFT, RIGHT,
         LAST_SWAP, HOLD    : integer
         SWAP, SORT_DONE    : boolean
         TABLE_SIZE            : integer, value = 10
   begin
         TARGET = TABLE_SIZE
         SORT_DONE = false
         while SORT_DONE = false
            SWAP = false
            LEFT = 1
            RIGHT = 2
            while RIGHT not > TARGET
               if TABLE_ITEM(RIGHT) < TABLE_ITEM(LEFT)
                     HOLD = TABLE_ITEM(RIGHT)
                     TABLE_ITEM(RIGHT) = TABLE_ITEM(LEFT)
                     TABLE_ITEM(LEFT) = HOLD . . . swaps items
                     SWAP = true
                     LAST_SWAP = LEFT
               end-if
               LEFT = LEFT + 1
               RIGHT = RIGHT + 1
            end-while
            if SWAP = false
               SORT_DONE = true
            else
               TARGET = LAST_SWAP
            end-if
         end-while
   end
```

The number of compare-and-swap operations required to sort the contents of an array sequence obviously depends on the initial sequence of the items before sorting.

The number of comparisons required to sort items into sequence via a bubble sort is in the order of $\frac{1}{2}N^2$, where N is the number of items to sort. This means that as N gets larger, the sorting procedure becomes exponentially less efficient. Because of the simplicity of its algorithm, however, a bubble sort remains the easiest method of sorting small volumes of data.

11.11   Selection sort

Like the bubble sort, a selection sort works on a compare-and-exchange basis. Assuming that the items are to be sorted in ascending sequence, the selection sort starts at the first item in the array and scans through the array looking for the smallest value. If that value is less than the first item, it is swapped with the first item. The sort now moves to the second item in the array and again scans forward to find the smallest item. If that item is less than the second element, it is swapped with the second item. This procedure is repeated for all the remaining items in the array.

Using the same values as in Figure 11.9, Figure 11.10 illustrates the procedure. It can be seen that in comparison to a bubble sort, a selection sort may need to make more comparisons but will usually make fewer exchanges of items.

As for the buble sort, the number of comparisons required to effect the sort is in the order of $\frac{1}{2}N^2$, where N is the number of items to sort.

Element number:	1	2	3	4	5	6	7	8	9	10
Initial contents:	14	6	23	18	7	47	2	83	16	38
After first pass:	2	6	23	18	7	47	14	83	16	38
After second pass:	2	6	23	18	7	47	14	83	16	38
After third pass:	2	6	7	18	23	47	14	83	16	38
After fourth pass:	2	6	7	14	23	47	18	83	16	38
After fifth pass:	2	6	7	14	16	47	18	83	23	38
After sixth pass:	2	6	7	14	16	18	47	83	23	38
After seventh pass:	2	6	7	14	16	18	23	83	47	38
After eighth pass:	2	6	7	14	16	18	23	38	47	83
After ninth pass:	2	6	7	14	16	18	23	38	47	83
After tenth pass:	2	6	7	14	16	18	23	38	47	83

Figure 11.10

An algorithm for the procedure is as follows:

```
Selection Sort
  local data
      TABLE_ITEM(10)         : integer array
      TARGET, INDEX, HOLD,
      SMALLEST, COMPARE  : integer
      TABLE_SIZE             : integer, value = 10
  begin
      TARGET = TABLE_SIZE
      INDEX = 1
      while INDEX < TARGET
          SMALLEST = INDEX
          COMPARE = INDEX + 1
          while COMPARE not > TARGET
              if TABLE_ITEM(COMPARE) < TABLE_ITEM(SMALLEST)
                  SMALLEST = COMPARE
              end-if
              COMPARE = COMPARE + 1
          end-while
          if SMALLEST not = INDEX
              HOLD = TABLE_ITEM(INDEX)
              TABLE_ITEM(INDEX) = TABLE_ITEM(SMALLEST)
              TABLE_ITEM(SMALLEST) = HOLD ... swaps items
          end-if
          INDEX = INDEX + 1
      end-while
  end
```

11.12   Shell sort

This sorting algorithm is named after its proposer, Donald Shell, and is another variation on the compare-and-swap principle of the bubble and selection sorts. It uses essentially the same approach as the bubble sort except that the span for comparing items starts at half the size of the array to be sorted and is halved again each time a pass is made through the array without needing to exchange the positions of any of the items. Finally, the span is reduced to a value of 1 and hence the final passes are identical with a bubble sort.

If an array of 100 items were to be sorted, the comparison span would start at 50 (100/2) and the algorithm would compare item 1 with item 51, item 2 with item 52, and so on. After a successful (i.e., requiring no swaps) pass at this span, the span would be reduced to 25 (50/2). The procedure would then compare item 1 with item 26, item 2 with item 27, and so on. The values of the span would then successively become 12,6,3,1 and finally terminate when 1/2 gave a value of zero.

The value of a Shell sort is its vastly superior performance compared with bubble and selection sorts as the size of the array to be sorted increases. The number of comparisons required for a Shell sort is the order of $1.5N\log_2 N$.

The work done in the sort is therefore a logarithmic function of the size of the array rather than an exponential function, as is the case with the previous sorts examined.

An algorithm for a Shell sort is as follows:

```
Shell Sort
    local data
        TABLE_ITEM(100)      : character array
        SPAN, COUNTER,
        TARGET, RIGHT, LEFT : integer
        HOLD                 : character
        PASS_DONE            : boolean
        TABLE_SIZE           : integer, value = 100
    begin
        SPAN = TABLE_SIZE / 2
        while SPAN > 0
            COUNTER = 1
            TARGET = TABLE_SIZE - SPAN
            while COUNTER not > TARGET
                LEFT = COUNTER
                PASS_DONE = false
                while PASS_DONE = false
                    RIGHT = LEFT + SPAN
                    if TABLE_ITEM(LEFT) < TABLE_ITEM(RIGHT)
                        PASS_DONE = true
                    else
                        HOLD = TABLE_ITEM(RIGHT)
                        TABLE_ITEM(RIGHT) = TABLE_ITEM(LEFT)
                        TABLE_ITEM(LEFT) = HOLD ... swaps items
                        if LEFT > SPAN
                            LEFT = LEFT - SPAN
                        else
                            PASS_DONE = true
                        end-if
                    end-if
                end-while
                COUNTER = COUNTER + 1
            end-while
            SPAN = SPAN / 2
        end-while
    end
```

Note: When calculating each value of SPAN; the division by 2 must produce an integer result which is rounded down, that is, $51/2=25$, $1/2=0$, etc.

Figure 11.11 provides a comparison of the performance of bubble, selection and Shell sorts for a variety of sizes of arrays. The times are those produced on an extremely well-known personal computer.

From these figures it is apparent that a Shell sort becomes imperative in the interest of efficiency as the number of items to be sorted becomes larger.

In Chapter 14, under a discussion of recursion, a further sorting algorithm (a Quicksort) is shown. Unless you are familiar with this technique and are using a language which permits recursion, that algorithm should be regarded as an academic exercise only.

Number of items sorted, N ($\frac{1}{2}N^2$) [$1\frac{1}{2}N \log_2 N$]	Bubble sort			Selection sort			Shell sort		
	Comparisons	Swaps needed	Time	Comparisons	Swaps needed	Time	Comparisons	Swaps needed	Time
10 (50) [60]	37	23	1 sec	45	7	1 sec	34	11	1 sec
20 (200) [150]	146	81	5 secs	190	17	3 secs	106	27	4 secs
50 (1250) [500]	1180	629	34secs	1225	45	20secs	341	121	16 secs
100 (5000) [1000]	4919	2642	2 mins	4950	96	1 m 20 sec	873	330	37 secs
500 (125000) [6700]	esti- mated 125000	esti- mated 63000	50mins	125500	450	33mins	7077	3355	5 mins

Figure 11.11 Comparison of sorting techniques

11.13 Conclusion

The construction, maintenance and manipulation of arrays is an essential skill for every programmer. It is one of the responsiblities of a programmer to be able to construct an appropriate storage structure for the data which has to be processed. A familiarity with a variety of types of arrays and the common processes associated with them should be regarded as a fundamental programming tool.

An appreciation of searching and sorting techniques and their relative effciency is important. A programmer, through ignorance of any sorting technique other than a bubble sort, might implement a program using that technique to accept an order from a user at a terminal and sort the order items into, say, product number sequence. If the order is small, the delay in sorting its contents is minimal. For orders of some hundreds of items, the delay would render the system inoperable.

11.14 Review questions

(1) A library has a computer system which records the borrowing and return of its books. Each time a loan or return is processed by a librarian, a record is written to a serial file containing the following data:

```
Book ID number   : character
Time (hhmm)      : integer (hours, minutes)
Transaction code : character (L = loan, R = return)
```

The time is recorded on a 24-hour clock basis, e.g., 3.25pm is recorded as 1525 hours. The file ends with a standard end-of-file sentinel and relates to the transactions of a single day.

Write the pseudocode for a program which will read the transaction file for a given day and output the hour of the day during which most transactions occurred. Hours are to be taken 0900 to 0959, 1000 to 1059, etc. Assume that the library is open from 0900 hours to 2159 hours.

(2) A serial file contains detals of the issues of goods from a group of 5 warehouses operated by a certain organization. The records on the file are in no particular sequence. Goods are identified by a series of 200 consecutive product codes ranging from 1000 to 1199.

Each record contains:

```
Product code     : integer (1000 . . . 1199)
Date of issue    : character
Warehouse code   : integer (1 . . . 5)
Quantity issued  : integer
```

The file ends with a standard end-of-file sentinel.

A report is required listing the total quantity of each product issued from each warehouse, together with a total for each product and grand totals for each warehouse and all products. The format of this report is to be:

Stock Issue Report

Product Code	Warehouses 1	2	3	4	5	Total Quantity
1000	100	0	0	300	0	400
1010	0	40	130	0	0	170
.	.	.	.	.	.	.
.	.	.	.	.	.	.
.	.	.	.	.	.	.
1199	50	0	70	0	30	150
	4000	2000	3000	1500	2600	13100

Write the pseudocode for a program which would read the file and produce the report without requiring the input data to be sorted.

(3) A serial file contains records relating to goods sold over a period of 12 months in six states. The records each contain:

Month (1-12);
State code (VIC, NSW, SA, WA, TAS, QLD);
Value of sale ($$$$.cc).

The records are in no particular sequence on the file and the month codes relate to a fiscal rather than a calendar year, hence month 1 is July and month 12 is June.

A program is required to read the file and produce a listing of the 72 totals (12 months for six states) in descending order of total value of sales, for example:

Sales report

Sales value	State	Month
674320	NSW	MAR
512306	SA	APR
493800	VIC	JAN
.	.	.
.	.	.
.	.	.
.		
1400	TAS	AUG
950	WA	MAY

You are required to design the data structure(s) needed to accumulate this information and write a pseudocode algorithm to read the file, accumulate the totals and print them in the required sequence.

(4) You are required to write a pseudocode algorithm for an insertion sort. The array to be sorted will need to hold a maximum of 100 integers. The numbers input to the sort will end with a value of 999 which is not to be part of the sorted array.

An insertion sort accepts incoming items in random sequence, determines the position at which the new item must be inserted in the array to maintain the sequence of the data, shifts other data along (if necessary) to make room for the incoming item and places the new arrival in its appropriate position. The following should indicate the procedure:

New item	Array
20	20
30	20, 30
15	15, 20, 30
25	15, 20, 25, 30
10	10, 15, 20, 25, 30
50	10, 15, 20, 25, 30, 50
18	10, 15, 18, 20, 25, 30, 50
etc.	

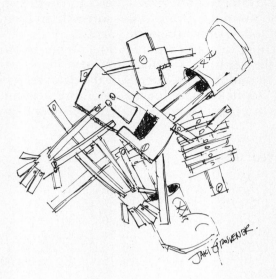

12 Abstract data structures

12.1 Introduction

One of the functions performed by data structures in a computer system is the internal representation, or modeling, of external entities in the world around us.

Programs are required to process, and, therefore, data structures are required to represent such situations as:

- seating plans for a theatre;
- a railway or road network;
- a queue of tasks awaiting processing;
- text comprising sentences, paragraphs and sections in a report (for 'word processing' applications);
- plots on a radar screen for radar operators' training simulation exercises;
- game playing situations: board games such as chess; tunnel-and-cave games such as 'Adventure'; and seek-and-catch games such as 'Space Invaders'.

In all these situations, a program must contain not only a suitable algorithm to perform the required data processing but also an appropriate data structure which most easily allows the program execute those operations which reflect the manipulation of the real-world entity.

12.2   Data abstraction

With the proliferation of more complex data structures there has been an increased use of data abstraction. The concept of data abstraction is that of defining a data structure and a series of possible operations on that structure and making the implementation of the process 'transparent' to the programmer. For example, we may define a stack as a series of similar elements which operate on a last-in-first-out principle whereby we may access only the most recently added item. We then define a 'push' as an operation which adds an element to the stack and a 'pop' as one which retrieves an element. It is then immaterial to the programmer whether the stack is maintained by a pointer moving along a linear array or by a list structure. Data base management packages are probably the most highly developed examples of data abstraction because a program may request the 'next' or 'prior' items in a set or the 'owner' of that set and be freed from the complexities (and made oblivious of the overhead!) of the processing required to retrieve the requested item.

The concept of data abstraction interlocks with that of structured programming which also deals with levels of abstraction. For example, we write a module of code which returns an item sought in a table. To the calling routine, the method of performing the search is immaterial. The search routine may then address itself more particularly to the data structure of the table and may be successively refined for efficiency without affecting the remainder of the program.

In looking at abstract data structures, we will define the abstraction which typified the data structure concerned, present a method of physically representing the structure and provide algorithms for common operations on the structures.

12.3   Queues

A queue is a data structure capable of holding a series of items to be processed on a first-in-first-out basis. It needs to be accessible at both its head (for removal of items) and its tail (for addition of items).

The operations usually required for queues are:

- *Initialize*: Set the initial conditions before the start of the queue's operation.
- *Insert*: Add a new item to the queue (provided that the queue is not full).
- *Remove*: Delete an item from the queue (provided that the queue is not empty).
- *Count*: Count the number of items currently in the queue.
- *Space*: Count the number of vacancies currently in the queue.

The queues with which we are familiar in the real world usually operate by moving each of their items one place forward whenever one is removed from the head of the queue. When representing queues inside a computer, rather than adjusting the position of items in a queue by physically moving them from element to element, a better approach is to maintain two pointers, one indicating the head of the queue and the other its tail. The pointers must therefore be capable of operating on the table on a wrap-around basis. A counter may be used to indicate the number of items currently in the table (see Figure 12.1).

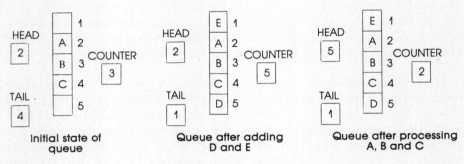

Initial state of queue   Queue after adding D and E   Queue after processing A, B and C

Figure 12.1

Note that it should not be necessary to physically delete items which have been logically removed. They will be over-written with new items added later as the queue operates.

The easiest method of physically representing a queue in a computer is with a linear array (although a linked list may also be used).

Algorithms:

global data
    QUEUE_ITEM(100)   : integer array
    COUNTER, HEAD, TAIL : integer
    QUEUE_SIZE   : integer, value = 100

Initialize   ... ready the queue for use
   begin
      COUNTER = 0
      HEAD = 1
      TAIL = QUEUE_SIZE
   end

Insert(NEW_ITEM, INSERT_OK)   ... add new item to end of queue
   local data
      NEW_ITEM : integer
      INSERT_OK : boolean
   begin
      if COUNTER = QUEUE_SIZE
         INSERT_OK = false   ... queue is full
      else
         COUNTER = COUNTER + 1
         TAIL = TAIL + 1
         if TAIL > QUEUE_SIZE
            TAIL = 1
         end-if
         QUEUE_ITEM(TAIL) = NEW_ITEM
         INSERT_OK = true
      end-if
   end

Remove(ITEM_REMOVED, REMOVE_OK)   ... remove item from head of queue

   local data
      ITEM_REMOVED : integer
      REMOVE_OK   : boolean
   begin
      if COUNTER = 0
         REMOVE_OK = false   ... queue is empty
      else
         ITEM_REMOVED = QUEUE_ITEM(HEAD)
         COUNTER = COUNTER − 1
         REMOVE_OK = true
         HEAD = HEAD + 1
         if HEAD > QUEUE_SIZE
            HEAD = 1
         end-if
      end-if
   end

Accessing COUNTER would provide a procedure with a count of the number of items currently in the queue, and the value of (QUEUE_SIZE − COUNTER) would indicate the space currently left in the queue.

A queue would be used by a program in a situation calling for the processing of a number of items in the order in which they are received. The queue does not have to be large enough to hold all items processed, but merely those waiting to be dealt with at any time. The space in the queue is hence constantly reused, but the programmer will need to be able to predict the maximum number of items the queue will need to hold.

12.4 Stacks

A stack is a data structure capable of holding a series of items to be processed on a last-in-first-out basis. It needs to be accessible only at its top. New items are added at the top of the stack and items are retrieved also from the top.

The operations usually required for a stack are:

- *Initialize*: Set the initial conditions prior to the operation of the stack.
- *Push*: Add a new item to the top of the stack (provided that the stack is not full).
- *Pop*: Delete an item from the top of the stack (provided that the stack is not empty).
- *Count*: Count the number of items currently in the stack.
- *Space*: Count the number of vacancies currently in the stack.

Figure 12.2 illustrates the use of a stack.

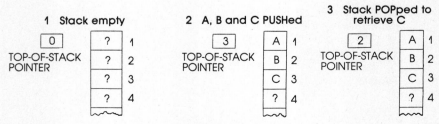

Figure 12.2

Note that retrieving items by POPping the stack does not physically remove them from the table; they will remain to be overwritten by the next item to be PUSHed.

Once again, the easiest method of physically representing a stack in a computer is by means of a linear array (although, as for a queue, a linked list may be used).

Algorithms:

```
global data
    STACK_ITEM(20) : integer array
    TOP_OF_STACK   : integer
    STACK_SIZE     : integer, value = 20

Initialize                          . . . ready the stack for use
    begin
        TOP_OF_STACK = 0
    end

Push(NEW_ITEM, PUSH_OK)             . . . add a new item to the top of the stack
    local data
        NEW_ITEM : integer
        PUSH_OK  : boolean
    begin
        if TOP_OF_STACK = STACK_SIZE
            PUSH_OK = false         . . . stack is full
        else
            TOP_OF_STACK = TOP_OF_STACK + 1
            STACK_ITEM(TOP_OF_STACK) = NEW_ITEM
            PUSH_OK = true
        end-if
    end

Pop(ITEM_REMOVED, POP_OK)    . . . remove an item from the top of the stack
    local data
        ITEM_REMOVED : integer
        POP_OK       : boolean
    begin
        if TOP_OF_STACK = 0
            POP_OK = false          . . . stack is empty
        else
            ITEM_REMOVED = STACK_ITEM(TOP_OF_STACK)
            TOP_OF_STACK = TOP_OF_STACK − 1
            POP_OK = true
        end-if
    end
```

Accessing the TOP_OF_STACK pointer will provide a procedure with a count of the number of items currently in the stack and the value of (STACK_SIZE − TOP_OF_STACK) will provide a counter of the number of vacant positions remaining in the stack.

A stack is used by a program in a situation in which items need to be processed in the reverse order to that in which they were encountered. An example will be seen later in this chapter when dealing with the processing of trees. In such a case, data items are dealt with in a sequence which requires the program to proceed as far as possible along a certain path before it can process an element in the data structure. The program must then retrace its steps, processing the items previously skipped over, in the reverse order to that in which they were encountered.

A program executing nested subroutines has the same problem at run-time. Procedure A calls procedure B which calls procedure C. Procedure C must return to B which must then return to A. Each time a subroutine is called, a program may store a return point on a stack. When a procedure reaches its exit, the return point at the top of the stack is retrieved (and then discarded) and the program branches back to that location.

Cave-and-tunnel games such as Adventure may also make use of such a technique. When the player arrives at a deadend, he or she may wish to turn around and retrace their steps. This is only possible if the game has stacked their previous locations and can return to them in the reverse order to that in which the player originally visited them.

12.5   Linked lists

A linked list is a data structure composed of a series of elements sometimes referred to as atoms and containing data together with a pointer to the next atom. A list will be associated with a list header which will contain a pointer to the first atom in the list. The last atom in a list may contain a null pointer to indicate the end of the data or may point back to the head of the list, in which case a circular structure is created which is often referred to as a chain or ring.

The advantage of such a structure is that elements may be inserted and deleted by manipulation of the pointers rather than by physical movement of the data.

A list of vacant atoms is maintained, called the free list, and additions to other lists are made by removing an atom (usually the first atom) from the free list and inserting it in or appending it to the other list. Similarly, atoms deleted from any list may be added back (usually at the front) to the free list either immediately upon release from their earlier list or by being flagged and picked up later by a 'garbage collection' operation. An example of these operations is shown in Figures 12.3 and 12.4.

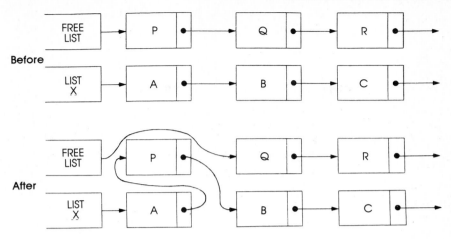

Figure 12.3 Inserting elements in a list

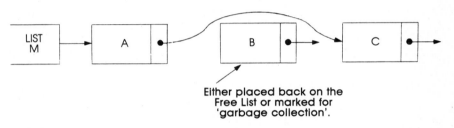

Figure 12.4 Deleting elements from a list

A list structure may be used to maintain a series of items in sequence without physically rearranging them as items are added to and deleted from the set. Figure 12.5 should illustrate the procedure.

A linked list may be physically represented in a computer by either a linear array of items, each of which is capable of holding a data item and a pointer, or by parallel arrays of data items and pointers such that the pointer in the nth element of the pointer array relates to the data item in the nth element of the data array.

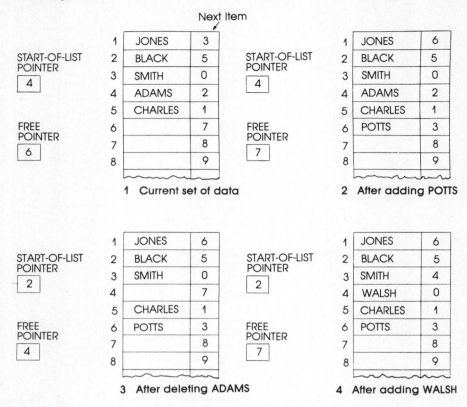

Next Item

1   Current set of data

1	JONES	3
2	BLACK	5
3	SMITH	0
4	ADAMS	2
5	CHARLES	1
6		7
7		8
8		9

START-OF-LIST POINTER [4]

FREE POINTER [6]

2   After adding POTTS

1	JONES	6
2	BLACK	5
3	SMITH	0
4	ADAMS	2
5	CHARLES	1
6	POTTS	3
7		8
8		9

START-OF-LIST POINTER [4]

FREE POINTER [7]

3   After deleting ADAMS

1	JONES	6
2	BLACK	5
3	SMITH	0
4		7
5	CHARLES	1
6	POTTS	3
7		8
8		9

START-OF-LIST POINTER [2]

FREE POINTER [4]

4   After adding WALSH

1	JONES	6
2	BLACK	5
3	SMITH	4
4	WALSH	0
5	CHARLES	1
6	POTTS	3
7		8
8		9

START-OF-LIST POINTER [2]

FREE POINTER [7]

Figure 12.5

In a situation in which items are continually being appended to an existing list, it is advantageous to maintain not only a Start-of-List Pointer but also an End-of-List Pointer. This latter pointer enables the position of what is currently the last element in the structure to be determined without a search through all of the list elements.

Typical operations required on linked lists are:

- *Initialize free list*: Before any list operations take place, the array must be initially created as free space.
- *Insert item in sequence*: A data item is to be added to a list (which may have to be created for the purpose) in a logical sequence which maintains the list in ascending order.

More complex list structures may be created in which:

(1) Each element contains both a pointer to the following element and one to the previous element. Such a list may be processed in either direction, as in Figure 12.6.

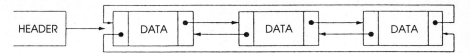

Figure 12.6 *A bi-directional list (circular)*

(2) Each element contains three pointers, a next and a prior pointer and in addition a pointer to the list header. In such a list, if any element is encountered at random, immediate access is available to the start of the list without having to traverse each intervening element, as in Figure 12.7.

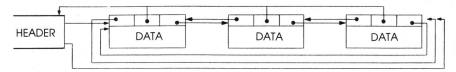

Figure 12.7 *Pointers maintained to prior, next, header*

Linked lists are used extensively in all facets of computing. Consider the following examples:

(1) A word processing application, by its nature, needs to be able to alter the physical sequence of sentences within a paragraph or paragraphs within a document. It needs to allow the operator to insert or delete words or sentences without the operator needing to re-key the entire work.

(2) A multiuser operating system needs to cater for, perhaps, hundreds of terminal users, each keying in text of varying and unpredictable length. The operating system cannot allocate a fixed amount of storage space in memory to handle the input from each terminal because the space required may be some dozens of characters or thousands of characters. The operating system may allocate a certain volume of storage space to allow the terminal user to get started and may then extend this space as required for as long as the user keys in data.

(3) A disk housekeeping system may need to allow a user to extend the sizes of many files stored on a single disk. The user may not be able to predict the ultimate size of any of these files and hence the housekeeping system cannot allocate a fixed (and inflexible) area for each file. Therefore, as the user extends files, additional areas of unused space must be located and associated with those areas currently holding the contents of the files.

All of these examples have common requirements of:

(1) an unpredictable environment;

(2) the need to extend and contract storage space dynamically as a task is being executed; and

(3) the need to maintain a sequence, or continuity, of data without having the ability to set aside a fixed area of storage and gradually fill it as data is accumulated over a period of time.

This is the type of environment suited for list processing. Linked lists provide the ability to maintain a data structure in a logical sequence without the necessity for that logical sequence to be implemented by a physical sequence.

12.6   Tree structures

A tree structure is one in which each element, frequently referred to as a 'node', contains one or more items of data and the possibility of two or more pointers. A tree may be referred to as being of order n where n is the number of subordinates (or 'children') possessed by each node. The value of trees, as was the case with linked lists, lies in their being able to represent a sequence or hierarchy by logical rather than physical means. As for lists, relationships are maintained by pointers and items may be added or deleted by adjustment of the pointers rather than the physical rearrangement of the other elements in the structure.

Tree structures are widely used in computing, often being implemented in system software functions providing 'transparent' facilities for application programs. The following discussion will provide an insight into their operation and sufficient explanation for the programmer to be able to implement the most useful tree structures in appropriate situations.

As for a list, a tree will usually make use of a free pointer to indicate the position of the next vacant node in which data may be placed.

Accessing items in a tree is often referred to as 'traversing' the tree and there are a number of common traversal strategies (the names of which may vary from one reference work to another):

```
In-order:   Left branches — Root — Right branches
End-order: Left branches — Right branches — Root
Pre-order: Root — Left branches — Right branches
```

The root of a tree is the first element accessed in the processing of the tree. It is the node from which all of the branches emanate.

A tree structure is recursive in the sense that the physical and logical construction of any part of the tree is identical to that of the tree itself.

Hence, an algorithm which can be applied to a whole tree structure may be applied to any part of the tree.

12.7   Binary trees (binary search trees)

A binary tree, more correctly referred to as a binary search tree, is of order 2. That is, each node contains data of its own and, in addition, contains two pointers to subordinate nodes. Such trees are normally used to hold a set of data in a desired sequence. The two pointers in a node then lead to a series of items which are respectively less than and greater than the item in that node itself. Figure 12.8 illustrates such a tree.

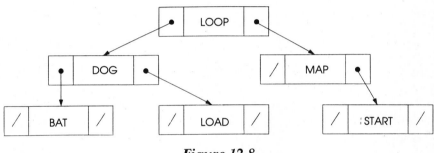

Figure 12.8

The advantages of such a table structure are:

(1) Additions and deletions may be handled by adjustment of pointers and hence the logical sequence of the items is maintained without physical movement of the data.
(2) Depending on how well 'balanced' the tree is, the access time to any item approximates that of a binary search.

'Balance', in this context, refers to the spread of the branches of the tree about its root. A balanced tree has the same distance to travel from the root to the furthest nodes ('leaves') in all directions. The physical representation of a tree structure may be implemented, as for a linked list, by means of a linear array in which each element contains a data item and two or more pointers or a group of parallel arrays for the data and pointer items. Physically, the table in the above diagram would appear as shown in Figure 12.9.

		Left pointer	Right pointer
1	LOOP	2	4
2	DOG	3	5
3	BAT	/	/
4	MAP	/	6
5	LOAD	/	/
6	START	/	/
7			

FREE POINTER

```
7
```

Figure 12.9

The handling of duplicated items in such a table is effected by either:

(1) rejecting them, if this is appropriate in the circumstances; or
(2) storing them on either the less-than or greater-than path, the choice being immaterial provided that it is consistent.

An in-order traversal of a binary tree will retrieve the elements in their logical sequence, that is, the least first and the greatest last.

Unless the tree structure was a 'threaded' tree (see Section 12.8) a stack would be needed to enable the algorithm to 'remember' the order in which it must retrace its steps up the tree.

A typical such algorithm would be:

```
global data
    BINARY_TREE (100)          : array of NODEs
    NODE                       : record of
        DATA_PART              : character
        LEFT_POINTER           : integer
        RIGHT_POINTER          : integer
    TREE_SIZE                  : integer, value = 100
    STACK (100)                : integer, array
    STACK_SIZE                 : integer, value = 100
    TOP_OF_STACK_POINTER : integer

Create Tree
    local data
        INDEX : integer
    begin
        INDEX = 1
        while INDEX not > TREE_SIZE
            DATA_PART (INDEX) = blanks
            LEFT_POINTER (INDEX) = 0
            RIGHT_POINTER (INDEX) = 0
            INDEX = INDEX + 1
        end-while
    end
```

(*Note*: To process an un-balanced tree, the depth of the stack may need to be equal to the size of the tree)

In-Order Traversal
    local data
        INDEX   : integer
        JOB_DONE : boolean
    begin
        TOP_OF_STACK_POINTER = 0
        INDEX = 1
        JOB_DONE = false
        while JOB_DONE = false
            while INDEX > 0
                do Push (INDEX)
                INDEX = LEFT_POINTER (INDEX)
            end-while
            if TOP_OF_STACK_POINTER = 0
                JOB_DONE = true
            else
                do Pop (INDEX)
                process DATA_PART (INDEX)
                (i.e. print it, etc)
                INDEX = RIGHT_POINTER (INDEX)
            end-if
        end-while
    end

Push (ITEM)
    local data
        ITEM : integer
    begin
        if TOP_OF_STACK_POINTER = STACK_SIZE
            output 'Stack full'
        else
            TOP_OF_STACK_POINTER = TOP_OF_STACK_POINTER + 1
            STACK (TOP_OF_STACK_POINTER) = ITEM
        end-if
    end

Pop (ITEM)
    local data
        ITEM : integer
    begin
        if TOP_OF_STACK_POINTER = 0
            Output 'Stack Empty'
        else
            ITEM = STACK (TOP_OF_STACK_POINTER)
            TOP_OF_STACK_POINTER = TOP_OF_STACK_POINTER − 1
        end-if
    end

The attraction of a binary-tree is that it may be used to maintain a series of items in a required sequence without the necessity to arrange those items physically in sequence as was the case with the sorting methods discussed in Chapter 11. The table can therefore be constructed dynamically as a program is executed and each item added to the tree automatically becomes 'sorted' into the sequence which the tree is maintaining.

12.8   Threaded trees

A threaded binary tree is one in which the pointers allow both downwards and upwards movement through the tree and hence remove the necessity for a stack to be used in its traversal. Downwards (or forwards) pointers will be positive values and upwards (or backwards) pointers will be negative.

The ability to dispense with the use of a stack provides a twofold benefit:

(1) the time taken to manipulate the stack is dispensed with; and
(2) the space required to implement the stack is saved.

This latter point is worth noting because the depth of a stack needed to process a binary tree is somewhat unpredictable. If the tree is balanced exactly, the maximum depth of the stack needed to process it (i.e., the number of items comprising the stack) is given by $\log_2 N$ where N is the number of nodes in the tree.

If the tree is so unbalanced, however, as to have each of its nodes pointing to, say, only an item in the less-than direction, the depth of the stack would equate with the number of nodes in the tree.

The following algorithms implement the insertion and retrieval of items in a threaded tree and use two implicit assumptions:

(1) the linked list of vacant elements is maintained via the right-hand pointer: and
(2) duplicated data items are placed to the 'left' of their equals.

```
global data
    TREE (100)            : array of ITEMs
    ITEM                  : record of
        DATA_PART         : character
        LEFT_POINTER      : integer
        RIGHT_POINTER     : integer
    FREE_POINTER          : integer
    TREE_SIZE             : integer, value = 100
```

Create Tree
    local data
        POINTER : integer
    begin
        FREE_POINTER = 1
        POINTER = 1
        while POINTER not > TREE_SIZE
            DATA_PART (POINTER) = blanks
            LEFT_POINTER (POINTER) = 0
            RIGHT_POINTER (POINTER) = POINTER + 1
            POINTER = POINTER + 1
        end-while
        RIGHT_POINTER (TREE_SIZE) = 0
    end
Insert New Item (NEW_ITEM, INSERT_OK)
    local data
        NEW_ITEM   : character
        INSERT_OK   : boolean
        NEW_POINTER : integer
    begin
        if FREE_POINTER = 0 (tree is full)
            INSERT_OK = false
        else
            INSERT_OK = true
            JOB_DONE = false
            NEW_POINTER = FREE-POINTER
            FREE_POINTER = RIGHT_POINTER (NEW_POINTER)
            DATA_PART (NEW_POINTER) = NEW_ITEM
            RIGHT_POINTER (NEW_POINTER) = 0
            LEFT_POINTER (NEW_POINTER) = 0
            if NEW_POINTER > 1
                do Link (NEW_POINTER)
            end-if
        end-if
    end

Link (NEW_POINTER)
    local data
        NEW_POINTER,
        COMPARE_POINTER : integer
        JOB_DONE   : boolean
    begin
        COMPARE_POINTER = 1
        JOB_DONE = False
        while JOB_DONE = false
            if DATA_PART (NEW POINTER)
              > DATA_PART (COMPARE_POINTER)
                if RIGHT_POINTER (COMPARE_POINTER) > 0
                    COMPARE_POINTER
                      = RIGHT_POINTER (COMPARE_POINTER)

```
              else
                  RIGHT_POINTER (NEW_POINTER)
                    = RIGHT_POINTER (COMPARE_POINTER)
                  RIGHT_POINTER (COMPARE_POINTER)
                    = NEW_POINTER
                  JOB_DONE = true
              end-if
          else
              if LEFT_POINTER (COMPARE_POINTER) > 0
                  COMPARE_POINTER
                    = LEFT_POINTER (COMPARE_POINTER)
              else
                  LEFT_POINTER (COMPARE_POINTER)
                    = NEW_POINTER
                  RIGHT_POINTER (NEW_POINTER)
                    = 0 - COMPARE_POINTER
                  JOB_DONE = true
              end-if
          end-if
      end-while
  end


  Retrieve Items in Sequence
      local data
          POINTER                  : integer
          JOB_DONE, STEP_DONE : boolean
      begin
          POINTER = 1
          JOB_DONE = false
          while JOB_DONE = false
              while LEFT_POINTER (POINTER) not = 0
                  POINTER = LEFT_POINTER (POINTER)
              end-while
              STEP_DONE = false
              while STEP_DONE = false
                  process DATA_PART (POINTER)
                  (i.e. print it, etc)
                  if RIGHT_POINTER (POINTER) > 0
                      POINTER = RIGHT_POINTER (POINTER)
                      STEP_DONE = true
                  else
                      if RIGHT_POINTER (POINTER) < 0
                          POINTER = 0 - RIGHT_POINTER (POINTER)
                      else
                          JOB_DONE = true
                          STEP_DONE = true
                      end-if
                  end-if
              end-while
          end-while
      end
```

	Data	Left pointer	Right pointer
1		0	2
2		0	3
3		0	4
4		0	5
5		0	6
6		0	7
7		0	8

FREE POINTER 1

1	HARRIS	2	3
2	CARNEY	0	−1
3	NOONE	0	0
4		0	5
5		0	6
6		0	7
7		0	8

FREE POINTER 4

1	HARRIS	2	3
2	CARNEY	4	−1
3	NOONE	0	5
4	BAKER	0	−2
5	STONE	6	0
6	QUIRK	0	−5
7		0	8

FREE POINTER 7

Figure 12.10 *The construction of a right-threaded binary tree*

12.9   N-ary trees

Trees may have more than two pointers in each node and may be used to represent a hierarchical table. The number of pointers in each node may be fixed or variable. A table holding items of expenditure is illustrated in Figure 12.11.

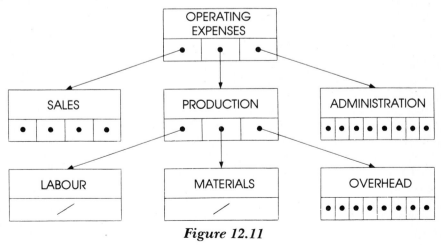

Figure 12.11

If a tree in which each node was able to hold several pointers was used to maintain a hierarchical data structure such as a chart of accounts or bill of materials (parts explosion) a pre-order traversal would enable its contents to be processed in their hierarchical groupings.

For example, such a traversal of the expenditure tree illustrated in Figure 12.11 would yield an output similar to:

```
Operating Expenses:
    Sales Expenses:
        Sales Representatives' Salaries
        Commission Paid
        Delivery Costs
    Production Expenses:
        Labor Cost
        Material Cost
    Manufacturing Overhead:
        Factory Rent
        Light and Power
        Depreciation on Machinery
    Administration Expenses:
        Office Salaries
        Printing and Stationery
        Depreciation on Fittings
```

A skeleton algorithm to effect this process would appear as:

Pre-order Traversal of an N-ary Tree
```
Initialize Stack
Pointer = address of root node (usually = 1)
Traversal Done = False
while Traversal Done = False
    if Pointer = Null
        Traversal Done = True
    else
        Push pointers in Element (Pointer) on the stack (from right to left)
        Process Data item (Pointer)
        Pop stack into Pointer
    end-if
end-while
```

It should be noted that any tree may be reduced to a binary format. The example in Figure 12.12 should illustrate the procedure.

These relationships consist of either:

(1) 'SUBORDINATES' — B, C, D, E are subordinates of A
                    — P, Q, R, S are subordinates of D; or
(2) 'PEERS' — B, C, D, E are peers
            — L, M, N are peers.

Therefore, the tree may be restructured with 'SUBORDINATES' to the left and 'PEERS' to the right, that is, a binary format (see Figure 12.13).

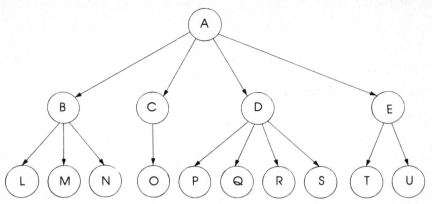

Figure 12.12 *An N-ary tree*

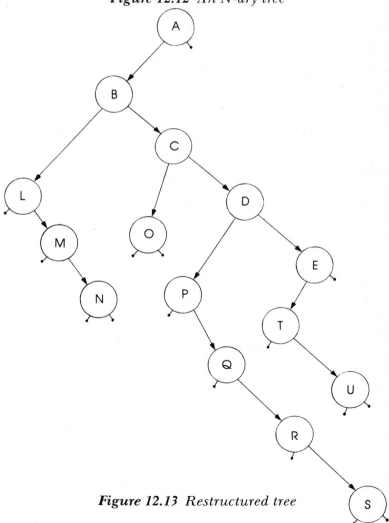

Figure 12.13 *Restructured tree*

12.10   B-trees

B-trees are a form of balanced tree often used to implement indexes to records on a file. In the foregoing examples of operations on tree structures, mention has been made of the advantages of having a tree which is balanced. This becomes even more imperative when the nodes of the tree are not held in memory but, rather, on an external storage device such as a disk. In such a case, the design of the structure would need to ensure that:

(1) the minimum number of nodes needed to be accessed were to be retrieved from the storage device in order to minimize peripheral transfer delays; and
(2) the time taken to locate any item in the tree (e.g., the key to any record in the index) did not differ significantly from one item to another.

A B-tree used to implement a file index will have in each node:

(1) the keys of several records and their associated positions on the file: and

(2) pointers to other nodes in which are located key values which fall between those keys in the node currently being examined.

A B-tree of order n has nodes, each of which may hold a maximum of n pointers and $(n-1)$ data items. In the case of a file index, each data item consists of a record key value and the position of that record on the file.

The tree, of order n, is continually balanced so that each node conforms to the following rules:

(1) the paths to the nodes farthest from the root are all of the same length;
(2) while the root node may have as few as one key and two pointers, all other nodes have a minimum of $n/2$ and a maximum of n pointers; and
(3) each node has one fewer keys than the number of pointers present in that node.

When an item is to be inserted into a B-tree, a search is made to determine whether or not the key already exists in the tree. If it does not, that is, a valid insertion may take place, the search will have terminated at a 'leaf' node (one farthest from the root). The item to be added is then inserted in that leaf in its proper sequence. If there was no room for the insertion because the leaf node was already full, the new value and those already in the leaf node are arranged in sequence and the middle data item is inserted in the parent node which pointed at the leaf node found to be filled.

The leaf node is now split into two new nodes, one containing the data items less than, and the other those greater than the item promoted to the parent node. If this promotion causes the parent node to overflow in the same fashion as the leaf node, the procedure will be repeated possibly causing a ripple effect right back to the root node itself. Figure 12.4 shows the creation of a B-tree from an initially empty state to one of holding the data values (possibly values of record keys on a file) shown. The order of inserting these values will be:

10, 70, 60, 20, 110, 40, 80, 130, 100, 50, 170, 90, 160, 200, 30, 120, 140, 180, 190, 150.

The tree is of order 5 and therefore each node may contain up to five pointers and four data items.

The number of accesses needed to locate a data item in a B-tree is approximately $\log_n T$ where n is the order of the tree and T is the total number of data items stored. Some examples of the efficiency which this permits were given in section 8.5.

12.11   Tree sorting

A tree structure may be used as a sorting device. The methods of sorting discussed in Chapter 11 required the physical rearrangement of data items. An alternative is to place the data in a binary tree and then retrieve them in sequence. This procedure has the advantage that items may be added to or deleted from the 'sorted' data without requiring any resorting.

12.12   Graphs

A graph structure consists of a collection of nodes which are joined together. Strictly speaking, a tree is a special case of graph; it is one which has no closed loops. Figure 12.15 illustrates a typical graph structure.

(1)   10, 70, 60, 20

```
10   20   60   70
```

(2)   110

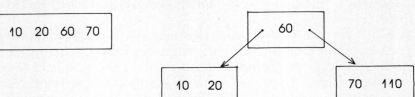

(3)   40, 80, 130

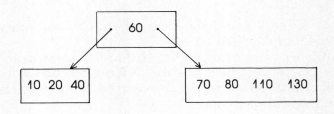

(4)   100

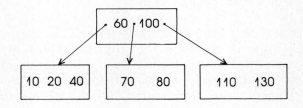

(5)   50, 170, 90, 160

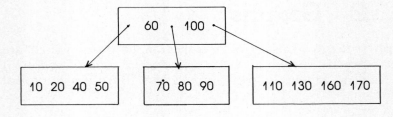

(6) 200

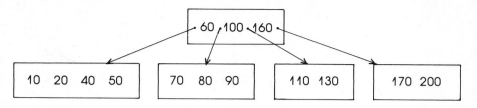

(7) 30, 120, 140, 180, 190

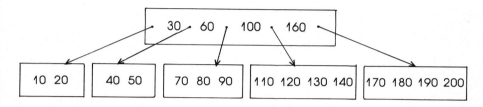

(8) 150

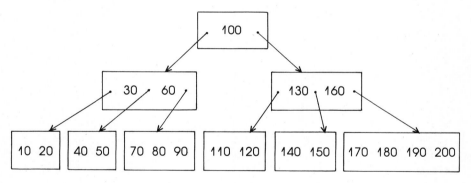

Figure 12.14 Growth of a B-tree

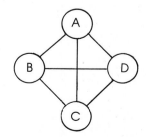

Figure 12.15 Graph structure

This graph consists of four nodes with connections between all of them. The connections may be regarded as one-way or two-way. The connection between A and B may indicate that movement is possible from A to B and B to A or it may be restricted to one of these directions only. In this latter case, the graph may be referred to as a directed graph or shortened to 'digraph'.

Two examples may serve to illustrate the usefulness of graph structures.

Figure 12.16 illustrates a data communications network between several cities. Each city is not necessarily connected directly to all others, although traffic is possible between any two cities by, if necessary, routing the message via one or more other nodes in the network. If duplex transmission is assumed, the traffic is assumed to be two-way along any of the connections. If any line is broken in the network, traffic may still reach its destination by a more circuitous route.

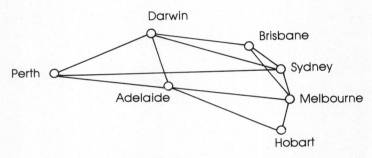

Figure 12.16 A communications network

A graph structure of this network held within a computer system would enable the possible traffic routes to be represented and alternative routes to be ascertained in the event of a direct connection being severed. By storing distances of each line (or 'edge') or costs associated with each connection within the structure, a program may calculate the shortest or least expensive route from one point to another. As a further example, an ambulance service may wish to store a grid of major roads covering a large metropolitan area. If such a grid could be represented within a computer system, it would be possible for the system to determine an optimum route for an ambulance to follow when proceeding from its current position to the scene of an accident or to a hospital. In addition to storing actual point-to-point connections, the data structure could hold data on roads temporarily closed for repairs, rail crossings rendering traffic temporarily impossible because of gates not operating, etc. In addition, it is obvious that for such a system, the possibility of a one-way road must be catered for. Hence, the connection between A and B does not necessarily imply that one may proceed from A to B as well as from B to A. Once again, distances or speed limits may be held within the structure and a program may calculate the shortest distance or the fastest route (these two may not necessarily be the same) between two points.

Figure 12.17 illustrates a directed graph with the direction of the edges indicated by arrows and the distance between the points noted on each connection. Associated with the graph is one method of representing the graph by a simple linear table.

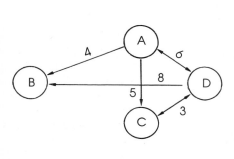

Possible connections		
From	To	Distance
A	B	4
A	C	5
A	D	6
B	D	8
C	D	3
D	A	6
D	B	8
D	C	3

Figure 12.17 A directed graph

The graph may be decomposed into a number of tree structures as illustrated in Figure 12.18.

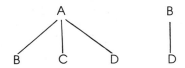 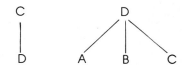

Figure 12.18 A directed graph decomposed into trees

An examination of this structure will show that a program could deduce from this data that there were multiple paths from A to C, for example:

(1) A-B-D-C (distance = 15)
(2) A-C (distance = 5)
(3) A-D-C (distance = 9)

It is also evident that in processing any such structure, a program must be able to detect that it has arrived at a point which it has already visited, for example, A-B-D-A, and must discard that route through the network.

12.13   Sparse arrays

A problem sometimes encountered in data processing is that of the sparsely populated array. A situation may exist where the possible dimensions of a structure are extremely large but, from the circumstances surrounding the problem, it is known that only a very small proportion of the possible elements will actually have any data in them.

Consider the case of a large retail organization with 100 stores selling a total product line of 500 items. The organization may require a program to collate statistics on the number and/or value of sales of each item in each store. If a two-dimensional array were to be declared to hold this data, it would need 50,000 elements requiring a total of up to one-half megabyte of memory! However, it may be known that only five stores stock the full range of 500 items and the others stock only an average of 100 items each — although not the same 100 items in every case. The number of elements is:

$$(5 \times 500) + (95 \times 100) = 12,000 \text{ elements}$$

The situation may be further complicated by the fact that the program may be run on subsets of the whole data from time to time and it is not predictable that every one of the 100 stores will have data present.

One possible solution to this problem is to construct the table as a list structure with each element holding two pointers as well as two items of data. Each element would have the format:

Key	Total	Pointer 1	Pointer 2

These components would store the following data:

Key: the identification of the store or product to which this element is related;

Total: blank for store elements (or could hold grand total for that store); total volume/value of sales in the case of a product element;

Pointer 1:   blank for product elements; a pointer to the next store in the case of store elements; and

Pointer 2:   in the case of store elements, a pointer to the first product element for that store; in the case of product elements, a pointer to the next product for that store.

Figure 12.19 shows a set of data which was accumulated from potentially thousands of transactions during a typical execution of the program and

Figure 12.20 shows the list structure that has grown during the program's execution. The items are shown in sequence of store and product for ease of recognition but this is not essential to the operation of the structure.

Store	Product	Total value
S10	P35	1000
	P47	2500
	P69	1500
S17	P10	6000
	P13	2000
	P20	3000
S24	P8	4500
	P99	7000

Figure 12.19 *Accumulated transaction data*

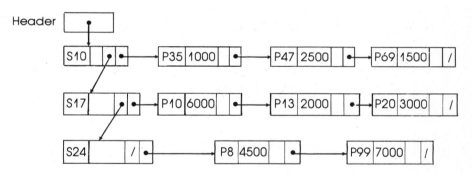

Figure 12.20 *List structure for sparse array*

It can be seen that the structure is expansible in both directions, that is, stores and products, and utilizes only those elements for which a combination of store and product is present. A penalty is paid for this efficiency of storage utilization in that each element in the list structure needs to be larger than the simple total which would have been all that was needed in the two-dimensional array. There will obviously be a break even point, determined by the size of pointers and key values, at which the list structure becomes more economical of storage than the array.

12.14   Conclusion

These definitions and algorithms illustrate two points:

(1) The abstract data structures are really linear arrays. The qualities which define them as stacks, lists, trees, and so on, lie in their behavior rather than in their physical construction.
(2) A variety of data structures exists; it should be the aim of the programmer to be familiar with their construction and manipulation and to be able to use them where appropriate.

Given that the aim of a computer system is to model the environment and behavior of real-world activities, a number of different types of data structures need to be implemented in application programs. The ability to choose an appropriate data structure for the solution of a problem is just as important a requirement for a programmer as the ability to construct an elegant algorithm.

12.15   Review questions

(1) Set out below is a representation of a binary search tree. Show the data and pointer values which would comprise the tree after inserting the following data items in the order given:

30, 65, 10, 3, 200, 47, 103

Data Item	Pointers	
	Less than	Greater than oir equal to

(2) The diagram below represents a right-threaded tree which uses the Less Than or Equal To pointer to maintain the free list. The data items in the table have been inserted in the physical sequence shown and element l is the root node.

State the values which the pointers 'a' to 'l' would have.

	Data Item	Pointers	
		Less than or equal to	Greater than
1	Evans	a	b
2	Marks	c	d
3	King	e	f
4	Quinn	g	h
5	Baker	i	j
6	Turner	k	l
7		8	0

(3) Two arrays are constructed as lists, each holding up to 50 items in ascending sequence. The first element in each array holds no data and its pointer indicates the first element in the list. The last element in each list has a pointer value of zero.

A pseudocode algorithm is required to output the contents of these two lists merged into a single listing in ascending sequence.

For example:

Input:

List 1

	Data	Pointer
1		3
2	Gnu	4
3	Ape	5
4	Hog	0
5	Dog	2

List 2

	Data	Pointer
1		4
2	Yak	0
3	Cow	2
4	Bee	3

Output: Ape, Bee Cow, Dog, Gnu, Hog, Yak

(4) A program is required to read a string of characters consisting of groups of up to 10 letters separated by '/' characters. The data will end with an asterisk.

Each of the groups of characters is to be output in reverse order and the '/' characters are to be removed.

For example:

Input string: A B C D / P Q R S / J K L M *

Output string: D C B A S R Q P M L K J

Decide on a suitable data structure to accomplish this task and write the pseudocode for the program.

13 Data-driven programs

13.1 Introduction

Data-driven programming techniques are derived from the premises that:

(1) Programs are constantly in need of amendment to make them cope with a changing environment.
(2) In general, it is easier to change data held in tables than it is to change program procedural code; and therefore:
(3) Programs which operate by following rules embodied in tables will be more amenable to modification than those which have their rules solely expressed in the instructions.

In this chapter we look at some of the techniques for constructing programs, or parts of programs, by:

(1) abstracting their governing rules and embodying these rules in tabular form; and
(2) driving the code by means of the data thus constructed.

13.2   Decision tables

Decision tables are an often-used aid in systems analysis and design and specify rules of logic required to solve a problem. They can be of assistance also in specifying the operation of a program.

The general format of a decision table is shown in Figure 13.1, together with an example of such a table used to specify the rules relating to a simple payroll.

	Rules			
Conditions				
Actions				

Figure 13.1 *General format of decision table*

If all possible rules resulting from n conditions are specified, the table must provide for 2^n rules although some (as in the case of rules 5 and 6) may not be possible (see Figure 13.2).

This format, containing only Yes/No combinations of rules, is known as a 'limited entry' decision table.

	1	2	3	4	5	6	7	8
Hours worked $>$ 40	Y	Y	Y	Y	N	N	N	N
Hours worked $>$ 60	Y	Y	N	N	Y	Y	N	N
Junior employee	Y	N	Y	N	Y	N	Y	N
Reject as error	X	X			X	X		
Replace hours by: 40+2 (Hours−40)			X	X				
Replace rate by: Rate x 0.875			X				X	
Compute pay=Rate x Hours			X	X			X	X

Figure 13.2 *A table showing all rules*

Rules 5 and 6 are logically impossible because they purport to relate to a situation in which the employee *has not* worked beyond 40 hours but *has* worked beyond 60 hours. Thus, rules 5 and 6 are eliminated as impossible:

	5	6	
Hours worked > 40	N	N	
Hours worked > 60	Y	Y	impossible!
Junior employee	Y	N	

It is possible to take rules which lead to the same action or group of actions and combine them in a single rule. Note that rules 1 and 2 lead to the common action 'Reject as error' and differ only in the result of the test for a junior employee. Clearly, the result of this test is immaterial because the action is taken whether or not the employee is a junior. Such an unnecessary test may be replaced by a 'dash' entry indicating that the test need not be made in evaluating that rule. Rules 1 and 2 are combined as follows:

	1	2		1
Hours worked > 40	Y	Y		Y
Hours worked > 60	Y	Y	becomes:	Y
Junior employee	Y	N		—
Reject as error	X	X		X

A simplified version of the table could be constructed by removing impossible conditions and introducing dash entries (see Figure 13.3).

	1	2	3	4	5
Hours worked > 40	Y	Y	Y	N	N
Hours worked > 60	Y	N	N	N	N
Junior employee	—	Y	N	Y	N
Reject as error	X				
Replace hours by:					
40 + 2 (Hours − 40)		X	X		
Replace rate by: Rate x 0.875		X		X	
Compute pay = Rate x Hours		X	X	X	X

Figure 13.3 A table with dash entries

Although the simplification of decision tables as shown in Figure 13.3 is of value in a documentation/analysis context, the tables are generally of more use as a programming aid if they are left in their fully expanded version. This has the additional benefit of ensuring that every possible combination of conditions has been considered and catered for.

If, in the case of the table incorporating all rules, each Y was replaced by a 1 and each N by a zero, the result would be as shown in Figure 13.4. Note that the actions have been simplified for the purpose of the example.

	1	2	3	4	5	6	7	8
Hours worked > 40	1	1	1	1	0	0	0	0
Hours worked > 60	1	1	0	0	1	1	0	0
Junior employee	1	0	1	0	1	0	1	0
Action 1	X	X			X	X		
Action 2			X	X				
Action 3			X				X	
Action 4			X	X			X	X

Figure 13.4

By ascribing a value of 4 to a 1 in the first row (i.e., a 'Yes' answer to the question 'Hours worked > 40'?), a value of 2 to a 1 in the second row (i.e., 'Yes' to 'Hours worked > 60'?) and a value of 1 to 1 in the third row (i.e., 'Yes' to 'Employee is a junior'?) the resulting table represents for each rule a number in the range 7 to zero.

Each number in the range can be obtained by satisfying only one pattern of results, that is, a 3 can be obtained only from a pattern of N, Y, Y as the result of the three tests, and a 6 can result only from answers of Y, Y, N.

The code to evaluate the three tests and drive the program logic accordingly can be implemented by a **case** statement:

```
RESULT=zero
if Hours Worked > 40
    Add 4 to RESULT
end-if

if Hours Worked > 60
    Add 2 to RESULT
end-if

if Employee is a junior
    Add 1 to RESULT
end-if
```

```
case of RESULT:
    7, 6, 3, or 2:    do Action 1

              5:    do Action 2
                    do Action 3
                    do Action 4

              4:    do Action 2
                    do Action 4

              1:    do Action 3
                    do Action 4

              0:    do Action 4
end-case
```

This technique is often referred to as 'rule matching'. It provides a neater solution in many cases to its alternative, the branching tree implemented by a series of nested **if**s, for example:

```
if Hours Worked > 40
    if Hours Worked > 60
        if Employee is a junior
            do Action 1
        else
            do Action 1
        end-if
    else
        if Employee is a junior
            do Action 2
            do Action 3
            do Action 4
        else
            .
            .
            .

            etc.
        end-if
    end-if
end-if
    .
    .
    .
```

An alternative format of decision table is that of an 'extended entry' table. Such a format moves away from relying completely on yes/no rules and allows for more descriptive text to be used in the specification of the rules. An example is shown in Figure 13.5.

This method of construction is included here in the interest of using decision tables as a form of program documentation. This format is not as generally useful in the generation of program code as that of a limited entry table. However, the latest versions of COBOL compilers contain an EVALUATE instruction which will implement extended entry tables.

Hours Worked	0 to 40		41 to 60		over 60
Type of employee	Junior	Other	Junior	Other	—
Reject as error					X
Replace Hours by: 40 + 2 (Hours − 40)			X	X	
Replace Rate by: Rate * 0.875	X		X		
Compute pay = Rate × Hours	X	X	X	X	

Figure 13.5 Extended entry decision table

13.3   State transition tables

A program may be considered as an algorithm which progresses from its current state (i.e., what it is currently doing) to one of many other possible states, depending on changes in its operating environment. The arrival at any one particular state, or process, depends on the combination of the previous state and the occurrence of a particular event.

Program control is effected by means of:

(1) a main driving module which performs as subroutines a series of processing modules;
(2) the processing modules, each of which addresses itself to one particular portion of the program's operation; and
(3) a state variable which is a data item, the value of which is potentially changed by the occurrence of events and used by the driving routine to direct the path of the program to the next appropriate module.

The following example is that of a routine which has the task of examining a character string, as it may have been input from an operator at a terminal, checking it for correctness of format (or syntax) and separating it into its discrete components.

A stock part identifier in a motor accessories application has the general format:

A/B/C

where *A* must be present and must be entirely numeric; the first '/' is permitted only if *B* and/or *C* follow; *B* may be omitted but, if present, it must be entirely numeric; the second '/' is permitted only if *C* follows; and *C* may be omitted but, if present, it must be either entirely numeric or entirely alphabetic (but may not contain blanks).

In addition to these rules, leading blanks (spaces) may occur before the start of *A*, and trailing blanks may occur after the last character, but blanks may not be embedded in the part identifier. A maximum of 30 characters is allowed on the screen for input of the entire identifier.

The following examples should illustrate the required operation of the program module in validating the format of the identifier and separating its components into their respective distinations:

Input text	Valid?	A	B	Numeric C	Alpha C
123/78/62	Yes	000123	000078	000062	blank
47/13	Yes	000047	000013	000000	blank
95//ABC	Yes	000095	000000	000000	ABC
46/XYZ	No				
46//145	Yes	000046	000000	000145	blank
/23	No				
57/13/AB96	No				
9481	Yes	009481	000000	000000	blank
376 42	No				

To embody the rules of syntax in a table, it is necessary to identify the states in which the algorithm may exist and the events which may result in a change from one state to another. The events in the example in Figure 13.6 will consist mainly of encountering various types of characters in the free-format input text string.

Algorithm states	Current character in input string					
	Digit	Letter	Blank	'/'	30 Characters processed	Else
1. Leading blanks	2	9	1	9	9	9
2. Processing A	2	9	8	3	10	9
3. Just after first '/'	4	9	9	5	9	9
4. Processing B	4	9	8	5	10	9
5. Just after second '/'	6	7	9	9	9	9
6. Processing numeric C	6	9	8	9	10	9
7. Processing alpha C	9	7	8	9	10	9
8. Trailing blanks	9	9	8	9	10	9
9. Error found, stop	Next state to which algorithm moves					
10. Format correct						

Figure 13.6 State transition table for stock identifier syntax

To implement these rules in an algorithm (and thence subsequently in a programming language) the following procedure is required:

(1) Build the state transition table as an array consisting of a row for each state other than the Error and Completed states and a column for each event required to be detected. The example in Figure 13.6 would produce the array shown in Figure 13.7.

Row	Column 1	2	3	4	5	6
1	2	9	1	9	9	9
2	2	9	8	3	10	9
3	4	9	9	5	9	9
4	4	9	8	5	10	9
5	6	7	9	9	9	9
6	6	9	8	9	10	9
7	9	7	8	9	10	9
8	9	9	8	9	10	9

Figure 13.7

It will be presumed that any component of the array in Figure 13.7 may be accessed by the name STATE and quoting appropriate values for ROW and COLUMN, for example:

STATE (ROW, COLUMN)

In the case where

ROW=5 and COLUMN=3
    STATE (ROW, COLUMN)=9

(2) Construct the algorithm of components which

(a) perform the initializing of variables and overall algorithm control;
(b) select the appropriate processing module (in those cases where processing is actually required) depending on the Current State; and
(c) detect the events which change the state.

The following algorithm implements the example above:

global data
    ID_CHARACTER (30) : character array
    STATE_TABLE (8)   : array of TABLE_ROWs
    TABLE_ROW (6)   : array of STATEs
    STATE   : integer
    (It is presumed that STATE_TABLE has been loaded with the state values.)
    A, B, NUMERIC_C   : integer
    ALPHA_C   : character
    ID_SIZE   : integer, value = 30

Validate Stock Identifier
  local data
        CURRENT_STATE, COLUMN,
         ROW, CHARACTER_TYPE, ID_INDEX : integer
  begin
        A = 0
        B = 0
        NUMERIC_C = 0
        ALPHA_C = blanks
        CURRENT_STATE = 1
        ID_INDEX = 0
        while CURRENT_STATE < 9
            do Check Next Character (ID_INDEX, CHARACTER_TYPE)
            COLUMN = CHARACTER_TYPE
            ROW = CURRENT_STATE
            CURRENT_STATE
                = STATE (ROW, COLUMN)
            case of CURRENT_STATE:
                2: A = 10 * A
                    + ID_CHARACTER (ID_INDEX)
                4: B = 10 * B
                    + ID_CHARACTER (ID_INDEX)
                6: NUMERIC_C = 10 * NUMERIC_C
                    + ID_CHARACTER (ID_INDEX)
                7: append ID_CHARACTER (ID_INDEX)
                    to current string of characters in ALPHA_C
            end-case
        end-while
        if CURRENT_STATE = 10
            .
            .
            .
        else
            .
            .
            .
        end-if
    end

```
Check Next Character (ID_INDEX, CHARACTER_TYPE)
    local data
        ID_INDEX, CHARACTER_TYPE : integer
    begin
        ID_INDEX = ID_INDEX + 1
        if ID_INDEX > ID_SIZE
            CHARACTER_TYPE = 5
        else
            case of ID_CHARACTER (ID_INDEX) :
                Digit  : CHARACTER_TYPE = 1
                Letter : CHARACTER_TYPE = 2
                Blank  : CHARACTER_TYPE = 3
                '/'    : CHARACTER_TYPE = 4
                else   : CHARACTER_TYPE = 6
            end-case
        end-if
    end
```

As well as using this simple algorithm, the programmer benefits from being able to implement many of the likely changes to the syntax rules for the Stock Identifier by changing some of the values in the state array without needing to change the processing algorithm. For example, consider the following changes to syntax rules:

(1) It is permissible for the whole item to be blank, that is, a null response from the operator is acceptable, but any identifier keyed in must conform to the prescribed rules.

(2) The two '/' characters are not invalid if they appear without being accompanied by a *B* or *C* identifier component, that is, 123/ or 123// is now to be valid.

(3) The component previously known as an alphabetic *C* may now contain any character at all providing that its first character is not a numeric digit.

The state table would appear as in Figure 13.8 after incorporating these above amendments.

	Column					
Row	1	2	3	4	5	6
1	2	9	1	9	10	9
2	2	9	8	3	10	9
3	4	9	9	5	10	9
4	4	9	8	5	10	9
5	6	7	7	7	10	7
6	6	9	8	9	10	9
7	7	7	7	7	10	7
8	9	9	8	9	10	9

Figure 13.8

When implementing such a technique in a program, care must be taken that sufficient documentation is provided to enable the reader to understand the purpose of the table. If this is not done, the algorithm will appear to be driven by 'magic numbers' which have no significance to anybody subsequently charged with the maintenance of the program.

13.4 Run-time interpreted tables

This technique involves the storing in tabular form of information concerning the operation of a program. It is essentially the same approach as that taken using state transition tables, except that it is extended to encompass more of the program's functions and more of the internal data items used by the program.

It is an extremely useful technique with which to specify a set of procedures which may be subject to frequent alteration at the request of a user or which may have to exist in several versions to cater for a variety of users, each of whom may require a degree of 'customizing' for his or her own environment.

Examples of situations suitable for such treatment are:

- Screen procedures for data input from source documents, the format of which may vary from one user to another. It is advantageous to be able to prompt for operator response in the sequence of the fields on the input document and to insert or delete fields for one of a number of users of a common system.
- Computer-assisted learning programs which function on a question-and-answer basis. At any time the program is required to present a varying set of questions, check the responses against a supplied list of answers, allow a varying number of retries at any question, and so on.

- Test file loaders which are parameter driven to prompt an operator to supply data for a variety of record types with a variety of fields, some of which may be subject to one of a number of edit constraints, for example, it must be numeric, must be a valid DDMMYY date, and so on.

The information contained in the table will be of three types:

(1) references to data items held in other tables;
(2) references to procedural routines to be executed within the program; and
(3) references to other items within the interpreted table itself.

References to data items held in other tables, for example, the text to be displayed as a prompt to a screen operator when requesting the input of a data item, will normally constitute the subscripts of those data items in their respective tables.

References to procedural routines to be executed in the program, such as a validation/edit procedure to be applied to a data field on its receipt from a screen operator, will be control variables associated with **Case** statements or computed branches.

References to other items in the controlling table will also be subscripts, this time to elements in its own structure, for example, the questions following and preceding a question to a screen operator.

Table maintenance

One method of maintaining interpreted tables in a program is by the conventional method of a programmer altering the contents of the control table or of any of its associated tables and recompiling the program each time the user requests a change. This procedure, however, does not either:

(1) enable the maintenance to be effected independent of program recompilation by the programmer or, preferably, by the user; or
(2) allow for the use of a program by a number of users, each of whom has a different requirement from his or her colleagues; for example, an order-entry procedure via a screen from order forms used by a number of branches of an organization, each of which may have a slightly different form design from the others.

A preferable maintenance technique is to remove the tables from the program and store them in one or more files. The contents of the tables may now be amended either by:

(1) the use of a standard text editor to vary the file/record contents; or
(2) the use of a specially written editor provided by the data processing staff to enable the user to effect the desired changes.

The second approach will involve the production of a special software tool, but the time spent on its implementation will be recouped many times over in the lifetime of the system.

Figures 13.9 and 13.10 illustrate the tables required for a typical procedure whereby an operator at a screen can be prompted for a series of responses, those responses validated where appropriate, an error message displayed if necessary, and the data thus captured written to an output file.

The purpose of each of the tables is as follows:

Control Table

This is the primary table which governs the operation of the driving algorithm in managing the dialog between the program and the screen operator.

- *Question details pointer*: The subscript of the entry in the Question Details Table which relates to the question being currently asked of the operator.
- *Reply edit pointer*: The subscript of the entry in the Reply Details Table which enables the operator's response to be accepted and validated.
- *Output format pointer*: The subscript of the entry in the Output Format Table which enables the operator's response, if valid, to be assembled in an output record to be written to a file holding the data input by the operator.
- *Next question if reply OK*: The subscript of the entry in the Control Table which contains details of the next question to ask the operator if the response to the current question is valid. Note that this need not necessarily be the adjacent question in the table. Different users may be asked the questions in different sequences depending on their operating environment.
- *Next question if reply not OK*: The subscript of the entry in the Control Table which contains the next question to be asked of the operator if the current response is invalid. This may be the repetition of the current question or any other suitable prompt.
- *Prior question*: The subscript of the entry in the Control Table which contains details of the question asked before the current question. This may be needed to allow the operator to return to previous questions to amend their responses.

Question Details Table

This table contains detailed information of each question referred to in the Control Table.

- *Prompt text pointer*: The subscript of the entry in the Prompt Text Table which contains the prompt to be displayed to the operator for any given question.

- *Prompt position*: The line and column on the screen at which the text is to be displayed.
- *Reply essential*: A Yes/No indication of whether the operator is obliged to input a response to a given question.

Prompt Text Table

This table holds the text of the prompts to be displayed to the operator.

Reply Details Table

This table contains information concerning the operator's response to each question.

- *Maximum size of reply*: The maximum number of characters to be accepted from the operator as a response to a given question.
- *Position to accept reply*: The line and column on the screen at which the operator's response is to be accepted.
- *Validation procedure*: An indicator which, if present, may be used in a **Case** statement or computed branch to select an appropriate processing procedure to validate the operator's response.
- *Position of error message*: The line and column at which an error message is to be displayed if the operator's response to a question is invalid.
- *Error message pointer*: The subscript of an element in the Error Message Text Table to be displayed as an appropriate message in the event of an invalid response.

Error Message Text Table

This table contains the wording of error messages to be displayed to the operator.

Output Format Table

This table contains details of the positioning of the operator's valid responses in a record constructed from the entire data input from one complete set of questions.

- *Output format*: This indicates whether the operator's response is to be right-hand or left-hand aligned in its receiving field in the record.
- *Position in output record*: This indicates the length of the field in the output record and its starting character position.
- *Special processing routine*: This may be used, if present, to select by a **Case** statment or computed branch a processing module which may perform one or more operations on the output field before its inclusion in the record.

	Output format	Position in O/P record		Special processing routine
		Start	Length	
1	R	1	12	
2	L	13	100	
3	R	113	6	7

OUTPUT FORMAT TABLE

1	Reply must be numeric
2	Date must be of DD/MM/YY format
3	Blank reply is not acceptable
4	Number must not exceed six digits

ERROR MESSAGE TEXT TABLE

Figure 13.9

Question number	Question details pointer	Reply edit pointer	Output format pointer	Next question if Reply OK	Next Question if Reply not OK	Prior question
1	1	1	1	2	1	0
2	2	2	2	3	2	1
3	3	3	3	4	3	2
.						
.						
50						

CONTROL TABLE

	Prompt text pointer	Prompt position		Reply essential
		Line	Column	
1	1	6	5	Y
2	2	7	9	Y
3	3	9	7	N

QUESTION DETAILS TABLE

1	Accession NO.
2	Title
3	Date acquired (DD/MM/YY)
4	Author

PROMPT TEXT TABLE

	Maximum size of reply	Position to accept reply		Validation procedure	Position of error message		Error message pointer
		Line	Column		Line	Column	
1	12	6	20	5	6	50	1
2	100	7	20		8	1	3
3	8	9	20	2	9	30	2

REPLY DETAILS TABLE

Figure 13.10

13.5   Conclusion

A large proportion of programming effort is spent on program maintenance. Alterations to programs are continually necessary to meet changing user requirements. Working from the premise that it is usually easier to change data than to change procedural code, it is worthwhile to incorporate as much as possible of a program's logic in a data structure. The foregoing approaches should provide an insight into the various means by which this may be accomplished.

13.6   Review questions

(1) An organization chooses its Southeast Asian sales representatives according to the following rules:

If a person has a degree qualification and has been employed by the organization for at least 5 years, they are eligible for immediate appointment. If they have a degree but less than 5 years' service, they are eligible for appointment if they can speak an Asian language. If the person has no degree qualification but has at least 5 years' service, they are first sent on an Asian language course, if they cannot already speak one, and then given an appointment. All other categories of applicants are rejected.

Draw a limited entry decision table incorporating these rules and simplify it to contain the minimum number of rules necessary.

(2) Each month, an organization pays its sales staff according to the following rules:

If the person's volume of sales does not exceed 1000 units, a base salary of $1500 is paid if the employee has been with the organization less than 5 years or $1800 if 5 years or more. No commission is paid in either of these cases. If the sales volume is greater than 1000 units but less than 2000, a base salary of $1800 is paid plus a commission of 4% on all sales provided that the sales person has achieved their budgeted sales quota; otherwise the commission is only 2% unless the employee has been with the organization for 5 years or more in which case the 4% is paid regardless of the quota. For sales of 2000 units or more, a base salary of $2000 is paid plus 5% commission on all sales if the budgeted quota has been achieved or 4% if the quota has not been reached.

Draw a decision table to embody these rules.

(3) The response to a question asked by a particular program to a terminal operator is to be an amount of money. To be valid, the response must conform to the following rules:

(1) A '$' may or may not preceed the monetary amount.

(2) An amount of dollars may or may not be present, but, if present, must be numeric.

(3) A decimal point is not needed unless an amount of cents is present but is not to be regarded as an error if no cents follow it.

(4) An amount of cents may or may not be present, but, if present, must be numeric. (There is no need to check that the amount of cents does not exceed 99.)

(5) No leading spaces are permitted before the monetary amount commences and no embedded spaces are permitted within the amount.

(6) An entirely blank response is acceptable.

Examples of valid responses are:

$47.36	$1234	$1234.
$.35	(blank)	1234
123.45	.20	1.2

Draw up a state transition table to incorporate these rules.

(4) One response required from an operator at a terminal during the running of a certain program is a street directory reference. The reference is in the format:

  map   row   column   (e.g. 106   B   10)

The rules for the format of the reference are:

(1) All components are essential.
(2) The map must be numeric and in the range 1 to 200 inclusive.
(3) The row must be alphabetic and one of the letters A to H,J or K.
(4) The column must be numeric and in the range 1 to 12.

The field into which the reference is accepted consists of a total of 10 characters. Leading spaces are permitted prior to the map number, one or more spaces may separate the row from the map and the column from the row or there may be no spaces between any of the components. For example, all of the following would be acceptable:

  37H4
  37   H 4
  37H 4
  37   H4

Draw a state transition table incorporating these rules and an algorithm driven by the table to check the syntax of any reference input from the terminal.

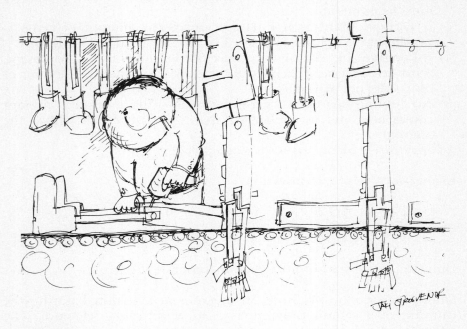

14 Program construction

14.1 Introduction

So far, emphasis has been placed on the logical construction of program code rather than the physical means of actually connecting the program modules. This chapter will deal with the alternatives available in programming languages for module implementation.

It must be noted that not all of these techniques are available in every language. Indeed there is probably no single language in which every one is permissible.

14.2 Macros

A macro is a single instruction, as written in the source code, which is expanded into several instructions during the process of compiling/ assembling into the object program. This compilation process is discussed more fully in the next chapter.

In a sense, all instructions in a high-level language are macros. Each instruction is converted by the compiler into a series of machine-level operations needed to accomplish the task of the instruction. In an assembler language, the programmer often has the facility of declaring additional instructions to be added to the repertoire of the assembler. With such a facility, the programmer can define an instruction such as PUSH which takes the content of a register and places it on the top of a stack. To do this the programmer supplies a number of known assembler instructions needed to accomplish the PUSH operation and the assembler program inserts these instructions in the object program wherever the PUSH appears.

By such a means, a programmer may effectively build up a customized, high-level language for a particular application.

Macros are also commonly found in the features offered by operating systems although they may be referred to by other names, such as command files. A programmer may define a series of operations such as loading a program from disk, executing the program and printing a file which the program produces. This series of operations can be placed in a file and the quoting of the file name causes the operating system to carry out the contained functions.

Situations in which macros are permitted vary in whether or not they allow nesting of such macros, that is, whether one macro may have another embedded in it and, if so, to what depth this nesting may occur.

14.3   Subroutines (procedures)

A subroutine, or procedure, is a section of code which carries out a self-contained task within a program. It is executed by being called from one or more points within the program and, upon completion, it returns to the instruction following its call. The calling, or invocation, of the subroutine may be via a specific instruction in the syntax of the language used, for example, a CALL, PERFORM, GOSUB, etc., or may be by using the name of the procedure as though it were an instruction. Return from the procedure to its point of invocation may be via an explicit instruction, for example, RETURN, EXIT, etc., or may be by merely reaching the physical end of its coding.

Programming languages differ markedly in their means of implementing subroutines. An examination of some of these features may serve to alert the programmer to the variations possible and ensure that he or she makes sure that the method used in any new language encountered is investigated.

(1) *Calling mechanism*: It is not uncommon for an assembler language to embed within the subroutine the address to which the program

must return upon the completion of the subroutine task. If this is the case, it will not be possible to call the procedure recursively (see Section 14.6 on recursion) as there is no provision for storing multiple return points.

Most subroutine calls in high-level languages are implemented by pushing the return address on a stack. In this way, nested or recursive procedure calls present no problem as each call deepens the stack and each return raises it as the program executes. A programmer may be made painfully aware of this procedure by inducing a bug in a program whereby a subroutine is repeatedly called in a 'runaway' loop and the program aborts with a message similar to 'STACK OVERFLOW'.

Whatever the calling mechanism used, it should be obvious that leaving a subroutine, except for the purpose of executing an embedded (nested) subroutine, by a GO TO-style branch rather than by the normal exit facility, will leave some form of unsatisfied return mechanism lurking within the program. This may cause a stack overflow or may be encountered in an inappropriate situation and cause a fatal condition during execution.

(2) *Parameters — local and global data*: The vast majority of subroutines are written to process data rather than to perform some completely independent task, for example, opening or closing files. This raises the question of how the subroutine determines on which data to operate during any invocation. One approach to solving this problem is to allow the subroutine to access data areas which are common to other, perhaps all other, procedures within the program. In such a case, the calling procedure leaves data in a predetermined area and the subroutine accesses that area to process the data. Such data, as we have seen in earlier chapters, is referred to as global data.

An approach to this problem regarded as more elegant is that of providing each procedure with its own local data areas which are then inaccessible to other procedures within the program. This ensures that a subroutine cannot access data in which it has no legitimate interest and cannot corrupt other data by a side effect of its own operation. The rules of syntax governing such access to data are known as scope rules and the scope of data within a program is the extent to which it is accessible by the procedures within the program.

Where a language permits nested procedures, the scope rules may permit an inner procedure to access the data items declared in its enveloping procedure but not vice versa. In languages making use of local data facilities, data is passed from a calling to a called procedure by means of explicit parameters in the calling mechanism, for example:

CALL TAXFORMULA (GROSS, TAX)

or

TAXFORMULA (GROSS, TAX)

In this example the calling procedure would place the gross pay in the variable GROSS and after return from the subroutine TAXFORMULA would expect the appropriate taxation to have been placed in TAX. For such a case, two further considerations must be clarified:

(a) What does TAXFORMULA expect to find in TAX when it is called? The probable answer is that its value is immaterial as it will be replaced by the result of the new calculation. However, the subroutine may have expected the calling procedure to have cleared TAX to zero before the call.
(b) What will be the contents of GROSS upon return from TAXFORMULA? Again, the probable answer is that it will still contain the value passed to the subroutine. There is the possibility, however, that the subroutine may have performed calculations on the value in GROSS and change that value.

When devising the specification for any procedure involving the passing of parameters, the contents of those parameters both before and after the call should be stated explicity and not left to the discretion of the programmer concerned.

(3) *Mechanism for parameter passing*: The concept of passing values between procedures by means of stated parameters is fairly simple. However, there are traps for the unwary which may arise from the actual passing mechanism adopted by the programming language and implemented by the compiler. While a number of subtle variations exist, the two basic means of passing parameters between procedures are a call by value and a call by name (or reference).

   Parameters passed via a call by value have their contents transferred to a separate data area within the space of the subroutine. Consider the case of one procedure executing subroutine calls:

CALL SUB (P,Q)
CALL SUB (X,Y)

and the subroutine declaration:

SUBROUTINE SUB (A,B)

Here, two parameters are passed between the procedures, the variables are known as P and Q or X and Y in the calling procedure. If the parameters are passed by value, at the time of calling SUB, the contents of P or X would be transferred to a data area named A within the subroutine and similarly Q or Y transferred to a different area B. At the conclusion of the subroutine, the reverse occurs and the contents of A are transferred back to P or X and B back to Q or Y.

If these parameters were to be passed via a call by name mechanism, there would be no movement of data from one area to another. Instead, the address of A within the subroutine would be equated with the address of P or X in the calling procedure and that of B with Q or Y. Hence, the subroutine, when executing an operation on, say A, is actually manipulating the contents of P or X directly.

In the case of a call by name, it is also important to know whether the address of the parameters are equated specifically when the subroutine is called or dynamically as the subroutine executes. Consider the following situation:

Procedure SENIOR contains an array of 100 elements, declared as TABLE (100). SENIOR executes the instructions:

```
N=16
CALL JUNIOR (N, TABLE(N))
```

The procedure JUNIOR is declared as:

```
SUBROUTINE JUNIOR (A,B)
```

On the calling of JUNIOR, the addresses N and A are equated and those of TABLE (N) and B are equated. Hence, A has an initial value of 16 and B is the sixteenth element in TABLE. If JUNIOR executes the instruction

```
A=A+1
```

the contents of A, and therefore N, become 17. The question now is: does this affect B? That is, is B still the sixteenth element in TABLE, as would be the case if the address equation was done only at the time of the subroutine call, or is B now the seventeenth element in TABLE, as would be the case if the addresses were dynamically equated as the program executes?

From these examples it can be seen that a programmer must be aware of the mechanism used to implement subroutine calls and pass parameters if errors are not to creep into programs because of misconceptions transported from other languages with which the programmer is familiar.

14.4   Functions

A function is something of a cross between a macro and a subroutine. In general, functions are executed as subroutines but their names may be used virtually as instructions in the manner of a macro. Many languages have inbuilt, or intrinsic, functions to perform mathematical or trigonometric operations. The function is supplied with a parameter value and its invocation returns the result of a calculation upon that value. This result must then be stored in a variable for subsequent use by the program. Typical such operations are:

```
A=SQR(B)  square root
X=LOG(Y)  logarithm
P=SIN(Q)  sine
```

Some languages provide the programmer with the facility to create functions; for example, FORTRAN would permit the definition of a function AREA to calculate the area of a circle given its radius:

```
FUNCTION AREA (RADIUS)
AREA=3.142*RADIUS**2
END
```

This function could then be used to provide the area of a circle by:

```
A=AREA (NUMBER)
```

or

```
A=AREA (34.46)
```

14.5   Co-routines

The mode of operation of a subroutine is such that when the calling procedure invokes the execution of the subroutine, the subroutine is entered at its first instruction and works its way through the instructions until the task is finished. The calling and called procedures are seen as being in a superior-inferior relationship with one another.

Some situations exist in which a pair of procedures transfers control back and forth between themselves, returning each time to the point from which they last left. In a sense, this is the way in which an operating system and an application program cooperate in a multi-programming environment. The application program halts from time to time because of a delay waiting for a peripheral transfer or because of the expiration of a time slice. When this occurs, control is passed back to the operating system which eventually returns to reactivate the application program at the point at which the interruption occurred. Consider a case involving the unpacking of eight-bit EBCDIC characters, held three per 24-bit word and translating them to a six-bit code to be stored four per 24-bit word. Three procedures are involved:

(1) GET, which accesses an eight-bit character from a word;
(2) TRANSLATE, which effects the code conversion; and
(3) PUT, which stores the translated code in a receiving word.

The procedure TRANSLATE may be regarded as a true subroutine of GET (or PUT) but GET and PUT can be regarded as co-routines. To differentiate a co-routine call from a subroutine call, an instruction EXECUTE will be used for the former and CALL for the latter.
   Basically the program would operate:

```
Procedure: GET                        Procedure: PUT
  ┌─► Pick up a word                    ┌─► Store first character in word
  │   Extract one character             │   EXECUTE GET
  │   CALL TRANSLATE                     │   Store second character
  │   EXECUTE PUT                        │   EXECUTE GET
  │   Extract second character           │   Store third character
  │   CALL TRANSLATE                     │   EXECUTE GET
  │   EXECUTE PUT                        │   Store fourth character
  │   Extract third character            │   EXECUTE GET
  │   CALL TRANSLATE                     └── Move on to next word
  │   EXECUTE PUT
  └── Back for next word
```

Each time one of the procedures encounters an EXECUTE it transfers control to the other at the instruction following the EXECUTE from which it last left. In this example it will be seen that the two procedures execute asynchronously.
   Each loop of GET invokes PUT three times whereas each loop of PUT invokes GET four times.

14.6   Recursion

This method of repetitively executing a series of instructions as dealt with so far in this book was referred to as iteration. We have seen that the repeated instructions can be placed in a subroutine and that subroutine may be called repetitively, for example,

```
while X < Y
    do Procedure-a
end-while
```

What has not been encountered to date is the ability of a procedure to call itself. This opeation is referred to as recursion and may be direct, in the case of a procedure calling itself explicitly, or indirect by a procedure calling another which then calls the original procedure. Many programming languages do not permit recursion (e.g., BASIC, COBOL, FORTRAN) whereas others make a feature of it (e.g., ALGOL, Pascal, PL/1)

There is nothing that can be done by recursion which cannot also be done by iteration. However, some situations lend themselves naturally to a recursive procedure. A commonly used example of a recursive mathematical operation is that of the factorial function. Factorial 4 is calculated, for example, as $4* 3 *2 *1 = 24$. Factorial n is $n*(n-1)*(n-2)$ ... for a total of n terms. Expressed somewhat differently, it can be stated that:

factorial n = n* factorial (n−1)

and of course,

factorial (n−1) = (n−1)* factorial (n−2)

and so on. This latter definition is recursive in that the definition of factorial makes use of factorial itself.

Given the requirement for a recursive function, FACTORIAL, with a parameter NUMBER for which the factorial value is to be calculated, the algorithm would be written:

```
FACTORIAL (NUMBER)
    if NUMBER=0
        FACTORIAL=1
    else
        FACTORIAL=NUMBER *FACTORIAL (NUMBER−1)
    end-if
```

It has been stated earlier that certain data structures, such as lists and trees are, recursive by nature, that is, each portion has the same structure as the whole. Hence, any algorithm which works on the whole will work on any portion and vice versa. The algorithm below illustrates a recursive procedure to perform the in-order traversal of a binary tree, printing the contents of the nodes in sequence.

The procedure is invoked by the instructions:

```
N=position of root node
do LIST (N)
```

The procedure algorithm would appear as:

```
LIST (N)
    if Left Pointer (N) not=null
        do LIST (Left Pointer (N))
    end-if
    Print contents of element (N)
    if Right Pointer (N) not=null
        do LIST (Right Pointer (N))
    end-if
```

Each time a recursive algorithm descends one further level of recursion, it must save the environment in which it was operating and restore it upon return to that level. This environment includes the variables which the algorithm was manipulating and the address to which the procedure must return upon exiting from that level. This storage and retrieval operation is effected via a stack as the saved information must be restored in the reverse order to that in which it was saved.

There is a sorting procedure called Quicksort which makes use of recursive techniques. It is a variation on the compare-and-swap sorts discussed in Chapter 11. A pair of pointers is used, one initially set to point to the left-most element in the array to be sorted and the other to point to the right-most. The two elements pointed to are compared and if the one on the left is greater than that on the right, they are swapped. If the left is not greater than the right, one of the pointers is moved one element toward the other, that is, the left is moved one place right or the right one place left. Whenever a swap is made, the pointer being moved is left stationary and the other pointer commences to move. Hence, by alternating the movement of these pointers after each swap, eventually a situation is reached where they meet at some point (not necessarily the exact center) within the array. At this stage, all the values to the left of the meeting point, the pivot, are smaller than any of those to the right.

The same procedure is now applied to each of the two segments of the array in turn. Each of these will now produce two segments, each of which will in their turn produce two segments, and so on, until eventually the array is completely sequenced.

It can be readily appreciated that the procedure for partitioning any segment of the array is precisely the same as that for the array as a whole. By using a recursive procedure which stacks the left and right ends of each of the partitions encountered, the sorting algorithm may be expressed more concisely than that of the iterative algorithms given in Chapter 11.

14.7 Re-entrant procedures

Re-entrant procedures, sometimes called pure procedures, are programs or program modules which do not alter their instructions in any way during execution and hence may be called simultaneously by a number of other programs. If this simultaneous calling occurs, the re-entrant procedure need be in memory once only, whereas otherwise a separate copy of the procedure would need to be in memory for each program making use of it.

Consider the case of a number of programmers each using a terminal to edit a source program. If a separate copy of the text editor needs to be resident in central memory for each programmer, we are faced with an extremely inefficient usage of the computer's resources. We are aware that at any one instant, only one of the programmers is being serviced by the editor. It appears to serve all programmers simultaneously only by sharing its time among them all under the control of the operating system. If one copy of the editor is going to service all of the programmers, it must be able to 'remember' where it was in each programmer's file when it returns to that programmer after dealing with all of the others. The editor cannot store information about any one user within its own working space, as that space would be overwritten while working for another user.

Re-entrant procedures will normally store all changing data within a user's own working space. This means that each serviced user is a self-contained entity which may be picked up and discarded as often as needed. When picked up, the user's working environment can be reaccessed by the re-entrant procedure and the task effectively recommenced at the point at which it was previously dropped. Just prior to dropping the user each time, the re-entrant procedure stores all transient data within the user's workspace.

It is common to find system software written as pure procedures because, by its nature, it must serve many users simultaneously and cannot afford the overhead in resources required to store multiple copies in memory.

14.8 Conclusion

One facet of program modularity is dealt with at a logical level and concerns the separation of functions, information hiding, etc. as discussed in Chapter 4. Another facet is concerned with the physical means by which the modularity is effected.

The facilities offered by various languages differ widely with respect to issues such as local and global data, the mechanism for passing parameters between procedures, the ability to define functions, the possibility of recursion, etc. These are all points to look for when approaching a new programming language and awareness of the possibilities which might be available in the starting point from which to examine the syntax of a language.

14.9   Review questions

(1) An organization pays its sales staff a bonus if the total of their local sales has exceeded $10000 in any month. The bonus is 5% on the local sales plus 10% on any overseas sales that month.

The following program code was written to perform this calculation:

```
    .
    .
    .
    do Calculate Bonus (LOCAL_SALES, OSEAS_SALES, BONUS)
    .
    .
Calculate Bonus (SALES_1, SALES_2, AMOUNT)
    local data
        SALES_1, SALES_2, AMOUNT : real
    begin
        if SALES_1 > 10000
            SALES_1 = SALES_1 + (2 * SALES_2)
            AMOUNT = SALES_1 * 5 / 100
        end-if
    end
```

Discuss any problems which this code msight cause in the running of the program.

(2) The Fibonacci Series consists of the numbers

1, 2, 3, 5, 8, 13, 21, 34, 55, . . .

The first two numbers are 1 and 2 and each following number is the sum of the preceeding two numbers. (As an aside, the series was originally formulated to calculate the breeding patterns of rabbits.)

Write pseudocode for a recursive function Fib (N) which will return the Nth number in the Fibonacci Series.

For example:

Fib (1) = 1
Fib (3) = 3
Fib (6) = 13
Fib (9) = 55

15 Programs at machine level

15.1 Introduction

When a program is running, it is resident in memory, wholly or in part, and is being executed by the control unit of the central processor. Although it is no longer necessary for programmers to write programs in machine code, an understanding of the principles of program operation at machine level assists programmers in understanding why certain features of some languages should be used or avoided in the interests of efficiency of execution. Such an understanding also helps to remove the mystique surrounding programs and exposes them as collections of numbers which have significance when interpreted by the control unit of the computer.

    The examination of program operation at this level requires the programmer to be on much more familiar terms with the workings of a computer than is necessary when using a high-level language. It is necessary, for example, to appreciate the internal representation of data and instruction formats and the limitations imposed on these by the number of bits allocated for the holding of their component parts.

15.2 Internal memory

The internal memory of any computer functions as though it were a very large collection of pigeon holes or locations which are capable of holding nothing other than a binary number. A binary system, based on two, is chosen in preference to the more familiar decimal system, based on ten, because of the engineering simplicity which the binary system permits. The size of the memory locations in any particular computer governs the ease with which data may be stored and manipulated and with which instructions may refer to, or address, a range of such locations in the course of executing a program. For a given number, N, of binary digits (bits) the range of combinations of the 1s and 0s is 2^N. These combinations may represent the magnitude of a numeric quantity or a system of codes by which numeric or non-numeric data is represented in the computer system.

Hence, a group of eight bits may represent the combinations ranging from 00000000 to 11111111. In a binary system, the values of the digits ascend in powers of two, hence the respective decimal equivalents of the above binary numbers can be calculated as follows:

2^7	2^6	2^5	2^4	2^3	2^2	2^1	2^0		
(128)	(64)	(32)	(16)	(8)	(4)	(2)	(1)		
0	0	0	0	0	0	0	0	=	0
1	1	1	1	1	1	1	1	=	255

By conventions adopted by the computer, bits could represent the decimal values 0 to 255, the decimal values -128 to $+127$ or a series of 256 separate characters representing numeric, alphabetic (both upper and lower case) and many special characters (e.g., $*/=;:$). The value thus represented could be interpreted as the whole or part of an item of data or a program instruction.

15.3   Storage of data

Depending on the size of the locations (i.e., the number of bits) in the memory of a computer, data items may be held within a single location or within a group of locations operated on as a unit or individually, depending upon the nature of the data. The types of data items manipulated by programs were outlined in Chapter 2.

The following outline covers the most significant features of each of the types of data:

(1) *Integers and fixed-point numbers*: These numbers will be held in pure binary format (i.e., as a true binary number rather than in a binary coded form) usually in a unit of at least 16 bits. This will enable a value to be held within the range of -32768 to $+32767$. Larger units of bits may be used with consequently larger values

being able to be held. A computer with a 32-bit location would be able to hold integer values within the range $\pm 2^{31}$ which is approximately ± 2 thousand million.

Negative values are held in a complementary format, either as 1s or 2s complements. The 1s complement of a number is obtained by inverting the bits, that is, the 0s become 1s and the 1s becomes 0s. The 2s complement of a number is the 1s complement plus 1. Figure 15.1 illustrates the format of complementary numbers.

Normally a computer will perform arithmetic on binary integers on the assumption that negative values are represented in 2s complement. To achieve this complementary representation, the left-most bit in the memory location must be excluded from the representation of the magnitude of the number.

Number, N (decimal equivalent)	−N 1s complements	−N 2s complements
011001 (25)	100110	100111
011111 (31)	100000	100001
000001 (1)	111110	111111
000000 (0)	111111	000000

Figure 15.1 Complementary representation

In absolute terms, the largest value able to be represented by a location holding N bits is $2^N - 1$. Hence, if N is 16, the value of $2^N - 1$ is 65535 and a 16-bit location may represent the values 0 to 65535. If negative numbers are required, however, only 15 bits of that location may represent the magnitude of any number, the sixteenth (left-most) bit will enable complementation to occur in the case of negative numbers. The range of numbers that can be represented is $+ (2^{15} - 1)$ to -2^{15}. There exists the ability to hold one more number on the negative scale than the positive scale. Figure 15.2 illustrates the bit pattern of binary integers represented with a unit of eight bits.

When arithmetic operations are performed on the contents of memory locations, it is possible to cause overflow or underflow. These conditions occur when the number of bits in the location is insufficient to represent the correct value of a calculation. This is a situation with which anybody using a digital calculator is familiar.

Binary number	Decimal equivalent
01111111	127
01111110	126
01111101	125
.	.
.	.
00000011	3
00000010	2
00000001	1
00000000	0
11111111	−1
11111110	−2
11111101	−3
.	.
.	.
10000011	−125
10000010	−126
10000001	−127
10000000	−128

Figure 15.2 Eight-bit binary integers

(2) *Floating point (real) numbers*: Floating point numbers will normally be allocated a storage unit of at least 24 to 32 bits, of which typically eight bits would hold the exponent and the remainder would hold the mantissa. Both the exponent and the mantissa are capable of being either positive or negative. This format allows for the storage of values of larger magnitude than those held in integer format but with a loss of accuracy in numbers which do not convert to an exact binary fraction.

Figure 15.3 illustrates a series of values held in floating point format using four bits for the exponent and eight bits for the mantissa. Each mantissa is a fraction and hence the bit pattern 01000000 represents a value of 0.1000000 or 0.5 on a decimal scale. The values of the fractional bits in a binary number, from left to right are, ½, ¼, ⅛, 1/16, 1/32, etc. However, the necessity to be able to represent negative values (of both the mantissa and exponent) requires that the left-most bit in each component does not count in the magnitude of that value but merely allows for complementation to occur when necessary. Hence, in the values shown in Figure 15.3, only three bits may effectively store the value of the exponent and seven bits the mantissa. Note that the mantissa for the last value, .65, is only an approximation. This fraction presents the equivalent problem, in a binary system, to 1/3 in a decimal system, that is, a repeating value.

Number as a decimal value	Floating point format	Binary representation	
		Exponent	Mantissa
1250	$.125 \times 10^4$	0100	00010000
−1250	$-.125 \times 10^4$	0100	11110000
12.5	$.125 \times 10^2$	0010	00010000
.000125	$.125 \times 10^{-3}$	1101	00010000
−.000125	$-.125 \times 10^{-3}$	1101	11110000
65	$.65 \times 10^2$	0010	01010011

Figure 15.3 *Floating point representation*

(3) *Characters*: Character, or string, data may consist of any alphabetic letter, numeric digits or special symbols, each of which will normally be allocated one eight-bit unit of storage usually referred to as a byte. The characters will be represented in a coding system such as ASCII (American Standard Code for Information Interchange, a seven-bit code) or EBCDIC (Extended Binary Coded Decimal Interchange Code, an eight-bit code). Numeric data held in this format will normally require conversion to binary integer format for the purpose of any mathematical operations. This will make the program larger because of the additional machine code operations needed to perform the conversion and slower because of the time taken for these instructions to be executed each time the data item is referenced.

(4) *Packed decimal*: Packed decimal numbers, also referred to as BCD (Binary Coded Decimal), are a variation on character storage. Each decimal digit is represented by a four-bit binary code, thus allowing two decimal digits per byte of memory. Such a representation is economic in its use of storage but, unless the computer is able to perform BCD arithmetic, will still need conversion to pure binary for computational purposes.

Negative values held in character or packed decimal format are indicated by either storing a minus sign character as part of the number's representation or by setting a bit in the leading or trailing digit to indicate the sign of the value.

(5) *Boolean*: Boolean variables are normally held in integer format. Two values only are needed and it is common to find True held as 1 and False as 0.

15.4   Storage of instructions

Depending on the size of a computer's memory location, instructions are held one per location, several per location or one may occupy several locations. There may be several formats of instructions in the repertoire of any one computer. The format of an instruction will typically contain:

- an operation code;
- one or more operands;
- an indication of register(s) used; and
- an indication of modified or indirect operations.

Given the need to store all of these components within the format of the instruction, there needs to be a compromise between them in terms of the number of bits allocated to each component. The larger the size of the locations of a computer, the more bits will be able to be allocated to each of these components of the instruction. The effect of this can be seen when we look at each component in turn:

(1) *Operation codes*: The operation code indicates the function to be carried out by the control unit in executing the instruction. Typical instructions at machine code level which are common to most computers are:

- load and store operations to transfer the contents of locations from one to another or to or from working registers;
- arithmetic operations to add, subtract, multiply and divide;
- compare operations to test the relative magnitudes of the contents of locations or registers;
- branch operations to transfer program control unconditionally or conditionally on the result of a test on the contents of a location or a register, to transfer control to a subroutine and arrange for the storage of a return address to the calling routine;
- shift operations to move the pattern of bits in a location or a register to the right or left by a specified number of positions;
- logical operations to perform Boolean AND and OR functions between the contents of locations and/or registers;
- input/output operations to transfer data between the internal memory and peripheral devices; and
- specialized instructions, for example to effect conversions between character and binary data or to operate on a hardware stack implemented within memory.

In addition to indicating the function to be performed, the operation code usually provides the addressing mode of the instruction. The addressing mode indicates the way in which the instruction interprets the operand. Typical addressing modes are:

(a) *Memory address mode*: The operand is interpreted as a memory location, the contents of which are to be operated on by the instruction.

(b) *Constant mode*: The operand is interpreted as a literal or constant value to be manipulated by the instruction.

(c) *No-address mode*: The instruction either needs no operand (e.g., stop) or the operand is inherent in the nature of the operation.

(d) *Indirect mode*: The operand is interpreted as an address which contains the actual operand to be used within the instruction.

(e) *Relative mode*: The operand is interpreted as a number which is to be added to (or subtracted from) the address of the instruction to obtain the address of the actual operand.

(2) *Operands*: An operand in any instruction is a constant, a memory location or register which is the object of the instruction's attentions. There may be none, one or several operands in an instruction depending on the format employed by a particular computer. This, in turn, is typically governed by the size of the computer's memory location. Larger locations contain more bits and may therefore be used to represent more than one operand in any instruction. This is referred to as a multi-address, as opposed to a single-address, instruction format.

If a computer has only one register in which to manipulate data, its use will be inherent in the operation. If several registers may be used, there must be some indication in the instruction as to which register is chosen. This may be by having the number of the register as part of the instruction, for example,

34 (ADM) 3   200

meaning add the contents of location 200 to register 3, or by having different operation codes for each register.

(3) *Index registers*: Most computers provide at least one index register which may be used in conjunction with most (but not necessarily all) instructions. Where such a facility is used, the effective operand of the instruction (i.e., the actual address the contents of which are manipulated) is obtained by adding together the operand quoted in the instruction and the contents of the index register at the time the instruction is executed. The use of the index register is normally signaled by the setting of a nominated bit in the location holding the instruction.

In this manner, the instruction may be placed in a loop and, by altering the contents of the index register each time through the loop, the instructions may be made to execute on a different effective operand in each iteration.

The following example of this procedure accumulates a total of the contents of a series of 100 locations commencing at location TABLE:

```
Index Register=0
TOTAL=0
COUNTER=100
while counter > 0
    TOTAL=TOTAL+TABLE (indexed)
    Index Register=Index Register+1
    COUNTER=COUNTER−1
end-while
```

In successive iterations of the loop in this algorithm, the effective operand accumulated in the total is TABLE+0, TABLE+1, TABLE+2, ... TABLE+98 and TABLE+99.

The effective operand obtained by adding together the quoted operand in the instruction, TABLE, in the above example, and the contents of the index register is formed in an address register, or operand register, within the control unit. This address register normally contains more bits than the operand in an instruction and hence may hold a larger value. This effect is often used to overcome the inability of the operand in an instruction to address a sufficiently large range of memory locations. For example, a 16-bit location may only be able to devote ten of its bits to holding the operand component of a contained instruction. The other six bits may be needed for the operation code, etc. In such a case, the maximum value of the operand is $2^{10} - 1$, that is, 1023. Hence, an instruction cannot directly access any locations other than those with addresses 0 to 1023 within the program space. Even a computer with a 32-bit location may be able to allocate only 16 of its bits to represent the operand in an instruction. This would permit the program to access directly 64K locations which, while not as trivial as the 1K in the 10-bit example, is certainly far short of a realistic operational program.

The means often used to overcome this limitation is that of a 'base + displacement' strategy. A base address of an area of memory is placed in an index register which may contain the same number of bits as the memory location of the computer. By using this index register to augment the operands within instructions, the instructions themselves need only hold as their operand the distance (displacement) of that operand from the base address.

15.5 Relocatable programs

In the early days of computing, programs were executed one at a time and had most of the internal memory to themselves. They were able to refer to absolute memory locations by their numeric addresses and could therefore refer to location 0 or location 400 and mean the first or 401st actual memory location. When multi-programming became the norm, programs had to share memory space cooperatively and their precise whereabouts in memory was no longer predictable. All memory locations then became relative rather than absolute addresses. Location zero now meant the first location within that program's space (wherever that was at the time) rather than the first location within memory as a whole. When a program is loaded into memory, the operating system records the 'datum' address from which its locations are allocated and this address is added to the value of the operand address within each instruction as it is executed.

In current systems using paged memory and non-contiguous storage of program segments, it can be appreciated that there is a large overhead involved in the execution of a program. This overhead is imposed by the necessity of having to translate the relative addresses of program operands to absolute memory locations by a complex table operation each time an instruction is executed.

The effect of this procedure is to ensure that programs are relocatable within memory, that is, their successful operation does not depend on their being loaded into memory at any particular address. In fact, during their operation, their position within memory may constantly change due to the time-sharing nature of the computing environment.

15.6 Program execution

Instructions are executed sequentially by the control unit with the aid of the program counter. The program counter is primed with the memory address of the first instruction when the program is loaded into memory and is thereafter incremented automatically as each instruction is decoded and executed by the control unit. The operation of branch instructions is to replace the contents of the program counter with the address of the instruction to be branched to.

Execution of an instruction involves the fetching of the instruction from the location or locations in which it is stored, decomposing it into its component operation code and one or more operands, and activating the mechanism by which the function is effected. This latter stage will involve opening the various electronic gates which enable the circuitry of the processor to execute instructions. It may also involve the execution of microcode, a series of very primitive machine operations which collectively perform one of the instructions in the computer's machine code repertoire. Such microcode is often held in read-only memory (ROM). Some computers are able to have their ROM changed by replacing one of their circuit boards and are thus able to emulate the mode of operation of an entirely different model of computer.

15.7 Program translation (compiling/interpreting)

Programs written in high-level languages such as COBOL, BASIC and Pascal are not in a form executable by the computer's control unit. To enable them to be executed they must be translated into the computer's machine code. This translation may be carried out in a single process referred to as compiling, as is typical with COBOL, or in two processes referred to as interpreting, as is usually the case with BASIC.

(1) *Compiling*: Compiling is the process of converting a source program written in a high-level language to an object program in machine code. The tasks of the compiler program are to:

(a) break up the source text into the statements comprising the syntax of the language;
(b) check each statement for correctness of format and report any error found for subsequent correction by the programmer;
(c) print (if possible) a listing of the source program together with any syntax errors discovered; and
(d) if the program has no syntax errors, generate an object program consisting of:

- memory locations allocated to the symbolic names used by the programmer for variables and constants;
- machine code instructions to accomplish the functions of the procedural statements in the source program, this process requires the generation of many machine code instructions for each source language instruction;
- library subroutines included in the object program to carry out complex functions such as input/output to and from peripherals, mathematical operations such as logarithms, and square roots and trigonometric functions such as sines, cosines and tangents.

    This phase is often referred to as linking and, depending on the compiler used, may be executed as an integral part of the compilation process or as a separate operation following a successful compilation.

The program is thereafter stored in its machine code version and needs to be recompiled only when amendments are made to the source program.

(2) *Interpreting*: Interpreting is the process of translating a source program into a format which is an intermediate stage between the syntax of the source language and the machine code of the computer. This will involve tasks (a), (b) and (c) of the compilation process but will stop short of the detailed machine code generation in task (d). This reduces the translation time, provides the programmer with a report of any syntax errors with less of a delay than is inherent in full compilation, and results in a smaller object program because of the elimination of the necessity to generate voluminous machine code.

Interpreting, however, results in programs which will be slower to execute than those which have been fully compiled. This is brought about by the necessity to generate machine code instructions (task (d) of the compiler) to accomplish the operation of the source instructions as the program is executing. Hence, a source instruction in a loop which is executed 100 times may be converted to machine code 100 times each time that loop is encountered in the running of the program.

As a general principle, interpreted programs will occupy less memory than compiled programs but will execute at a slower rate.

15.8   Assembler languages and machine code

All computers ultimately work on the basis of machine language programs. The central processor has a series of possible operations, each of which is allocated a numeric code and has a particular format. Between this level of programming and that of the high-level languages with which we are familiar lies a level of assembler programming languages.

Assembler languages usually have a one-for-one relationship with their machine code, that is, each assembler instruction generates only one machine code instruction. However, assembler languages have mnemonic (aid to memory) operation codes consisting of a few alphabetic characters indicative of the operation and addressing mode of the instruction. They also permit the use of symbolic address names whereby the programmer can assign meaningful names, for example, COUNTER, TOTAL, etc., to memory locations. They also typically have 'pseudo operations' which are not translated to machine code but rather give information to the assembler program which translates the assembler language to machine code. These pseudo operations are usually concerned with assignment of symbolic names to locations or the reservation of blocks of storage.

Appendix E gives the specifications for a hypothetic computer and its assembler language. A sample assembler language program is also provided.

15.9   Polish notation

To facilitate the execution of mathematical expressions, compilers commonly reduce them to a notation formulated by a Polish mathematician, Lukasiewicz, and hence the technique is known as Polish notation. It is a technique of rearranging the terms in an expression so as to place the operators after the operands to which they refer. In this way, $A + B$ becomes $AB +$ and $A * (B + C)$ becomes $ABC + *$. Polish notation eliminates ambiguities in expressions and the need for brackets to resolve the order of evaluation.

The terms of an expression in normal algebraic format, for example, $X = Y * Z + W$ are referred to as being in 'infix' notation and when reduced to Polish form, $XYZ * W + =$, are referred to as 'postfix' notation. Mathematical operators are assigned a hierarchy of precedence, from high to low:

- exponentiation (** or ↑);
- multiplication and division (*, /);
- addition and subtraction (+, −);
- replacement (assignment) (=).

Within each of the groups, the order is left-to-right.

The execution of expressions in Polish form is accomplished by the use of a stack. Terms are pushed on a stack until an operator is encountered. This operation is applied to the two operands at the top of the stack. These two operands are then discarded and replaced by the result of the operation. This procedure continues until the Polish string is exhausted.

The following is a skeleton algorithm to transform infix to postfix notation:

Polish Notation
 Initialize operator stack to empty
 while there are terms in the infix string
  if the next infix element is an operand
   Place the operand in the postfix string
  else (i.e. term is an operator)
   while operator is not greater than the operator at the top
   of the stack (and stack is not empty)
    Remove operator at top of stack and place it
    in the postfix string
   end-while
   Push infix operator on top of stack
  end-if
 end-while
 Pop any remaining operators from stack and place in postfix string.

This algorithm may be modified to handle brackets by incorporating the following modification:

- When a left bracket is encountered in the infix string, push it on the operator stack (i.e., as though it had highest precedence) and continue with the normal scanning of the infix string. Operators subsequently compared with such a bracket at the top of the stack should be regarded as being of higher precedence than the bracket and therefore pushed on top of it.

- When a right bracket is encountered, pop operators from the stack and place them in the postfix string until a left bracket is encountered. Both the right and left brackets are now discarded and the scanning of the infix string continues.

Using the above procedure, the following transformation would be effected:

 $W = A + B * C - D / E \uparrow 2$

becomes

 $WABC* + DE\,2\uparrow/-=$

and

 $W = (A+B) * (C-D/E)\uparrow 2$

becomes

 $WAB + CDE/-2\uparrow*=$

15.10   Conclusion

This is a brief summary of the background of knowledge needed by a programmer when faced with the choice of using:

(1) integers as opposed to floating point variables in BASIC or Pascal, or the choice between DISPLAY and COMPUTATIONAL variables in COBOL; or
(2) a fully compiled, as opposed to an interpreted, version of a programming language; or
(3) a microcomputer with replaceable ROM enabling it to run software written originally for a different computer.

High-level languages have removed much of the tedium otherwise associated with writing programs at machine level, but they have also removed the intimacy between programmer and computer which promotes a fuller understanding of what actually happens when a program executes.

15.11   Review questions

(1) The ICL 1900 Series computers had 24-bit memory locations.

(a) The format of branch instructions held in these locations was:

```
bits 0 - 2    register indicator
bits 3 - 8    operation code
bits 9 - 23   operand location
```

(i) What span of locations is directly addressable by these branch instructions?
(ii) How many registers could be tested by the branch instructions?

(b) The format of instructions other than branches was:

```
bits 0 - 2     register indicator
bits 3 - 9     operation code
bits 10 - 11   index register indicator
bits 12 - 23   main operand
```

(i) How many operation codes could this instruction set have?
(ii) How many registers could instructions address?

  (iii) How many index registers could instructions use, and
        what might they be used for?
  (iv) What span of memory locations is directly addressable by
        these instructions?

(c) If the 24-bit location were to be used to hold positive and negative
    integers (assuming that negative values were held in 2's
    complements), what range of integers could be held?

(2) Convert the following infix expressions to Polish notation:

(a) X = A + B * C − D / E
(b) X = (A + B) * (C − D) / E
(c) X = A + B ↑ C − (D + E) * F ↑ G / H
(d) X = (A + B) ↑ (C − D) + E * F ↑ (G / H)
(e) X = ((A + B ↑ (C − D)) * (E ↑ (F * G))) / H

  Notes: The symbol ↑ indicates exponentiation.

Appendix A   COBOL

A1   Algorithm implementation

Implementation of the program control structures of sequence, iteration and selection is possible through syntax which is extremely close to that of the pseudocode used to express the algorithm from which a program will be coded.

Sequence

As COBOL instructions are executed in the order in which they occur in the source program, no further technique is required to implement a series of sequential operations, for example:

```
ADD 1 TO TOTAL
MOVE TOTAL TO ANSWER
DISPLAY "RESULT IS" ANSWER
```

Iteration

The pseudocode construct used was **While** condition statement(s).

Because the PERFORM ... UNTIL ... feature in COBOL usually allows only for the execution of a separate module, or subroutine, the statement(s) to be executed must be placed in a separate section or paragraph within the Procedure Division. It must be remembered that the PERFORM ... UNTIL ... construct implies a leading decision technique. This means that the condition controlling the loop is evaluated before executing the performed procedure for the first time and thereafter before each subsequent execution. Hence, if the condition is satisfied before the loop operation starts, there will be no execution of the instructions within the loop.

There are two basic methods of controlling a loop in COBOL, illustrated by a routine designed to examine each element in a table and to count the number of such elements containing the value zero.

The algorithm expressed in pseudocode would be:

```
Total=zero
Counter=1
while Counter ≤ size of table
    if Number (Counter)=zero
        Total=Total+1
    end-if
    Counter=Counter+1
end-while
```

There are two basic means of implementing this loop in COBOL:

(1) **Internal control of the loop:**
```
PERFORM COUNT-ZEROS
    .
    .
    .

COUNT-ZEROS SECTION.
    SET COUNTER TO 1.
    MOVE ZERO TO TOTAL.
CZ1.
    IF NUMBER (COUNTER)= ZERO
        ADD 1 TO TOTAL.
    IF COUNTER < TABLE_SIZE
        SET COUNTER UP BY 1
        GO TO CZ1.
```

(2) **External control of the loop:**
```
MOVE ZERO TO TOTAL
SET COUNTER TO 1.
PERFORM COUNT-ZEROS
    UNTIL COUNTER > TABLE_SIZE
    .
    .
    .

COUNT-ZEROS SECTION.
    IF NUMBER (COUNTER)= ZERO
        ADD 1 TO TOTAL.
    SET COUNTER UP BY 1.
```

or alternatively

```
MOVE ZERO TO TOTAL
PERFORM COUNT-ZEROS
    VARYING COUNTER FROM 1 BY 1
    UNTIL COUNTER > TABLE-SIZE.
  .
  .
  .

COUNT-ZEROS SECTION.
    IF NUMBER (COUNTER)=ZERO
        ADD 1 TO TOTAL.
```

Of the two methods, external loop control provides a cleaner program and is in keeping with the general approach of structured programming. Internal loop control has the added disadvantage that it needs a branch (GO TO) instruction to implement it, and the prolific use of these instructions, and the labels (paragraph names) which they necessitate, is extremely harmful to program clarity.

More recent COBOL compliers provide for in-line PERFORM sequences. These eliminate the necessity to place the code performed in a paragraph or section remote from the controlling PERFORM statement. An in-line PERFORM is written as:

```
MOVE ZERO TO TOTAL.
SET COUNTER TO 1.
PERFORM UNTIL COUNTER > TABLE-SIZE
    IF NUMBER (COUNTER) = ZERO
        ADD 1 TO TOTAL
    END-IF
    SET COUNTER UP BY 1
END-PERFORM.
```

or alternatively

```
MOVE ZERO TO TOTAL
PERFORM VARYING COUNTER FROM 1 BY 1
      UNTIL COUNTER > TABLE-SIZE
    IF NUMBER (COUNTER) = ZERO
        ADD 1 TO TOTAL
    END-IF
END-PERFORM.
```

Selection

Selection in COBOL is basically implemented by the IF . . . [ELSE] . . . construction, for example:

```
IF TOTAL = ZERO
    DISPLAY ERROR-MESSAGE.
IF HOURS-WORKED > WORK-LIMIT
    PERFORM ERROR-PROCEDURE
ELSE
    PERFORM COMPUTE-PAY.
```

Multiple tests may be implemented by a series of IFs and ELSEs, for example:

```
IF SKILL-CODE = CARPENTER-CODE
    MOVE CARPENTER-RATE TO PAY-RATE
ELSE IF SKILL-CODE = FITTER-CODE
    MOVE FITTER-RATE TO PAY-RATE
ELSE IF SKILL-CODE = CLERK-CODE
    MOVE CLERK-RATE TO PAY-RATE
ELSE IF SKILL-CODE = SUPERVISOR-CODE
    MOVE SUPERIOR-RATE TO PAY-RATE
    .
    .
    .
```

The concept of a **Case** statement may be implemented by means of the EVALUATE verb, another recent addition to the COBOL repertoire:

```
EVALUATE SKILL-CODE
    WHEN CARPENTER-CODE
        MOVE CARPENTER-RATE TO PAY-RATE
    WHEN FITTER-CODE
        MOVE FITTER-RATE TO PAY-RATE
    WHEN CLERK-CODE
        MOVE CLERK-RATE TO PAY-RATE
    .
    .
    .

    WHEN OTHER
        MOVE ZERO TO PAY-RATE
        PERFORM ERROR-PROCEDURE
END-EVALUATE.
```

Program modules

The pseudocode also introduced the concept of a module or subroutine comprising a free-standing task to be accomplished as part of a larger job and executed via a **Do** command.

Such modules in COBOL should comprise a SECTION or paragraph and should be executed by a PERFORM verb. Examples of this have been given in the above illustrations.

A2 Program structure

Programs should be written in modules, each of which should be a Section in the Procedure Division. The first Section should contain the mainline, or driving, logic of the program. Program termination, via the STOP RUN instruction, should occur at only one point in the program, that point being at the end of the first Section in the Procedure Division.

Execution of any but the mainline Section should only be by means of a PERFORM, never by a GO TO or by 'falling through' the program from a prior Section.

Each Section should contain or control a separate task within the program and, hence, there should be no need for the use of the PERFORM . . . THRU . . . variant.

An EXIT verb within a paragraph at the end of a Section should not be necessary unless that Section contains an 'escape' branch (via a GO TO). Such a procedure should be regarded as an exceptional rather than a customary procedure.

If GO TO instructions are used they should not in any circumstances branch outside their own Section.

Care should be taken to separate 'managing' from 'working' Sections and the descent of the hierarchy of Sections within a program should reflect a transition from manager to worker instructions.

This progression is illustrated below by skeletal coding to implement the payroll algorithm in Chapter 3.

```
PROCEDURE DIVISION.
MAINLINE SECTION.
    PERFORM PROGRAM-INITIALIZATION.
    PERFORM OBTAIN-CORRECT-WORK-DETAILS
        UNTIL DETAILS-OK=TRUE
            OR END-OF-DATA=TRUE.
    PERFORM PROCESS-PAYROLL
        UNTIL END-OF-DATA=TRUE.
    PERFORM PRINT-FACTORY-TOTALS.
    PERFORM PROGRAM-FINALIZATION.
    STOP RUN.
*
*

PROCESS-PAYROLL SECTION.
    PERFORM PAY-CALCULATION.
    PERFORM UPDATE-HISTORY-RECORD.
    PERFORM PRINT-PAY-DETAILS.
    PERFORM OBTAIN-CORRECT-WORK-DETAILS
        UNTIL DETAILS-OK=TRUE
            OR END-OF-DATA=TRUE
    .
    .
    .

PAY-CALCULATION SECTION.
    IF HOURS-WORKED NOT > NORMAL-PERIOD
        MOVE HOURS-WORKED TO PAYABLE-HOURS
```

```
ELSE
    COMPUTE PAYABLE-HOURS
            =NORMAL PERIOD
            +OVERTIME PERIOD
            *(HOURS-WORKED-NORMAL-PERIOD)
COMPUTE GROSS-PAY=PAYABLE HOURS*
                    HOURLY-RATE.

PERFORM TAX-FORMULA.
COMPUTE NET-PAY=GROSS-PAY-TAX-AMOUNT.

PERFORM COINAGE-ANALYSIS.
ADD GROSS-PAY TO FACTORY-TOTAL-GROSS.
ADD TAX-AMOUNT TO FACTORY-TOTAL-TAX.
ADD NET-PAY TO FACTORY-TOTAL-NET.
```

Note that in this example, MAINLINE and PROCESS-PAYROLL Sections are managerial by nature because they only contain directives to other modules to perform certain tasks. The PAY-CALCULATION Section is partly managerial (i.e., IFs and PERFORMs) and partly working because it accomplishes several arithmetic calculations. We could infer that the COINAGE-ANALYSIS Section would entirely consist of working instructions.

A3 Module design

It should be a major consideration in program design that each functional task, consisting of one or more Sections, should operate as independently as possible of other tasks in the program.

Although data in a COBOL program is global by nature, it is possible to allocate a specific data area to the task of communicating with a procedural module. The allocated area will contain items which will be data and/or status variable parameters. The following is an example of the implementation of the Check Product ID Number algorithm in Chapter 4.

```
01 CHECK-PRODUCT-ID-WS.
    03 PRODUCT-TO-CHECK      PIC 9(6).
    03 PRODUCT-NAME          PIC X(30).
    03 PRODUCT-FOUND         PIC 9.
    .
    .
    .
```

```
MOVE INPUT-PRODUCT-ID TO PRODUCT-TO-CHECK.
PERFORM CHECK-PRODUCT-ID.
IF PRODUCT-FOUND=TRUE
    .
    .
    .

    ELSE
    .
    .
    .

CHECK-PRODUCT-ID SECTION.
    SET TABLE-INDEX TO 1.
    MOVE FALSE TO PRODUCT-FOUND.
    MOVE SPACES TO PRODUCT-NAME.
    PERFORM CHECK-PRODUCT-LOOP.
        UNTIL PRODUCT-FOUND=TRUE
            OR TABLE-INDEX > TABLE-SIZE.
CHECK-PRODUCT-LOOP SECTION.
    IF PRODUCT-TO-CHECK=TABLE-PRODUCT-ID (TABLE-INDEX)
        MOVE TRUE TO PRODUCT-FOUND
        MOVE TABLE-PRODUCT-NAME (TABLE-INDEX) TO
        PRODUCT-NAME
    ELSE
        SET TABLE-INDEX UP BY 1.
```

An alternative solution for the table search routine is given below, together with an illustration of suitable comments which would aid internal documentation.

```
CHECK-PRODUCT-ID SECTION.
*   -----------------------------------------------------------------------------------------
*       TO USE THIS PROCEDURE:
*       PLACE PRODUCT ID TO BE CHECKED IN
*       'PRODUCT-TO-CHECK'
*       IF PRODUCT ID IS MATCHED AGAINST A
*       PRODUCT IN THE TABLE OF VALID CODES
*           'PRODUCT-FOUND' IS SET TO 'TRUE'
*           'PRODUCT-NAME' WILL CONTAIN THE
*           NAME OF THE RELEVANT PRODUCT
*       ELSE
*           'PRODUCT-FOUND' IS SET TO 'FALSE'
*           'PRODUCT-NAME' WILL CONTAIN SPACES

    SET TABLE-INDEX TO 1.
    SEARCH PRODUCT-TABLE VARYING TABLE-INDEX
        WHEN PRODUCT-TO-CHECK=TABLE-PRODUCT-ID (TABLE-INDEX)
        MOVE TRUE TO PRODUCT-FOUND
        MOVE TABLE-PRODUCT-NAME (TABLE-INDEX) TO
        PRODUCT-NAME
    AT END MOVE FALSE TO PRODUCT-FOUND
        MOVE SPACES TO PRODUCT-NAME.
```

This example makes use of TRUE and FALSE as values for status variables. These are user-defined items and should be used for setting and testing all such variables. Avoid the use of 88-level condition names for this purpose because they provide less clarity to the reader than the use of TRUE and FALSE. The following example should illustrate this point:

The use of an 88-level status item implementation typically appears as:

```
01 CODE-STATUS              PIC 9
   88 CODE-ERROR-FOUND      VALUE 1.
   88 CODE-CORRECT          VALUE 0.
```

Consider the instruction:

```
IF CODE-A IS NOT=CODE-B
   MOVE 1 TO CODE-STATUS.
```

Without cross-reference to the Data Division 88-level entry, it is not apparent to the reader whether the status value of 1 represents the finding of an error or the finding of a correct situation.

The testing of the status item offers no help,

```
IF CODE-ERROR-FOUND
   PERFORM CODE-ERROR-PROCEDURE.
```

There is no apparent connection between the placing of a value of 1 in CODE-STATUS and the testing of the condition CODE-ERROR-FOUND.

The preferred method of implementing all status items within a program should be by declaring global condition names and values, for example:

```
01 STATUS-VALUES
   03 TRUE                  PIC 9 VALUE 1.
   03 FALSE                 PIC 9 VALUE 0.
```

The chosen PIC clauses and VALUEs are immaterial provided that all subsequent variables have the same PIC clause, for example:

```
01 CODE-ERROR-FOUND         PIC 9.
```

The setting and testing of such status variables is now self-explanatory to the reader of a program:

```
IF CODE-A IS NOT=CODE-B
   MOVE TRUE TO CODE-ERROR-FOUND.
```

and

```
IF CODE-ERROR-FOUND=TRUE
    PERFORM CODE-ERROR-PROCEDURE.
```

A4   Programming standards

The following are suggested as minimum standards for the writing of
COBOL programs:

Program function

The Identification Division should contain comments or a REMARKS
section explaining the function(s) of the program and its interaction
with any other program(s) in a system.

Coding format

DIVISIONs and major SECTIONs must commence on a new page.

Related groups of statements in the Data Division and Procedure
Division should be separated from one another by * lines for clarity of
presentation.

Commence successive ASSIGN, PIC and VALUE clauses at the same
column, for example:

```
SELECT          X-FILE   ASSIGN TO 'ABC'
SELECT          Y-FILE   ASSIGN TO 'PQR'

01 AAA          PIC X    VALUE 'A'
01 BBB          PIC 9    VALUE 6.
```

Indent elementary items comprising a group item by 4 character
positions and advance their level numbers by at least 2, for example:

```
01   A.
     03   B              PIC 9.
     03   C.
          05   D         PIC X.
          05   E.
               07   F    PIC 9(2)
               07   G    PIC 9(5)V9(2).
     03   H              PIC X(4)
```

Use bracket notation for multiple characters in PICTURE clauses,
for example:

```
PIC 9(3)   not   PIC 999
```

When using long alphanumeric literals, start the literal on a new line, for example:

```
01  MESSAGE        PIC X(40)      VALUE
    '......ETC.......................................................................'.
```

A VALUE clause should be used to define a constant, not to initialize a variable, for example

```
01  PAGE-SIZE      PIC 9(2)       VALUE 60.
```

correctly defines an item of data which does not alter during the execution of the program, whereas

```
01  ERROR-COUNTER      PIC 9(2).
```

and later

```
MOVE ZERO TO ERROR-COUNTER
```

correctly initializes a variable, the contents of which may change many times as the program runs.

In the interests of efficiency, Index Variables should be used (and the related SET instructions) as subscripts to arrays (tables). In addition, each array should be accompanied by a size variable to be used in testing/controlling operations in the procedural code, for example:

```
01  TABLE
    03   ITEM                 PIC 9(4)
                              OCCURS 20 TIMES
                              INDEXED BY ITEM-INDEX.
01  TABLE-SIZE                PIC 9(2) VALUE 20.
```

and later

```
PERFORM 40-CLEAR-TABLE   TABLE-SIZE TIMES.
```

or

```
IF ITEM-INDEX IS NOT > TABLE-SIZE
        < action(s) >
```

Heavily used arithmetic items should be held in **COMP** format for efficiency.

Program structure

Programs should be written in modules, each of which will be a SECTION, the first module being the mainline or driving logic for the program.

Execution of any but the mainline SECTION may only be by a PERFORM, never by a GO TO or by 'falling through' the program from a previous SECTION.

Do not use the PERFORM . . . THRU . . . variant.

Indent IF/ELSE sequences to ensure that their function is clear, placing the IF < condition > and ELSE on lines by themselves, for example:

```
IF A=B
    ADD P TO Q
    MOVE R TO S
    IF C=D
        ADD M TO N
    ELSE
        NEXT SENTENCE
ELSE
    ADD V TO W.
```

Note: An acceptable format for multiple IFs is:

```
IF < condition >
    action-1
    action-2
ELSE IF < condition >
        action-3
        action-4
ELSE IF < condition >
        action-5
        action-6
        .
        .
        .
ELSE IF < condition >
        action-99
        action-100.
```

In the Procedure Division, write only one instruction per line and never break a data-name across two lines.

Naming conventions

Data division:

(1) All data names must be meaningful and hyphenation must be used to facilitate readability, for example, GROSS-PAY.

(2) Abbreviation of names is not a virtue; for example, use **GROSS-WEEKLY-WAGE**, not **GR-WK-WGE**.

(3) Always use the same basic name for an item of data wherever it is found in the DATA DIVISION. Duplication of data-names may be overcome by the use of Qualifiers or avoided by the use of identifying prefixes or suffixes on the names, for example:

```
FD MAG-TAPE—FILE
    .
    .
    .

01   MT-CUSTOMER
     03   MT-CUSTOMER-NUMBER
     03   MT-CUSTOMER-NAME
     03   MT-CUSTOMER-ADDRESS
FD DISK-FILE
    .
    .
    .

01   DISK-CUSTOMER.
     03   DSK-CUSTOMER-NUMBER
     03   DSK-CUSTOMER-NAME
     03   DSK-CUSTOMER-ADDRESS
```

but *never* the use of several variants on a name for what is essentially the same data item but appearing in several records, for example:

```
CUSTOMER-NMBR
CST-NO
CUST-NUMBER
    etc.
```

(4) Avoid the use of generalized global data items. Where possible, each procedural module should have allocated to it its own local data items.

Procedure division:

(1) **SECTION** names must be meaningful and, unless the **SECTION**'s purpose is self-explanatory, each must start with sufficient comment lines to make its purpose clear to the reader, for example:

```
READ-CUSTOMER-RECORD SECTION
    .
    .
    .
```

```
CALCULATE-NET-PAY SECTION.
    .
    .
    .

FIND-CODE SECTION.
*  THE TABLE OF VALID CODES IS
*  SEARCHED VIA A BINARY CHOP TO
*  MATCH THE CODE IN THE EMPLOYEE RECORD.
```

(2) An **EXIT** paragraph for a **SECTION** should not be syntactically necessary unless that **SECTION** contains an 'escape' branch.

(3) A program should contain only one **STOP RUN** instruction and that should be in the mainline **SECTION**.

(4) The use of **GO TO** instructions and Paragraph names should be confined to the handling of exceptional circumstances and not considered to be part of normal control structures.

If **GO TO** instructions are used, under no circumstances may they reference paragraphs outside their own **SECTION**.

Further points of programming style

When possible, use 88-level condition names and avoid multiple testing by IFs, for example:

```
03   RECORD-TYPE                 PIC 9.
     88   VALID-TYPE VALUES      1, 3, 4, 6.
```

A program should contain only one **OPEN**, **CLOSE**, **READ** or **WRITE** for each file. These will normally be in a **SECTION** which may be **PERFORM**ed whenever required.

Literals should not be used in the **PROCEDURE DIVISION**. Literal values should be given symbolic names and placed in the **DATA DIVISION**, for example:

```
MOVE CASUAL-EMPLOYEE-TYPE TO RECORD-TYPE
```

rather than

```
MOVE 12 TO RECORD-TYPE
```

In particular, subscripts should *never* be tested against literal values, for example use:

```
IF SUBSCRIPT < TABLE-SIZE
ADD 1 TO SUBSCRIPT
    etc.
```

never

```
IF SUBSCRIPT < 25
    etc.
```

Avoid complexity in compound and nested IF statements. In particular, avoid the use of compound tests linked by NOT; for example, many programmers have trouble in understanding why

```
IF CODE IS NOT=1 OR NOT=2
    PERFORM REJECTION-ROUTINE
```

rejects every code, including 1 and 2! As a rule of thumb, if a compound/nested IF . . . ELSE . . . sequence is sufficiently complex that you feel the need to have somebody else check your logic, then it is too obscure! Break it up into smaller components and, if necessary, push some of the testing back into a subroutine.

Appendix B   BASIC

Note: A problem which arises in illustrating programs in BASIC is the variety of dialects of BASIC which are available. What has been chosen here is a very 'basic' BASIC which has none of the features which made the various forms of extended BASIC a much more elegant language. The reader should compare these features with those in the BASIC he or she is using and try to improve on these examples.

B1   Algorithm implementation

BASIC by nature has few facilities to aid elegant program construction. Whatever structure is incorporated in the program must be the result of a discipline of coding style brought to bear by the programmer.

Sequence

As BASIC instructions are executed in the order in which they occur in the source program, no further technique is required to implement a series of sequential operations, for example:

```
100 READ A
110 B=2*A
120 C=3*A
130 PRINT A, B, C
```

Iteration

The pseudocode construct used was **While**.

If a loop is to be executed a predetermined number of times, a FOR ... NEXT ... construct may be used, for example, to set to zero each element in an array of N elements:

```
100 FOR K=1 TO N
110   E(K)=0
120 NEXT K
```

To implement a loop of an unknown number of interactions, a branch (GO TO) instruction is needed, for example, to read and print a series of numbers until a value of zero was encountered:

```
100 READ N
110 IF N=0 THEN 140
120 PRINT N
130 GOTO 100
140 . . .
```

Note that in such a case the concept of a priming read may provide a neater solution, for example:

```
100 READ N
110 IF N=0 THEN 150
120   PRINT N
130   READ N
140 GOTO 110
150 . . .
```

The latter solution is in closer conformity with the concepts of structured programming.

For the sake of program clarity, program loops of either of the above types should not span more than, say, six to eight lines. If the task requires more than that amount of code, it should be committed to a subroutine, for example:

```
100 FOR K=1 TO N
110   P=E(K)
120   GOSUB 500
130 NEXT K
      .
      .
      .

500 REM   THIS SUBROUTINE PERFORMS A NUMBER
510 REM   OF CALCULATIONS ON 'P' AN
520 REM   ELEMENT EXTRACTED FROM AN ARRAY
      .
      .
      .

690 RETURN
```

Many current implementations of BASIC contain a WHILE statement which controls a series of operations terminating with a WEND (or sometimes a NEXT), for example,

```
110 READ N
110 WHILE N < > 999
120   T=T+N
130   READ N
140 WEND
```

Selection

Selection is implemented by the IF command, but the construction in most BASICs allows for only a single instruction to follow the evaluation of the IF condition and allows for no ELSE construction.

For all but the most simple of situations, the program relies on a branching technique to effect the selection procedure, and it is essential to ensure that, to conform to the principles of structured programming, both the 'true' and 'false' branches of the IF resume processing at a common point, for example:

```
100 IF A=B THEN 160
110 REM    WHEN A < > B:-
120        P=Q+R
130        W=T*V
140        C=D/E
150        GOTO 200
160 REM    WHEN A=B:-
170        P=Q-R
180        W=T/V
190        C=D*E
200 PRINT P, W, C
    .
    .
    .
```

Note the use of indentation to highlight the two sets of actions emanating from the IF and the REM statements to provide additional documentation for the reader.

If there are more than, say, six to eight instructions consequent on either branch of an IF, they should be placed in a subroutine and executed by a GOSUB instruction, for example:

```
100 IF A=B THEN 140
110 REM    WHEN A < >B:-
120        GOSUB 400
130        GOTO 160
140 REM    WHEN A=B:-
150        GOSUB 500
160 READ A, B, C
    .
    .
    .
```

Multiple selection may be implemented by an ON instruction where the range of values being tested is consecutive. Once again, the various branches should all terminate at a common point before proceeding with the rest of the program, for example:

```
100 ON A GOTO 110, 150, 190
110 REM      A=1
120            .
130            .
140            GOTO 220
150 REM      A=2
160            .
170            .
180            GOTO 220
190 REM      A=3
200            .
210            .
220 PRINT A, B, C
     .
     .
     .
```

The use of REMs and identation will again provide clarity for the reader.

Program modules

The concept of a free-standing module or subroutine introduced by the pseudocode **Do** command should be implemented by a GOSUB. The module of code executed should always terminate by a RETURN, and under no circumstances should a routine executed in this manner do anything else other than, on completion, return to the instruction following the initiating GOSUB, for example:

```
100 IF A=B THEN 120
110     GOSUB 800
120
  .
  .
  .

800 REM THIS ROUTINE IS EXECUTED WHEN A < > B
810
     .
     .
     .
     .

890 RETURN
```

B2   Program structure

Programs should be written in logical sections, the first containing the mainline or driving logic of the program and the others each performing a self-contained task.

Execution of any but the mainline section should be by means of a GOSUB rather than by GOTOs or by 'falling through' the program from a previous section.

As a language, BASIC does not give much help to the programmer in maintaining a visible logical structure in a program. The success of the technique depends entirely on the discipline imposed by the programmer on his or her coding style.

Because sections of a program have no means of being assigned a meaningful procedure name, much more importance is thrust on internal comments statements than is the case in many other languages.

To further avoid confusion, care must be taken to separate 'managing' from 'working' modules, and there should be a hierarchy of such segments in the program.

This procedure is illustrated below by skeletal coding to implement portions of the payroll algorithm in Chapter 3:

```
100 REM      OBTAIN CORRECT WORK DETAILS
110 GOSUB 300
120 REM      CHECK FOR END OF JOB
130 IF S1 = 1 THEN 250
140 REM      PAY PROCEDURE LOOP
150          REM PAY CALCULATION
160          GOSUB ...
170          REM UPDATE HISTORY RECORD
180          GOSUB ...
190          REM PRINT PAY DETAILS
200          GOSUB ...
210          REM OBTAIN CORRECT WORK DETAILS
220          GOSUB 300
230          REM REPEAT FOR NEXT EMPLOYEE
240          GOTO 130
250 REM      PRINT FACTORY TOTALS
260 GOSUB ...
270 STOP
280 REM      * * * * * * * * * * * * * * * * * * * * * * * * * * * * * * * * * * * * * * * * * * * * * * * *
290 REM
300 REM      OBTAIN CORRECT WORK DETAILS:-
310 REM      ACCEPT EMPLOYEE NUMBER FROM OPERATOR
320 GOSUB 400
330 REM      CHECK FOR END OF JOB
340 IF S1 = 1 THEN 370
350 REM      ACCEPT HOURS WORKED FROM OPERATOR
360 GOSUB ...
```

```
370 RETURN
380 REM      * * * * * * * * * * * * * * * * * * * * * * * * * * * * * * * * * * * * * * * * * * * * * *
400 REM
400 REM      ACCEPT EMPLOYEE NUMBER AND VERIFY
410 REM      BY RETRIEVING EMPLOYEE RECORD
420 REM      USING EMPLOYEE NUMBER AS KEY
430 REM      A ZERO INPUT AS EMPLOYEE
440 REM      NUMBER SIGNALS END OF JOB
450 PRINT 'EMPLOYEE NUMBER PLEASE'
460 INPUT E
470 IF E < > 0 THEN 500
480 S1 = 1
490 GOTO 590
500
    .
    .
    .
    .
    .
    .
    .
    .
    .

590 RETURN
```

B3 Module design

It should be a major consideration in program design that each functional task should operate as independently as possible of other tasks in the program.

Although data in a BASIC program is global by nature, it is possible to allocate specific variables to the task of communicating with a procedural module. These designated variables will contain data or status parameters. The method by which the procedural module accomplishes its task is then immaterial to the remainder of the program.

This concept is amply illustrated by the intrinsic functions available in BASIC, for example:

```
X = SQR(Y)
```

This acknowledges the existence of a routine named SQR, the task of which is to evaluate the square root of any non-negative variable passed to it. The user of the procedure may have no knowledge of the means by which the evaluation is effected. This independence of function should be sought in all program construction. Sufficient documentation must be included in the program to explain to a reader the means by which each program module may be used. The example below illustrates a procedure for calculating the area of a triangle from the lengths of its three sides.

```
500 REM     CALCULATE AREA OF TRIANGLE
510 REM   VARIABLES USED: S, S1, S2, S3, A, F
520 REM     TO USE THIS ROUTINE PLACE THE
530 REM     SIDE LENGTHS OF ANY TRIANGLE IN
540 REM     S1, S2 and S3
550 REM     IF THE DIMENSIONS ARE IMPOSSIBLE
560 REM         F WILL BE SET TO ZERO
570 REM          A, THE AREA, WILL BE SET TO ZERO
580 REM     ELSE
590 REM         F WILL BE SET TO 1
600 REM         A WILL CONTAIN THE AREA
610 REM
620 S=(S1+S2+S3)/2
630 IF (S-S1) < 0 THEN 700
640 IF (S-S2) < 0 THEN 700
650 IF (S-S3) < 0 THEN 700
660 F=1
670 S=S*(S-S1)*(S-S2)*(S-S3)
680 A=SQR(S)
690 GOTO 720
700 F=0
710 A=0
720 RETURN
```

A typical use of this routine would appear as:

```
100 S1=X
110 S2=Y
120 S3=Z
130 GOSUB 500
140 IF F=0 THEN 170
150             PRINT 'AREA=' A
160             GOTO 180
170 PRINT 'IMPOSSIBLE TRIANGLE'
180     .
        .
        .
```

B4 Programming standards

The following are suggested as minimum coding standards for BASIC programs:

Program function

Comment statements at the beginning of the program should clearly state the function of the program and its interaction with any other program in a system.

Dictionary of variables

Comment statements should list all variables used in the program and explain what each represents. This should be done at the start of the program for global variables and at the start of each subroutine for local variables.

Coding format

Where permitted by the BASIC system, use statement indentation to delineate sections of code which form a logical grouping. Illustrations of this are given earlier in this appendix. Write one instruction per line. Use comments statements liberally throughout the code as BASIC has little inherent self-documentation.

Program structure

Construct the program using small task-oriented self-contained subroutines with local data items.

Execute the functional subroutines by means of an hierarchical structure of controlling modules, overall control being vested in a mainline module.

Keep all program modules small: no more than 20–30 executable statements.

Overall control should be by GOSUB calls to modules rather than GOTOs. If GOTOs are used they should never branch beyond their own module.

Each program module should have one entry point and one RETURN point.

It is important to remember that BASIC often has no in-built facilities for handling structured programming. The elegance of a program depends entirely on the discipline brought to bear by the programmer.

Appendix C   Pascal

C1   Algorithm implementation

As Pascal is a relatively modern programming language, it has been designed from the outset to possess features which facilitate the principles of structured program design.

The program control structures of sequence, iteration and selection are able to be implemented by syntax identical to the pseudocode used to formulate an algorithm.

Sequence

Pascal instructions are executed in the order in which they occur in the source program. No further technique is therefore required to implement sequential operations, for example:

```
read (a, b, c);
s : = (a + b + c)/2
temp : = s*(s − a)*(s − b)*(s − c);
area : = sqrt (temp);
writeln (area);
```

Iteration

The pseudocode construct used for iteration is:

While condition
    statement(s)
end-while

This construct implies a leading decision-making strategy, that is, the governing condition is evaluated before the execution of each iteration of the loop, and if the condition is true when the statement is encountered, the loop will not be performed at all.

Pascal provides for such an iteration construct in the **while . . . do . . .** command, for example:

```
sum:=0;
read (number);
while number > 0 do
    begin
    sum:=sum+number;
    read (number)
    end;
```

This code will read and accumulate the sum of a series of numbers until one (which may be the first) is read which is not greater than zero.

In addition to the **while** command, Pascal also provides a **repeat . . . until . . .** construct which implements a trailing decision-making strategy. A loop controlled by such a means would always be executed at least once. In this case, the following coding would not necessarily produce the same sum as that above:

```
sum:=0;
read (number);
repeat
    sum:=sum+number;
    read (number)
until number < =0;
```

In the latter case an initial *number* which was not greater than zero would be added to *sum* before the termination of the loop. Unless a particular reason exists for the use of a **repeat** in preference to a **while**, the **while** should be regarded as the normal means of implementing iteration.

A variation on the **while** is the **for** command which also implements a leading decision, for example:

```
sum:=0;
for n:=1 to limit do
    sum:=sum+n;
```

If the initial value of *limit* was less than one, the *for* loop would not have been executed.

Selection

Simple selection in Pascal is implemented by the **if . . . then . . . (else)** command, for example:

```
if number < target then
    begin
    number:=number+1;
    total:=total+number
    end;
```

```
if counter > 0 then
    average:=total/counter
else
    writeln ('invalid data');
```

Multiple selection is implemented by the **case** statement, for example:

```
range:=grosspay div 10000;
if range > 6 then
    range:=6;
case range of
0, 1, 2: percentage:=10;
3, 4: percentage:=25;
5, 6: percentage:=35
end;
tax:=grosspay*percentage/100;
```

Program modules

The concept of a program module as executed by the **do** construct in pseudocode may be implemented in Pascal by a **begin . . . end** block of in-line commands, by the execution of a free-standing subroutine, by the use of a named procedure or by the declaration of a function with the attendant transfer of parameters at the time of its invocation.

Unless a task can be expressed in no more than six to eight lines of code, it should be constructed as a function or procedure rather than a **begin** block; **begin** blocks which comprise lengthy amounts of code obscure the overall structure and readability of programs.

C2   Program structure

Programs should be written in modules, each of which should be a declared procedure. Overall control of these procedures should be the task of a mainline or driving module which, by the nature of a Pascal program, will be the last procedure to be declared.

Care should be taken to avoid placing too much coding in any one procedure and to separate 'managing' from 'working' procedures.

This procedure is illustrated below by skeletal coding to implement the payroll algorithm in Chapter 3.

```
begin
    paycalculation;
    updatehistoryrecord;
    printpaydetails;
    while (notendofdata) or (not truedetails) do
        obtaincorrectdetails;
```

```
end;
procedure printfactorytotals

       .
       .
       .

end;
    (*mainline program procedure*)
    while (not endofdata) or (not truedetails) do
        obtaincorrectdetails;
    while not endofdata do
        processpayroll;
    printfactorytotals;
end;
    (*end of program*)
```

C3   Module design

It should be a major consideration in program design that each functional task, consisting of one or more *procedures,* should operate as independently as possible of other tasks in the program.

Pascal provides the facility for both local and global data and strict rules encourage their correct usage.

Data may be exchanged between a procedure and its controlling module (or block) by means of global variables or parameters to the procedure.

Parameters in the procedure declaration (or heading) may be any of four kinds, namely:

- value parameter;
- variable parameter;
- procedure parameter; or
- function parameter.

Here we are concerned only with value parameters and variable parameters.

```
program payroll;
var  .
     .
     .
     .

    procedure processpayroll;
    var

      .
      .
```

```
    procedure paycalculation;
var        .
           .
           .

    procedure calculatetax;
           .
           .
           .

    end;
    procedure analyzecoinage;
           .
           .
           .

    end;
begin
    if hoursworked not > normalperiod
        payablehours:=hoursworked
    else
        payablehours:=normalperiod
                      +overtimefactor*
                      (hoursworked−normalperiod);
    calculatetax;
    netpay:=grosspay−taxamount;
    analyzecoinage;
    factorytotalgross:=factorytotalgross+grosspay;
    factorytotaltax:=factorytotaltax+taxamount;
    factorytotalnet:=factorytotalnet+netpay;
end;
procedure updatehistoryrecord;
    .
    .
    .

end;
procedure printpaydetails;
    .
    .
    .

end;
procedure obtaincorrectdetails;
    .
    .
    .

end;
```

A *value* parameter (sometimes known as an input parameter) is one which is local to the procedure and is used to pass a value to the procedure. Although the value of a parameter may change during the execution of the procedure (although this is to be discouraged), it will return to its original value following the execution of the procedure.

A *variable* parameter (sometimes known as a throughput or output parameter) is one used primarily to pass a value back to the controlling module. Its value may be altered during the execution of the procedure and the parameter will retain the newly calculated value after the procedure has been executed.

C4   Programming standards

The following are suggested as minimum coding standards for Pascal programs:

- Comments should appear in each procedure where an explanation of the function would assist the reader.
- Indentation of embedded procedures, **if/else, case** and **while/do** constructs should follow the example of the pseudocode.
- Meaningful names should be used for all variables.
- Constants used within the program should be assigned to variables with meaningful names and those variables used within the procedural statements rather than the constants themselves.
- Boolean values of true and false are provided in the syntax of the language and should be used in operations involving status variables.

Appendix D   dBASE III

D1   Algorithm implementation

The procedural code used by dBASE is syntactically very close to that of the pseudocode used in this text.

Sequence

As dBASE executes instructions in the order in which they are written, no further technique is required to implement a series of sequential operations, for example:

```
USE ORDERS
APPEND BLANK
REPLACE ORDER_ID WITH ORDER_NO
REPLACE ORDER_QTY WITH NEW_QTY
```

Iteration

The **DO WHILE . . . ENDDO** construct in dBASE corresponds with the **While . . . end-while** in pseudocode, for example:

```
USE CUSTOMER INDEX CUSTINX

@ 3, 1 SAY 'Please input Customer ID' GET CUST_ID
READ
DO WHILE CUST_ID # 0
    SEEK CUST_ID
    @ 4, 1 SAY, CUST_NAME
    @ 3, 1 SAY 'Please input Customer ID' GET CUST_ID
    READ
ENDDO
```

Selection

The IF . . . ELSE . . . ENDIF construct in dBASE equates with the **if** . . . **else** . . . **end-if** in pseudocode, for example:

```
IF NEED_SORT = 'Yes'
    USE CUSTOMER
    SORT ON CUST_ID TO NEWCUST
ELSE
    @ 4, 1 SAY 'No sort will be done'
END-IF
```

A multiple selection as in the **case** . . . **end-case** construct in pseudocode is implemented by the dBASE DO CASE, for example:

```
@ 10, 1 SAY 'choice please' GET CHOICE
DO CASE
    CASE CHOICE = '1'
        DO NEXTMENU
    CASE CHOICE = '2'
        DO INVOICE
    OTHERWISE
        @ 12, 1 SAY 'Invalid choice'
        WAIT
ENDCASE
```

Program modules

The pseudocode concept of subroutines executed with data passed as parameters is implemented in dBASE by means of a DO . . . WITH . . . , for example:

```
PROCEDURE ONE
    .
    .
    .
DO TWO WITH VALUE1, VALUE2
    .
    .
    .
RETURN

PROCEDURE TWO
PARAMETERS NUMBER1, NUMBER2
    .
    .
    .
RETURN
```

In this case, when procedure ONE calls procedure TWO via the DO command, the contents of VALUE1 and VALUE2 are transferred to NUMBER1 and NUMBER2 respectively. When procedure TWO returns control to ONE, the contents in NUMBER1 and NUMBER2 are retransferred to VALUE1 and VALUE2 and these will now contain any new values which may have then computed during the execution of procedure TWO.

D2   Program Structure

Programs should be written in single-task-orientated procedures with the first being the mainline or driving logic. Sub-procedures should be invoked by means of DO commands and parameters passed by means of the DO . . . WITH and PARAMETERS features.

D3   Relational Operators in dBASE

The relational algebra operations of Restrict, Project, Join and Append are implemented in dBASE either directly, as in the case of JOIN and APPEND, or indirectly as in the case of the COPY command.

Restrict and Project

These operations are effected by means of the COPY command. For example, to restrict a table of students to only those rows which contained a code of 'LAW' in the COURSE column:

```
USE STUDENTS
COPY TO LAWFILE FOR COURSE = 'LAW'
```

To project the STUDENTS table to a new table containing only the students' names and id numbers:

```
USE STUDENTS
COPY TO NEWFILE FIELDS ID, NAME
```

A combination of these commands would achieve a restrict and project in the same operation, for example:

```
USE STUDENTS
COPY TO PARTFILE FOR COURSE = 'LAW' FIELDS ID, NAME
```

Append

The append operation is effected by the dBASE APPEND command, for example:

```
USE STUDENTS
APPEND FROM ENROLLMENTS
```

The rows in the ENROLLMENTS table will now be added to the end of those already existing in the STUDENTS table.

Join

The join operation is implemented by the JOIN command in dBASE and is a somewhat cumbersome operation, for example:

```
SELECT 1
USE STUDENTS
SELECT 2
USE LECTURERS
JOIN WITH STUDENTS TO NEWFILE
    FOR SUBJECT = STUDENTS – > SUBJECT
```

Once again, a project operation could be combined with a join by adding to the above JOIN command the statement:

```
FIELDS NAME, SUBJECT, TEACHER
```

Appendix E
A hypothetical computer and its assembler language

E1   Computer characteristics

- 64K (i.e. 65536) 16-bit locations;
- one 16-bit accumulator, the A-Register;
- one 16-bit index register, the I-Register;
- one 16-bit program counter, the P-Register;
- arithmetic performed in integer mode only, negative values held in 2s complements;
- instruction format:
    operation code: 5 bits (bits 0–4)
    index flag: 1 bit (bit 5)
    operand: 10 bits (bits 6–15)
    (bit 0 is left-most, bit 15 right-most in each location);
- program space commences from relative address zero and the P-Register is set to zero when the program is loaded.

E2   Instructions

Addressing modes

C   Constant mode — operand is a positive integer within the range of 0 to 1023;
    Note: If a symbolic label is used as an operand in these instructions, the operand will be the *address* of that label *not* its contents.
M   Memory address mode — operand is a memory location within range 0 to 1023;
N   No address mode — operand is inherent in the operation code and bits 6 to 15 are set to zero.

Instruction format

(Label) op code (,I) operand

where label is optional and, if present, has a maximum of five alpha numeric characters, the first of which must be alpahabetic;

op code — see table below:

,I   is optional, and if present, indicates that the instruction is indexed, that is, the effective operand is the sum of the operand in the instruction plus the contents of the I-Register — this applies *only* to memory address mode instructions;

operand is a numeric constant within the range 0 to 1023 or a label.

Instruction set

Mnemonic op. code	Machine code	Addressing mode(s)	Function
Arithmetic			
ADC	00	C	Add operand to A-Register.
ADM	01	M	Add contents of address to A-Register.
SBC	02	C	Subtract operand from A-Register.
SBM	03	M	Subtract contents of address from A-Register.
MPY	04	M	Multiply the contents of the A-Register by the contents of an address (answer in A-Register).
DVD	05	M	Place in the A-Register the unrounded integer quotient obtained by dividing the contents of the A-Register by the contents of an address.
AOR	06	N	Add 1 to the A-Register.
NGR	07	N	Negate the contents of the A-Register. (I's complement)
AOI	08	N	Add 1 to the I-Register.
Data transfer			
LDC	09	C	Load a constant into the A-Register.
LDM	10	M	Load the contents of the address into the A-Register.
STM	11	M	Store the A-Register in the address.
LDI	12	N	Load the I-Register into A-Register.
STI	13	N	Store A-Register in the I-Register.

Mnemonic op. code	Machine code	Addressing mode(s)	Function
Test/branch			
JMP	14	M	Branch unconditionally to the operand address.
SRJ	15	M	Store the address of the next instruction in the operand address and branch to the operand address + 1 (i.e. subroutine branch).
JPI	16	M	Branch to the address contained in the operand address (i.e. indirect branch/subroutine exit).
JPZ	17	M	Branch to operand address if A-Register contents are zero.
JPN	18	M	Branch to operand address if A-Register contents are negative.
Shift/rotate			
SRR	19	C	Shift bits in A-Register right by the number of bits indicated by the operand. Zeros enter at left.
SRL	20	C	Shift bits in A-Register left by the number of bits indicated by the operand. Zeros enter at right.
RRR	21	C	Rotate bits in A-Register right by the number of bits indicated by the operand.
RRL	22	C	Rotate bits in A-Register left by the number of bits indicated by the operand.

(*Note*: Shifting 'drops bits off' the A-Register, rotating treats the bits as though they were on a circular belt.)

Logical/Boolean			
AND	23	M	Perform a logical AND between the contents of the A-Register and those of the operand address.
IOR	24	M	Perform a logical inclusive OR between the contents of the A-Register and those of the operand address.

(*Note*: The result is formed in the A-Register.)

Mnemonic op. code	Machine code	Addressing mode(s)	Function
Miscellaneous			
NOP	25	N	No operation.
HLT	26	N	Terminate the program and return to the operating system.
CAB	27	N	Convert the right-hand byte in the A-Register from ASCII to an equivalent binary numeric value, the left-most byte is lost in the process.
CBA	28	M	Treat the contents of the A-Register as a binary value and convert it to five ASCII characters to be stored in three locations (the first two holding two characters each and the third holding one character) starting from the operand location.
Input/output			
INP	29	M	Transfer from the screen the number of characters indicated by the contents of the A-Register and store them, two per location, in a series of locations starting at the operand address.
OUT	30	M	Transfer to the screen the number of characters indicated by the contents of the A-Register from a series of locations, holding two characters each, starting at the operand address.
MVC	31	N	Move the screen cursor to the position specified by the contents of the A-Register where bits 0 and 7 hold the line number and bits 8 to 15 hold the column number.

Notes on Input/Output Instructions:

(i) *Screen I/O*
An MVC instruction executed with the A-Register set to zero will cause the screen to be cleared and the cursor moved to the top left-hand corner.

(ii) *Printer Output*
If an indexed OUT instruction has the I-Register set to zero, the output will be directed to the printer.

(iii) *Disk I/O*
 • If the INP and OUT instructions are indexed, they will operate on a disk file rather than the screen. The disk file will be treated as a relative file and the content of the I-Register will be taken as the record number to be accessed on the disk. All records must be of equal length in any file.

- If a disk file is used, it will have the same name as the assembler source program file plus a .DSK extension (e.g., PROG1.DSK).
- Writing a record to a position already occupied will cause the new record to be written in place of the old record.
- Writing a blank record to a position on the disk file will cause the record at that position to be deleted.
- If a disk file already exists for any program, it will be opened and extended/amended by that program; otherwise a new file will be created at the execution of the first disk I/O instruction.

Pseudo instructions

label	NUM	n	Place a numeric constant, *n* in a location identified by the label.
label	ASC	'....'	Place the string of ASCII characters between quotes in a series of locations, starting at the location identified by the label.
label	TBL	n	Allocate a series of *n* consecutive locations starting at label (i.e. creates an array).

Comments

A comment may be inserted on any line of code provided that the comment commences with an asterisk, for example,

```
SPOT  ADM  TOTAL    *    Add TOTAL to A-Reg.
```

E3 Sample program

Task required: Accept a series of numbers in the range one to nine from the screen, and display their total and average. The series will end when the operator inputs a zero. The total will not exceed 999. The program should check that the character accepted is within the range specified. The screen should be cleared as the first operation of the program.

Algorithm:
```
    do Clear Screen
    Total=0
    Counter=0
    do Get Valid Digit
    while Digit is not=0
        Total=Total+Digit
        Counter=Counter+1
        do Get Valid Digit
```

end-while
if Counter=0
   Average=0
else
   Average=Total/Counter
end-if
Display Average and Total
Stop

Assembler program

Label	Op-code	Operand	Comments
	JMP	START	*Branch to first instruction

*The following are the data items needed in the program.

Label	Op-code	Operand	Comments
TOTAL	NUM	0	*Total of digits
COUNT	NUM	0	*Counter of digits
AVGE	NUM	0	*Average of digits
TALLY	NUM	0	
REPLY	NUM	0	
*			
PRMPT	ASC	'DIGIT PLEASE (0-9)'	
ANSR1	ASC	'TOTAL='	
ANSR2	ASC	' '	*2 space characters
NUMBR	ASC	' '	*6 space characters
ZERO	ASC	'0'	
NINE	ASC	'9'	
*			

*This is the start of the procedural instructions.
*

Label	Op-code	Operand	Comments
START	LDC	0	*clear screen
	MVC		
	LDM	ZERO	*isolate the zero ..
	SRR	8	*.. and nine characters
	STM	ZERO	
	LDM	NINE	
	SRR	8	
	STM	NINE	
	SRJ	GETD	*Subroutine gets value of digit in
			*A-Register
LOOP	JPZ	CALC	*Terminate if digit=0
	ADM	TOTAL	*Add this digit . . .
	STM	TOTAL	* . . . to Total
	LDM	COUNT	*Get contents of Counter . . .
	AOR		* . . . add 1 to it, and . . .

Label	Op-code	Operand	Comments
	STM	COUNT	*... put it back
	SRJ	GETD	*Get next digit
	JMP	LOOP	*Back to start of loop
*			
*When loop terminates upon digit=0:-			
*			
CALC	LDM	COUNT	*Get Counter
	JPZ	DISP	*To DISP if counter=0
	LDM	TOTAL	*Get Total
	DVD	COUNT	*Divide Total by Counter ...
	STM	AVGE	*... result in AVGE
*			
DISP	SRJ	RSLT	*Subroutine to display results
*			
	HLT		*Terminate program

* *

*Subroutine to accept a character from the screen, check that it is a numeric
*character from 0 to 9 and prompt for another character if that check fails.
*

Label	Op-code	Operand	Comments
GETD	NOP		*Leave room for return address
	LDC	10	*Move cursor to ...
	SRL	8	*... line 10, col 1 ...
	AOR		*... to display prompt
	MVC		
*			
PRMPT	LDC	22	*Display the prompt ...
	OUT	PROMT	*... for the digit
*			
	LDC	1	*Get character in left-most ...
	INP	REPLY	*... byte of REPLY
	LDM	REPLY	*Put character in A-Reg ...
	SRR	8	*... and move to right-most byte
	STM	REPLY	*Store back in REPLY
*			
	SBM	ZERO	*Subtract char value of 0
	JPZ	ALTER	*To ALTER if char=0
	JPN	PRMPT	*Back if char < zero
*			
	LDM	REPLY	*Get reply again
	SBM	NINE	*Subtract char value of 9
	JPZ	ALTER	*To ALTER if char is ...
	JPN	ALTER	*... 9 or less, otherwise ...
	JMP	PRMPT	*... back for another char
*			
ALTER	LDM	REPLY	*Get reply again
	CAB		*Convert to binary value
*			
	JPI	GETD	*Exit from subroutine

* *

Label	Op-code	Operand	Comments
*			
*Subroutine to display the Total and Average			
*			
RSLT	NOP		*Leave room for return address
	LDM	TOTAL	*Get value of TOTAL and . . .
	CBA	NUMBR	*. . . change it to ASCII
*			
	LDC	15	*Move cursor to . . .
	SRL	8	*. . . line 15, col 1 . . .
	AOR		*. . . to display Total
	MVC		
	LDC	8	*Display message for . . .
	OUT	ANSR1	*. . . value of Total
*			
	LDC	5	*Display Total value . . .
	OUT	NUMBR	*. . . in ASCII chars
*			
	LDM	AVGE	*repeat this procedure for
			*Average
	CBA	NUMBR	
	LDC	17	
	SRL	8	
	AOR		
	MVC		
	LDC	10	
	OUT	ANSR2	
	LDC	5	
	OUT	NUMBR	
	JPI	RSLT	*Exit from subroutine
*			

* *

Appendix F Diagrammatic representation of algorithms

F1 Introduction

Algorithms in this text have been presented in pseudocode format because:

(1) it is by far the most common international and inter-disciplinary medium for program design documentation and expression;
(2) it allows for data declaration as well as procedure specification;
(3) by limiting its control syntax (do, while . . . end-while, if . . . else . . . end-if) one can force the expression of an algorithm to be in a format which allows its implementation in a target language using only the structured concepts of sequence, selection and iteration;
(4) by allowing statements to be written in prose form rather than being forced into diagrammatic boxes, a more natural English expression of the problem may be obtained; and
(5) it is more amenable to the trial-and-error, cut-and-paste activity associated with program design.

However, in an argument something akin to the right vs left brain hemisphere theories, many people find it more natural to express logic by means of diagrams rather than (structured) prose. It is for this reason that this Appendix has been included.

Let me start with some guidelines for prospective users of N–S diagrams.

(1) Whatever technique is used as an aid to designing the logic of an algorithm, it must be useful as a *design* tool not a *documentation* tool. As I have stated earlier in the text, pseudocode, flowcharts, N–S diagrams, etc, are not worth keeping as on-going documentation for

programs. They are too detailed and therefore become outdated too quickly. If a maintenance programmer wants that level of detail, they will go straight to the source code of the program. A structure diagram is worth keeping because it gives an overall picture of structure rather than logic.

From this it follows that there is no point in drawing a logic diagram *after* the program has been written. In a classroom situation, this might score some points from the teacher but in a working, professional environment it is not worth the time.

(2) The contents of the symbols in a logic diagram must be expressed in English, not in the syntax of the target programming language. Remember, the diagram is an aid to writing the program, not an alternative form of expressing the program once it has been coded.

Hence, a step in a program such as

$$\boxed{\text{MCOUNT} = \text{MCOUNT} + 1}$$

is useless. What does MCOUNT count? A far better statement of the process would be

$$\boxed{\text{Add 1 to males counter}}$$

Similarly, a decision shown as

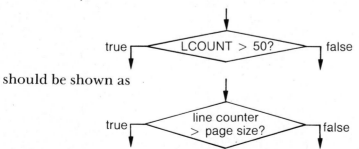

should be shown as

There is no need to have a symbol in a logic diagram for every line of code ultimately required in the program.

Hence, instead of

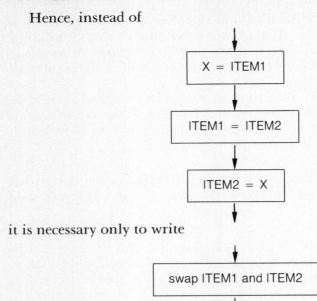

it is necessary only to write

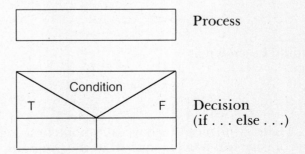

F2   Nassi-Shneiderman (N-S) diagrams

N–S diagrams are essentially flowcarts without the necessity for arrows to indicate the flow of logic. The arrow symbol in flowcharts allows programmers to design solutions which do not conform to the structured programming concepts of sequence, selection and iteration. Flowcharts which break these rules may only be implemented in program coding by the use of GO TO instructions and a consequent loss of control over the program structure.

The symbols used in N–S diagrams are:

Process

Condition	
T F	

Decision
(if . . . else . . .)

```
case of:

value 1   value 2   . . . .   else        (case . . . end-case)
```

```
while                                       Iteration
                                            (while . . . end-while)
```

```
                                            a called
                                            Procedure/Subroutine
```

The flow of logic is indicated by joining symbols together so that the steps are executed by reading from top to bottom.

The following examples are taken from earlier chapters in this book and should serve as a set of graded examples to illustrate the techniques involved in drawing N–S diagrams.

Chapter 1

Example 1.1

Request a positive integer from an operator at a terminal and output all of the powers of 2 from 2 to 2 to the power of that integer.

Powers of 2

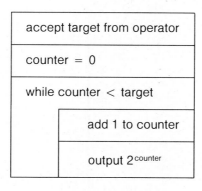

```
accept target from operator

counter = 0

while counter < target

       add 1 to counter

       output 2^counter
```

Example 1.2

Read and print all of the records on a personnel file. The file ends with a standard end-of-file sentinel.

Print Records

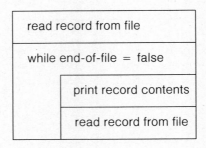

Example 1.3

A large table holds, in each of its elements, the salary of a person in a particular company. The precise number of such persons, and therefore of such salaries, is unknown but the last salary is followed by a dummy value of 999999 to indicate that no more data follows. An algorithm is required to calculate and print the average of all these salaries.

Average Salary

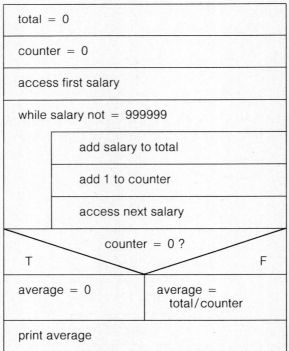

Example 1.9

Examine Table

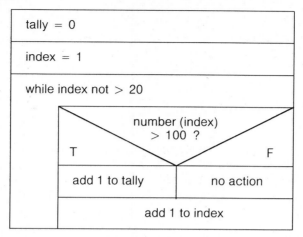

Where procedures are called and have parameters passed to them (see Chapter 2), the procedure call symbol may be used to indicate the name of the procedure and the parameters may be shown in brackets.

Chapter 2

Example 2.1

A program is required to accept pairs of integers from an operator at a terminal and to display their sum and average. The program is to terminate when a pair of zero values is entered.

Total and Average

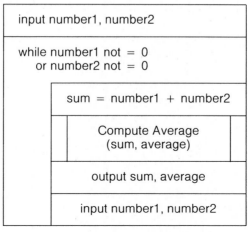

Compute Average (sum, average)

$$\boxed{\text{average} = \text{sum} / 2}$$

Example 2.3

A program is required to input 10 integers from an operator at a terminal and to output a counter of those integers whose value is greater than the average value of the input numbers.

Process Numbers

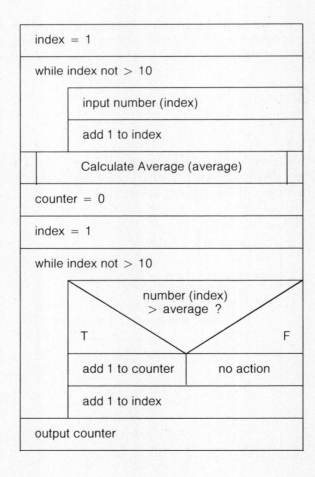

Calculate Average (average)

```
┌──────────────────────────────────────────────┐
│ total  =  0                                    │
├──────────────────────────────────────────────┤
│ index  =  1                                    │
├──────────────────────────────────────────────┤
│ while index not  >  10                         │
│      ┌─────────────────────────────────────┐  │
│      │ add number (index) to total         │  │
│      ├─────────────────────────────────────┤  │
│      │ add 1 to index                      │  │
│      └─────────────────────────────────────┘  │
├──────────────────────────────────────────────┤
│ average  =  total / 10                         │
└──────────────────────────────────────────────┘
```

Example 2.4

A program is required to process a file containing details of students enrolled in a college. Each student record contains an identification number, the student's name and the codes of up to four subjects in which that student is enrolled. The program is to print each student's name together with a counter of the number of subjects in which the student is enrolled. If a student is enrolled in fewer than four subjects, the unused subject codes will be blank. The file ends with a standard end-of-file sentinel.

Student Enrollments

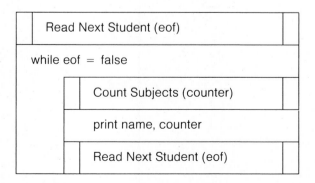

Read Next Student (eof)

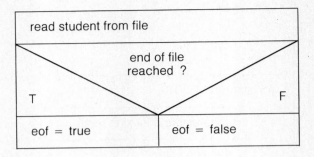

Count Subjects (counter)

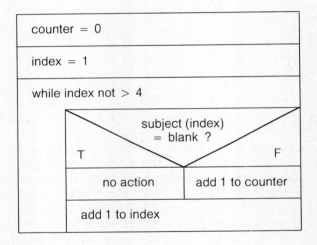

Glossary of terms

abstract data structure
a set of items of data which is defined by its behavior rather than its physical structure, e.g., a queue or a tree.

accumulator — *see* **register**

addressing mode
a direction to the central processor as to how to interpret the operand in a machine code or assembler language instruction.

algorithm
a set of instructions or steps to solve a problem.

argument — *see* **parameter**

bit
a binary digit, 0 or 1.

boolean variable
a variable within a program which is able to hold only two values, 'true' or 'false'.

byte
a group of 8 bits, usually representing one encoded character in a computer system.

character
a letter, digit or special symbol able to be represented within a computer system.

cohesion
a measure of the logical connection among the instructions comprising a program module.

compiler
a program which converts instructions from a high-level language to the machine code of a particular computer.

constant
an unchanging, or literal, value in a program, e.g., 123, 'HAPPY NEW YEAR'.

control break
a change in the value of a key field used to produce totals in report program.

333

co-routine
one of a number of procedures which transfer control asynchronously from one to the other during the execution of a program.

coupling
a mutual inter-dependence of program procedures on one another's operations.

database
an arrangement of data within a computer system so as to eliminate redundancy and allow a variety of access paths.

debugging — *see* **testing**

decision table
a tabular presentation of conditions to be tested, actions arising from those conditions and the rules connecting the actions to the appropriate combination of conditions.

decomposition
the systematic subdivision of a program's functions into an hierarchical structure of task-oriented modules.

file
a collection of related records held within a computer system.

floating point number — *see* **real number**

flowchart
a diagrammatic representation of the logic comprising the operations of a program.

function
a program module, usually with parameters, which, when invoked within a program, returns a value to be assigned to a variable, e.g., the square root function in BASIC is invoked as $X = SQR(Y)$.

global data — *see* **scope rules**

graph
an abstract data structure consisting of 'nodes' connected by 'edges' often used for representing network structures.

hash-addressed files
files, the records in which, are accessed by using an identifier which is computed by a formula applied to their key field.

hashing algorithm
the formula applied to the key of records in a hash-addressed file to compute their location.

index
a pointer to an element in an array or a set of pointers to records within a file.

index register
a register, the contents of which, are added to an operand in an instruction at its time of execution.

indexed file
a file, the records in which, are able to be accessed by means of an index which relates the record keys to the positions of those records in the file.

information hiding
the process of defining a program module in terms of what it does, not how it operates.

integer
a whole number, positive or negative, held within a computer's memory.

interpreter
a program which dynamically converts the source code of a high-level language to machine code as the program executes.

iteration
the repetitive execution of one or more program instructions until a nominated condition becomes true or ceases to be true.

key
a field within a record which uniquely identifies that record or on which the record is sequenced within its file.

linked list
an abstract data structure in which each element, often called an atom, consists of data plus one or more pointers to other elements in the structure.

list — *see* **linked list**

local data — *see* **scope rules**

logical record — *see* **record**

loop — *see* **iteration**

macro
a program instruction which is expanded to perform a number of tasks at either compile time or execution time.

module
a group of instructions forming a logical unit within a program and organized to perform a given task.

normalization
the reduction of a set of data to a number of relations which contain no repeating items and, in each of which, all items are directly dependent on the key.

object program
the machine code generated by a compiler.

operand
the component of a computer instruction which indicates the function to be performed (and usually the addressing mode) at execution time.

overflow
the result of attempting to store in a memory location a value too large to hold for the the number of bits comprising the location.

parameter
a value passed between a calling procedure and a called subroutine or function during the execution of a program.

physical record — *see* **record**

Polish notation
a form of postfix mathematical notation which eliminates the necessity to use brackets to determine the sequence of mathematical operations.

pop
a procedure which returns the latest item pushed on a stack.

procedure
a series of program steps to achieve a specified result.

program
the combination of an algorithm and its associated data structures which produces a specified result when executed.

pseudocode
the expression of an algorithm in a form of 'structured' English embodying only the constructs of sequence, selection and iteration.

push
a procedure which places a new item in a stack.

queue
an abstract data structure which operates on a first-in-first-out principle.

real number
a numeric value held within a computer system and represented by a mantissa holding the significant digits comprising the number and an exponent holding a scaling factor in terms of the base number used in the representation.

record
a collection of related items of data comprising a unit for manipulation with a computer system; the record may be a logical record e.g., all of the items comprising, say, one customer or one employee, or a physical record comprising the amount of data read from or written to a peripheral device in one physical operation, e.g., a block or sector.

recursion
the calling of itself as a subroutine by a program procedure in the course of its execution.

re-entrant procedure
a program, or program module, capable of serving several users with a single copy of itself.

register
a device used by a computer to hold specific contents such as instructions or data.

relational algebra
procedural operations which manipulate normalized tables of data.

relational calculus
non-procedural operations which manipulate normalized tables of data.

relative file
a file, the records in which, are accessed by a position number rather than a key value.

scope rules
rules relating to the access to data from procedures within a program; global data is accessable by all procedures whereas local data is accessable only by the procedure in which it is declared.

selection
a point at which a program makes a choice between two or more alternative courses of action.

sequence
the execution of program instructions one following the other as written in the source program.

software
the programs containing the functions which comprise a computer application.

sorting
the arrangement of data, logically or physically, in a particular sequence.

source program
program instructions in a high-level language as originally written by the programmer.

stack
an abstract data structure which operates on a last-in-first-out basis.

state transition table
a tabular arrangement of values which embody rules to enable a program to operate as a finite state automaton, i.e., a device which moves from one task to another as the result of some external event.

string
a group of characters with no structure which is apparent to the computer.

structure diagram
a diagram which represents the modules comprising a program as an hierarchically organized group of entitities.

structured programming
writing programs which have their procedures expressed only in terms of the logic constructs of sequence, selection and iteration together with a top-down decomposition into task-oriented modules which conform to the precepts of cohesion, coupling and information hiding.

subroutine
a stand-alone procedure, usually with passed parameters, which performs a specific task on a given set of inputs to produce a specific output.

subscript
an index which indicates the position of a given element in an array.

table — *see* **array**

testing
the process of executing a program with the deliberate intention of attempting to detect errors in its execution.

tree
an abstract data structure consisting of elements, usually referred to as nodes, each of which contains data plus pointers to two or more subordinate elements.

underflow

the result of attempting to store in a memory location a value too small to be represented by the number of bits comprising the location; in such a case, the computer will normally store a value of zero instead of the true value of the operation.

updating

usually applied to files to describe the process of applying transaction data to master records to keep their content up-to-date.

variable

a data item used in a program to hold varying values as the program executes, e.g., a counter or a total.

walkthrough

the process of, usually, a group of people jointly examining the code comprising a program with the intention of discovering errors in logic or deficiencies in style.

Index